— PRAISE FOR —
We Buried Dad in a Leisure Suit

"A clear and crisp vision of growing up in rural Iowa through the eyes of a young boy trying to make sense of life in a struggling American family. The rich detail of each family member jumps off the pages and leaves the reader to reflect on their family histories."

—Sheila Kelley, Actor in *LA Law, Gossip Girls, The Good Doctor, Singles, Nurse Betty*; Founder/CEO of S Factor

"Douglas Rife is a born storyteller and this rollicking, hilarious and poignant story of his family will make you laugh, cry and most of all marvel at his ability to bring his unique family to life on the page."

—Donna Hayes, Former CEO of Harlequin

"The characters leap off the page resurrected by storytelling that has passed through generations, and one son's hunger to uncover the reasons a family thrives or survives. As Douglas tumbles back through time, guided by the milestones of his father's family history, we are along for the ride of one man's lifetime: the hungers, loves, losses, hopes, and ultimate resilience that drive his motto: to bite down hard on life."

—Juliet Hart, Director of Education/TimeLine Theatre Company/Chicago, Illinois

"*We Buried Dad In a Leisure Suit* is an insight into a whole side of America that many others will barely know or imagine.

This is a book full of memorable characters. The dad—the Great Santini of the book, incorrigible but ultimately still lovable despite his immense imperfections. Uncle Ron and his remarkably hardworking but unsuccessful career as a criminal. His brother's fire and its aftermath—the "mummy" scene is a brilliant mixture of pathos and farce. And the mom, blousy, brassy, and feisty. The exotic dancers—voluptuous Toulouse-la-Trec icons of natural beauty and raunchy quasi porn-stars combined that bordered between sexual freedom and exploitation.

There is alcoholism, abuse, pornography, exotic dancing, violent crime, tragedy, love, and persistence with all kinds of things despite incredible obstacles. It's a testament to survival and to life itself in some of its most extraordinary forms."

—Andy Hargreaves, Director of CHENINE (Change, Engagement and Innovation in Education) at the University of Ottawa in Canada, and Emeritus Professor at Boston College, and member of the National Academy of Education.

We Buried Dad in a Leisure Suit

DOUGLAS M. RIFE

Mechanicsburg, PA USA

Published by Sunbury Press, Inc.
Mechanicsburg, PA USA

www.sunburypress.com

Copyright © 2025 by Douglas M. Rife.
Cover Copyright © 2025 by Sunbury Press, Inc.

Sunbury Press supports copyright. Copyright fuels creativity, encourages diverse voices, promotes free speech, and creates a vibrant culture. Thank you for buying an authorized edition of this book and for complying with copyright laws. Except for the quotation of short passages for the purpose of criticism and review, no part of this publication may be reproduced, scanned, or distributed in any form without permission. You are supporting writers and allowing Sunbury Press to continue to publish books for every reader. For information contact Sunbury Press, Inc., Subsidiary Rights Dept., PO Box 548, Boiling Springs, PA 17007 USA or legal@sunburypress.com.

For information about special discounts for bulk purchases, please contact Sunbury Press Orders Dept. at (855) 338-8359 or orders@sunburypress.com.

To request one of our authors for speaking engagements or book signings, please contact Sunbury Press Publicity Dept. at publicity@sunburypress.com.

FIRST SUNBURY PRESS EDITION: December 2025

Set in Adobe Garamond | Interior design by Crystal Devine | Cover by Victoria Mitchell | Edited by Abigil Bunner.

Publisher's Cataloging-in-Publication Data
Names: Rife, Douglas M., author.
Title: We buried dad in a leisure suit / Douglas M. Rife.
Description: First trade paperback edition. | Mechanicsburg, PA : Sunbury Press, 2025.
Summary: The book tells the story of two brothers' raucous retelling of their father's life on the way to his funeral. There is alcoholism, abuse, exotic dancers, crime, tragedy, love, and persistence with all kinds of things despite incredible obstacles. It's a testament to survival and to life itself in some of its most extraordinary forms.
Identifiers: ISBN : 979-8-88819-362-4 (softcover).
Subjects: FAMILY & RELATIONSHIPS / Dysfunctional Families | FAMILY & RELATIONSHIPS / Divorce & Separation | FAMILY & RELATIONSHIPS / Death, Grief, Bereavement | HUMOR / Topic / Marriage & Family.

Designed in the USA
0 1 1 2 3 5 8 13 21 34 55

For the Love of Books!

To my wife, Huma,
the glue that holds our family together,
and to our three wonderful children—
Aliya, Zain, and Sofi

Contents

Acknowledgments ix
Foreword xi

CHAPTERS

1   The Phone Call 1
"If I can't dance, I don't want to hear the music."

2   The Long Ride Home. 12
"The closer to the bone, the sweeter to the meat."

3   Clyde and Ada 18
"I'd just as soon hear a dawg howl."

4   Living with Annie Rife 30
"She was no bigger than a pint of soap after two weeks of washin'."

5   Harry Hatheway 42
"Gramma fried them taters offin' that grease from Howard Bly and Lish McQueen."

6   Dead Cat 52
"He's a gritty little guy."

7   In Search of a Home 58
"I hope he grows up to be a cop."

8   Shanty Town 62
"She could eat watermelon through a picket fence."

9   Beer at Uncle Dave's 75
"Give me a nickel, or I'll pee in your beer—again."

10   The Army 80
"I joined for three hots and a cot."

11   Marriage 90
"The first one can come any time; the rest take nine months."

12 Luck 102
"If there weren't two kinds of luck, we wouldn't have any."

13 Ashes 108
"For your information, it starts with a w."

14 The Farmer's Northside Tavern 122
"I don't know how they make it so good and sell it so cheap."

15 Barflies and Butterflies 136
"When they're nose to nose, his feet is in it, and when they're toes to toes, his nose is in it."

16 Uncle Ron Returns 141
"If they didn't have a pussy, I wouldn't even talk to them."

17 The Divorce 152
"She got the gold, and I got the shaft."

18 City Hall 159
"She had more meat showing than a butcher's window."

19 Yesterday's Dream 178
"When it rains I think of you, drip, drip, drip."

20 The Unexpected Benefactor 187
"Douglas, oh, Douglas, we got lumps."

21 Buying a Plot, Picking the Casket 194
"For all I care, you can run my body up a flagpole after I die."

22 Cleaning the Trailer 208
"Boys will be boys, if girls will let 'em."

23 The Last Chapter 225
"I ain't never seen a hearse followed by an armored car. You can't take it with ya."

Epilogue 240
"The gun was in the waste of his pants."

About the Author 260

Acknowledgments

One evening at a business dinner with Donna Hayes, who was then the CEO of Harlequin, those gathered around the table began sharing stories about their families. There were people there who were the sons or daughters of prominent professionals, even a descendant of General Meade, and they themselves were highly successful—investment bankers, publishers, financial analysts, and me. After we went around the table, it fell on me to share about my family. I started by saying that my parents were in the same business, "My dad plastered walls and my mom plastered people." I told some quick stories and when I finished, Donna said I needed to write my stories down. I want to thank her—she was the first to encourage me to write this book.

I also would like to thank the following relatives and family friends for sharing information and their stories about Dad, many of whom I interviewed on several occasions while I was working on the book:

Connie Chapman
Alice Clark
Gladys Kuehler
Great Aunt Myrtle Anderson Brooks
Great Aunt Pearl Richards Rife Caldwell
Great Aunt Dora Rife Chapman
Jack Mansel Hampton
Leona Hampton
Great Aunt Emmogene Rife Harper
Bessie (Granny) Haynie
Uncle Rolland (Ron) Keith Gillett aka Art Procter

My brother, Clyde "Deke" Rife
My brother, Brian Rife
Uncle Frederick (Fred) Clyde Rife
My mother, Shirley Rasmussen Rife

Thanks to Connie Trier for her expert research assistance—detective work, really—in helping me track down many obscure but important dates and bits of information.

I want to thank Cassandra Love, my first writing coach on this book, who helped me find my voice in the first few chapters. I also want to thank two great editors: Rachel Rosalina who first read my manuscript and shared her reader's notes with me for my second draft. And Lesley Bolton who gave my second draft a first-rate edit. And, lastly, to my wife, Huma, who turned out to be a damned good editor and gave thoughtful and insightful suggestions throughout her reading of the book.

I would like to thank John Jordan who was an early advocate for my book to be published at Sunbury Press. Lastly, I'd like to thank Lawrence Knorr and his yeoman team—Abigail Bunner, an expert and precise editor who found errors and typos I read right over; Crystal Devine who designed the interior pages and made the words come alive on the page; and Victoria Mitchell who designed an eye-catching cover that gives the reader a promise of what's to come when they open the pages and read the story!

Foreword

A note: The story is true. When my dad died, my brother, Brian, and my girlfriend, Kitty, made the trip to Iowa State University at Ames to pick me up and drive me back the two and a half hours to my hometown of Logan, Iowa. While we did retell many family stories about my father, it wasn't his whole story—we did not retell his story from birth to death in chronological order. Just as the car took corners, swerves, and detours, so did our conversation. But, the car ride is my *vehicle* for retelling his life story as it unfolded chronologically.

I have used my recollections, newspaper articles, and taped interviews, and have consulted with family members and other sources to check facts when my memory was faulty. In many places in the manuscript there is dialogue. These are either my recollections of the dialogue as best as I can remember it or my memory of dialogue described to me—some modified from taped interviews. While the words may not be exact, the tone and tenor and meaning are true. In order to maintain the anonymity of some, I have changed the names of certain individuals.

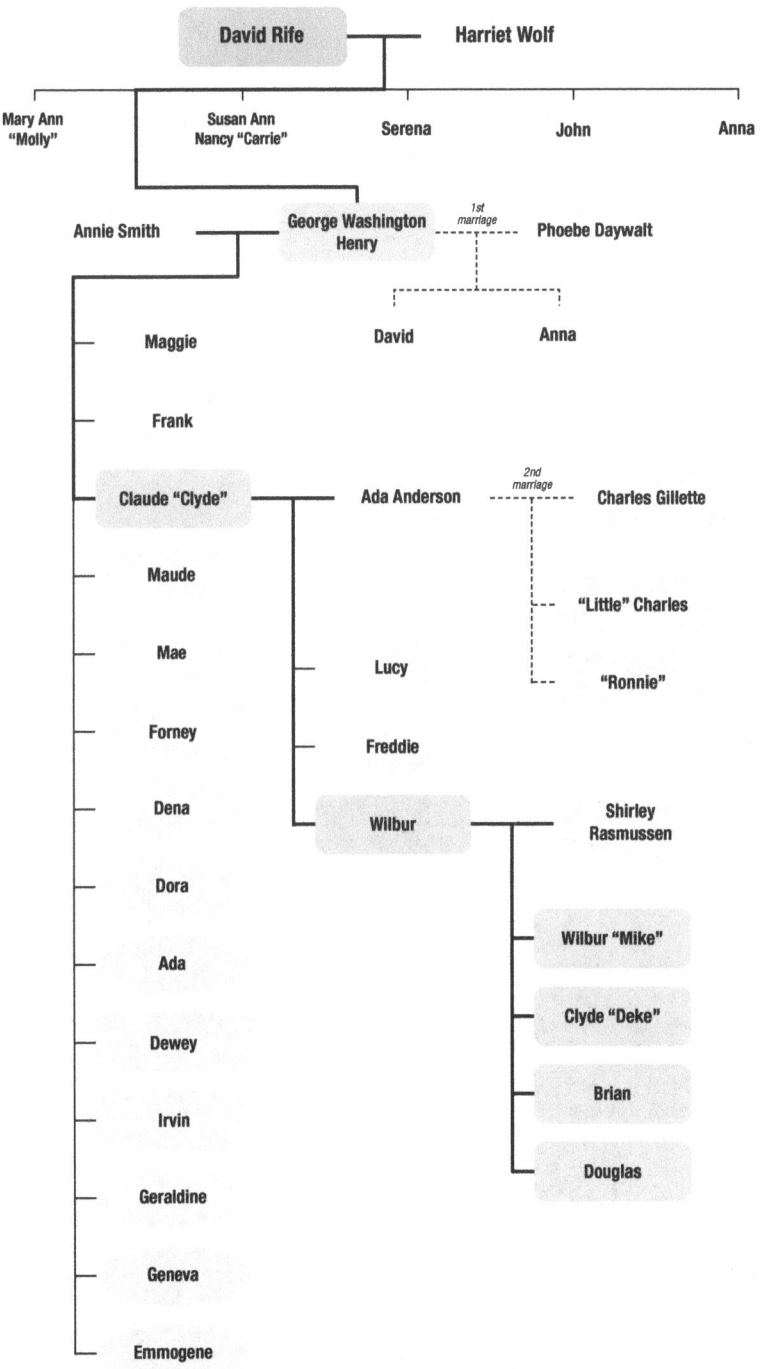

Douglas Rife at Iowa State

1

"If I can't dance, I don't want to hear the music."

The Phone Call

The room looked like the inside of a college student's upset stomach, painted lime green bile. The walls held the dirt from a decade of students who had lived in the room and endured the bargain color.

I had been the third man into that dorm room in Merrill Hall on the Iowa State University campus in Ames. Last man in took what was left, and I had no say where I could put my things. I came in at the beginning of the second quarter, too late to lay a claim. I was the oldest of the three of us in the room by five years, though it seemed more like a generation.

I had been convinced that I wouldn't be able to succeed in college. I didn't think I had the mental aptitude to make it, but after meeting my new college roommates, I was sure if they could do it, I would do just fine.

When I got to the room, my two roommates, dubbed Uncle Fester and Lurch, were finishing a pizza. Nearly everyone in college gets a nickname; we had one kid who was a psych major on the floor nicknamed ESP—Eat, Sleep, and Puke.

The room smelled of pepperoni and Pepsi—and, of course, the sophomoric farting and belching of these two titans of moronic humor. I was jealous that they had money for Pepsi and pizza but repulsed by the constant flow of gases that were released with utter joy into the room by these two. Flatulence sent them into riotous laughter. I didn't play along, and that made me a freak. And they thought even less of me when I yelled at them for their childish and repugnant behavior.

When I got my mother's call early on that Tuesday morning, we had been roommates for two months.

The incessant ringing of the telephone broke the morning silence. My roommates were still sleeping, so I hopped out of the loft to answer the phone. It was 6:00 a.m., early by dorm standards. I picked up the phone and answered, "Hello?"

My mother was on the other end.

"There is no easy way for me to tell you this," she said. Her words were slow, measured, and emotional. I had that sinking feeling in my stomach that you get when you drive your car over a dip real fast.

"There is no easy way to tell you this," she repeated. Breath. Gulp. "Your father died this morning."

I had just seen him in the hospital on the previous Sunday. My brother Brian and I had driven down to Omaha to visit Dad in the veteran's hospital. Brian was working at Dubuque Pack in Denison, Iowa, trimming hams on the ham line. Mom was working there, too. A girl there, Lonnie, had taken to Brian. Women were always attracted to him. Brian wasn't interested in women, especially this one, but she persisted nearly to the point of being a stalker. He was weak and gave in. Lonnie came with us to see Dad that Sunday.

Dad was sitting on the edge of his bed in a white dressing gown and cowboy boots when we walked into the ward. He had a flattop haircut, steel gray eyes, and big, full, round jowls. There was a scar from the corner of his right bottom lip halfway down his neck where a car window had cut it open. The wound was not so noticeable anymore; its color had faded like his hair, which was now gray, too. Dad wasn't tall but had presence because of his deep, loud voice, the kind of voice that could penetrate a room and make babies cry. He was incapable of whispering. Often, even kindness coming out of Dad's mouth sounded like anger.

When my cousin's boy, David, was little, Dad offered him a piece of candy. "WANT SOME CANDY?" he bellowed. David, then about five years old, looked up at Dad in terror.

Dad stared at David with his arm extended, the piece of candy in his muscular fingers. "HERE, TAKE IT!"

David's eyes teared up. He grabbed the candy and made a quick escape.

Dad's build supported the big voice. His arms and chest were muscular, and even though he had a paunch, he was stout from thirty-five years of lifting plaster.

Dad looked up when we walked into the room. He was expecting us.

We both gave him a hug. Brian's stalker friend stood back, uninterested.

Dad said, "LOOK, MY UNION SENT ME UP SOME MONEY FOR DIRTY BOOKS. HAMPTON'S BEEN UP HERE, TOO. MY WATCH BROKE, AND HAMPTON BROUGHT ME A NEW ONE."

Jack Hampton had been Dad's best friend since his army days. They met in basic training at Fort Robinson, a barren army outpost in the sand hills of the Nebraska panhandle. The army trained horses and mules for the cavalry there during World War II. After the war, they got an apartment together. Jack Hampton and Dad were more like brothers than friends. I called him Uncle Jack until I was about sixteen, when I realized that he wasn't really my dad's brother.

He showed us the watch. Dad was animated as he told us about some of the veterans in the ward with him. Dad was fifty-six, young compared to the World War I and even some of the World War II veterans in the hospital with him. He had lied about his age so he could get into the army when he was seventeen.

He saw the army as a good place to get regular meals. When he was sent to Fort Robinson for basic training to train horses, he had plenty to eat. Finally.

He, along with so many others, endured poverty and hunger. He had been haunted by hunger since his parents divorced in 1927, when he was four years old. He began working early for food. Sometimes he would work all day for a pound of bacon or a loaf of bread. Sometimes when things were really bad, the county would come by with "commodities" and a pair of shoes. It was always just enough to stave off the hunger for a few days. It usually consisted of a sack of sugar, a sack of flour, and a crate of citrus fruit. The army gave him three squares a day and a roof over his head. Private Wilbur Merle Rife was regular army now, and to him that meant regular food.

"How are you feeling?" Brian asked.

"ALL THAT SALTPETER THEY GAVE ME IN WORLD WAR TWO IS STARTING TO TAKE HOLD." Dad grabbed his crotch and laughed. "THE DOCTORS CAME IN TODAY AND GAVE ME AN INSULIN SHOT. THEY TOOK ME OFF MY PILLS. AIN'T HAD ONE OF MY PILLS FOR THE WHOLE TIME I'VE BEEN IN HERE. BUT TODAY I GOT A SHOT."

The veterans were laid out in beds in rows like sardines in a can, and the ward had a bad smell—a mixture of urine and Lysol.

"What's that smell?" I asked.

"OH, SOME OF THE OLD BOYS IN HERE DON'T HAVE VERY GOOD CONTROL OF THINGS. DID I EVER TELL YA ABOUT MY THREE WORST SMELLS?" Dad asked. It was not really one of those questions that needed an answer; he was going to go ahead and tell us anyway.

Lonnie was completely disinterested by this time. She walked over to the window. The sun was cascading in, so her shadow cast a wide column of darkness over three hospital beds. I was sure that the old soldiers lying in them thought nightfall had descended. They pulled up the covers almost in unison and rolled over.

She stared out the eighth-floor window—her overripe chest rising up and down as she expelled heavy, breathy sighs to punctuate her impatience. We hadn't been there ten minutes and she was ready to leave.

"SEE, WHEN I WAS A KID, I RAN A TRAP LINE. I TRAPPED MUSKRAT ON THE LITTLE SIOUX RIVER. I'D TRAP 'EM, SKIN 'EM, AND SELL THE PELTS."

I had never heard that dad was a trapper as a kid. I knew he'd been quite a fisherman, but this was the first time I'd heard this story.

"WELL, ONE TRAP THAT I HAD SET OUT HAD CAUGHT A SKUNK. I'D NEVER CAUGHT ME ONE BEFORE. I SET OUT TO SKIN THAT SKUNK. I SAW A LITTLE SACK AND I GUESS I PRESSED IT AND IT BROKE. IT WAS THE SCENT SACK. IT SPRAYED ME RIGHT 'TWEEN THE EYES. I THOUGHT IT HAD BLINDED ME. I SMELLED AWFUL FOR DAYS. NO ONE WOULD COME NEAR ME AND GRANDMA WOULDN'T LET ME IN THE HOUSE 'TILL THE SMELL WORE OFFIN ME."

Brian leaned forward and said in disgust, "Oh, my gawd, that musta been a horrible smell."

"THEN SEE, WHEN I WAS IN GREENLAND, AT THE THULE AIR FORCE BASE, I RAN HEAVY EQUIPMENT. I RAN SEVERAL KINDS UP THERE. WHATEVER THEY NEEDED ME TO DO AT THE TIME. SIDE BOOMS, FRONT END UNLOADERS, BIG GRATERS, YOU KNOW, BIG STUFF. ANYWAY, UP THERE, BIG TANKS HAD BEEN BURIED UNDERGROUND TO COLLECT THE WASTE FROM THE CAMP. I HAD TO DIG THEM UP FOR SOME REASON, CAN'T REMEMBER WHY. ANYWAY, I WAS DIGGING AROUND ONE OF THEM TO GET IT READY TO LIFT UP, AND I PUNCTURED ONE OF THOSE TANKS AND THE PISS STARTED POURING OUT. MY EYES BURNED LIKE HELL."

We were living part of the story with burning eyes and bad smells right there on the eighth floor of the VA hospital.

"MY THIRD WORST SMELL WAS IN HOT SPRINGS, SOUTH DAKOTA, OF ALL PLACES. I HAD STRUCK UP A CONVERSATION WITH THIS CUTE LITTLE WOMAN. OVER A COUPLE OF HOURS WE GOT TO TALKING ABOUT THIS AND THAT. 'FORE TOO LONG WE WERE IN THE BACKSEAT OF MY CAR. WE WERE STARTING TO GET AFTER IT WHEN I SLIPPED HER PANTIES DOWN. I WAS ALL READY TO GO, BUT I GOT ONE WHIFF OF THAT AND THE PARTY WAS OVER. UP WENT HER PANTIES AND OUT SHE WENT!"

I wasn't sure how to respond, and there was a bit of awkward silence after he finished. I mean, what are you supposed to do, top it? Besides, who in God's name wants to hear any story that has the possibility of one of your parents having sex?

"YOU KNOW, ALL THAT SALTPETER, THEY GAVE ME IN WORLD WAR TWO IS STARTING TO TAKE HOLD," he said again with a chuckle. "HELL, WHEN I GET OUTTA THIS PLACE, I'M GOIN' TO HAVE TO GET SOME SPRAY STARCH."

"You think that'll fix it?" Brian asked.

"OR MAYBE A SPLINT."

I said, "I doubt it's the saltpeter. Don't you think it might have something to do with the sugar diabetes?"

"WELL, I S'PPOSE," he said, grinning.

Brian's fat stalker was getting more restless. She probably wanted something to eat. She asked when we were going to go, and I snapped, "Why don't you go look out the window some more until we are ready to leave?"

I couldn't stand this girl. She was Gothic before Gothic was cool. She had jet black hair, eye makeup that made her look like an overstuffed Elvira, baggy black jeans, and a black T-shirt. I wasn't sure if her dark brooding personality was part of the act or if that was actually her. She was a pain in the ass.

Dad was in a talkative mood. He said, "YOU KNOW, ONCE HAMPTON AND I RETIRE, WE ARE PLANNING ON MOVING UP TO SOUTH DAKOTA."

"Really? What are you going to do up there?" Brian and I asked, almost in unison.

"WE THOUGHT WE'D GET A LITTLE FARM PLACE AND RAISE HOGS."

"Why do you want to do that?" Brian asked.

I suppose Dad didn't really care what he did as long as it was with Hampton.

We stayed and talked to Dad for quite a while before we finally gave in to Lonnie's sighs. Besides, I had to get back to college and still had a two-and-a-half-hour drive ahead of me.

Just as we were ready to get into the car, we turned and looked up. Dad was standing in the window. We waved. He waved back. I felt an unexpected shudder of fear and sadness wash over me. Somehow I knew it was going to be the last time I saw him.

Brian sensed it. "What's wrong?" he asked.

"I don't know why, but I don't think he is coming home."

* * *

I couldn't believe he was dead.

I looked toward my desk in the corner. On top was the last Christmas card I got from him. Dad wasn't much on buying Christmas presents, but he'd bring cards to the house and throw them on the tree Christmas morning with the same kind of gusto with which he attacked everything else. Inside, he'd write a line or two and stuff money in the cards. The amount varied from year to year, depending on how he was doing financially—this last year, it was fifty dollars.

I thought about what he wrote on my card last Christmas—less than a month ago:

Good God what a wonderful son you are.
How lucky can one dad be anyway?
All my love, Dad.

How much those words meant to me. Now he was gone.

Dad had boundless energy. He got up every morning at 5:00 no matter how late he went to bed. Dad never missed work, and he worked like he was killing snakes when he was on the job. Even on that Sunday, the last time I saw him, he was energetic as he told us about the old veterans.

I thought he was indestructible. He was rough as a cob—the strongest man I knew. Even though he was only five-foot-seven, he was still the strongest. He was a plasterer, and for thirty-five years, he mixed mud and plastered walls and ceilings. The labor had made his chest and arms huge, and his fingers were fat and thick and muscular. His fingers looked like sausage links with hair and fingernails.

Silence.

"What happened?"

"We don't know all of the details, yet. But the vets' hospital called this morning about five-thirty. Brian answered, and they told him that his father had died. They wanted to know if they could have permission to do an autopsy."

"So, what happened? We were just there Sunday. Dad was fine. He was supposed to get out today."

"I don't know, honey." There was another pause.

One of my roommates pushed the pillow off his head and screamed, "Who the fuck is on the phone this early in the morning?"

"My father died," I said faintly. I wanted to stuff a sock in his mouth and beat his head with a shoe, but I was still dazed and trying to process what my mom was telling me.

He covered his head with his pillow and rolled over. My other roommate got up and bolted from the room. Neither of them had ever had a relative die. Neither of them had ever even been to a funeral. Their lives had been untouched by death.

I was from a small town in which Mom ran a tavern. We knew nearly everyone in Logan one way or another. In small towns we all turned out for funerals. Everyone showed up for the viewing of the body the night before the funeral. We sent food to the grieving family's home—a pie, a cake, cookies, or a ham, something. And then the day of the funeral we gave the family a card with money in it. Usually it wasn't a lot but something to help out. In her tavern, Mom always put out a money jar with the dead person's name taped to it and then sent the collection to the family to help pay for funeral expenses.

"Do you think we should go ahead with the autopsy?" Mom asked.

"I suppose. I don't know," I answered.

My thoughts turned to more practical matters. I didn't have a car. How was I going to get home for the funeral? How could I get home the quickest possible way? I didn't want to take the bus. Ames was only 131 miles from Logan on the highway—the Lincoln Highway. On a clear day with dry roads, it only took a little more than two hours to drive home, but on a bus, it took five and a half hours.

For years, a sign outside of town proclaimed boldly and proudly: "Logan, the whitest town in the U.S.A." This is what greeted the odd traveler as he traversed the old Lincoln Highway through Logan. I say *through* Logan because there isn't much to stop for these days. Logan had been a thriving town with five banks, three grocery stores, a dry goods store, a movie theater, the Candy Kitchen where fine caramels and chocolates were hand-dipped by Italian immigrants, an opera house, the Lusk Hotel, and a train depot before the stock market crash of 1929. Only one bank survived and only because the family who owned it could squeeze an Indian-head nickel so tight the buffalo on the flip side would fart. Man, were they tight.

I thought about how lonely and desolate it was to sit on the bus, watching the lights of each little town and farmstead pass by on my way home. It was hard enough to take the waiting during just a regular trip home. I knew it was going to be terribly hard thinking about dad being dead for five and a half hours with no family on the bus to talk to about it.

Mom said she had to get a hold of my other brothers, Mike and Deke, and that she would call me back quickly. I sat down in the dark to wait. It was January, and the sun hadn't risen yet, though it was beginning to get lighter. You could begin to see the garish lime green walls in my room.

The phone rang again. My roommate turned over. "Mom?" I asked.

"Yes," she said into the phone. "Brian is going to come and get you."

"I can take the bus, Mom," I protested weakly. "It's such a long way for him to drive just to pick me up, and then we have to turn right around and drive back."

"No," she argued, "he says that he wants to come and get you."

While I waited for Brian to come, I decided to write notes to my professors. I sat at my desk in near darkness, so as not to disturb the sleeping mental giant who had pulled the pillow over his head.

After I had the notes written out, I slipped them into envelopes, bundled up, and headed out of the dorm to deliver them. I put a roll of Scotch tape in my pocket, so I could tape the notes to the office doors for each professor.

It was before 8:00 as I walked to their offices. I headed toward Ross Hall, a tall office building of concrete boxes stacked on top of one another with windows. The 1970s was a bad decade for design—any design—oversized bow ties, plaid pants, autumn-colored shag carpeting, avocado appliances, plump cars with hatchbacks, and buildings that looked like glass and concrete boxes. This building was proof of that. Ross Hall looked out of place on campus. It is to the left and slightly behind Curtis Hall, a stately old building of stone, and next to the Farm House, the oldest building on campus. I was taking a history survey class at Marston Hall, and my professor's office was in Ross Hall. I went up to the eighth floor and taped the note to his door, then went down the elevator and out.

I made the turn to the walkway that led to Central Campus and trudged across it. I walked to the Design Center and left a note for my drawing teacher. That was the furthest I had to walk. I circled back to leave the rest of the notes on my way back to the dorm. I stopped in the library. I was taking an art class there and also Library 186. That was an easy class everyone had to take so they could look things up in the library using the Library of Congress system. No more Dewey Decimal once you got to college. I stopped at Pearson Hall. Pearson was a three-story brick building next to Marston and behind Beardshear, the neoclassic old administration building with Corinthian columns. I was taking French and Speech 211 in Pearson. I had gotten into speech early because the woman I had rented from my first two quarters at college had worked on campus for twenty years. She told me if I gave a certain woman in Beardshear a bottle of wine, she would get me into Speech 211. It was nearly impossible to get into when you were a freshman.

Then it was back to the dorm.

As I walked back, I was just wishing I could be home. I just wanted to be with people who knew Dad, people who loved him. I wanted to talk about our memories of him and how much we missed him. I felt a terrible emptiness.

I walked along the sidewalks at Iowa State and heard the snow crunching under my feet.

U.S. Highway 30 into Logan, Iowa

2

"The closer to the bone, the sweeter the meat."

THE LONG RIDE HOME

Brian showed up at about 11:00 in the morning. It took nearly two and a half hours to drive the 131 miles from Logan to Ames along U.S. 30, the old Lincoln Highway.

When Brian got there, he was with Kitty, my girlfriend at the time, though our relationship was starting to fall apart—a great hazard in the family. Kitty was beautiful and spirited. She had dark brown, shoulder-length hair and clear, big, bright blue eyes. She had high cheekbones, the kind you'd expect to see on a model, and an aquiline nose. Her skin was perfect—smooth, creamy white, and flawless. Kitty's five-foot-five frame didn't weigh more than 110 pounds soaking wet. Two of her most attractive features, though, were her long, thin, shapely legs.

Kitty was four years older than I was. I knew Kitty long before we started dating. I knew nearly everyone in town—everybody knew everybody. She pulled her car up next to me one Sunday night while I was out for a walk.

"Say," she said, "do you want to go for a ride?" I did, so I got in.

She was wearing a blue and white gingham shirt and Daisy Dukes. She was forward. I was shy. From that point on, we were dating.

Over the following months, we got to know each other.

Ounce for ounce, Kitty was the most hot-tempered woman I'd known, outside of any girl or woman in my family, of course. The Rifes grew them fairly hot tempered, too.

Kitty was driving her 1972 copper and white, two-tone Ford Mustang, the last year the Mustang still looked sporty. I knew the car intimately—inside and out, you might say.

During one of our many arguments, she tried to run me over—successfully, I might add. One hot summer afternoon, Kitty suggested that I mow her yard. We were watching a Bob Hope special of some kind on television. Neither of us was really paying much attention to it.

"Since it is a nice day, I think it would be a good time for you to mow," she said.

"I would rather do something else today. Let's enjoy the day. I can mow tomorrow." I really wasn't in the mood to mow.

"It might not be as nice tomorrow as it is today."

"Since I do the mowing, don't you think that I should decide when to mow?"

That all seemed quite logical to me. I just wanted to enjoy the day and do nothing. I could tell, though, that the conversation was heating up.

"Besides," I said, "I am watching Bob Hope."

"You've got to be kidding," she said. "You are a little young to be a Bob Hope fan."

"I think Bob Hope is timeless."

"I think his jokes are stale. Why don't you mow?"

"I don't feel like mowing. I told you that," I said. I could feel myself digging in. The argument was escalating.

Kitty sprang to her feet and bolted out to the garage.

The argument elevated to a monumental scale, and before I knew it, it had taken on a life of its own, moving from the little light-green house she was renting to the garage. We were shouting at each other all the way. She hopped into the car, slammed the door, and backed out of the garage and into the street. I ran in front of the car to offer a much-too-late compromise.

By this time, our raised voices had caught the attention of her neighbor across the street, and he came out of his garage to watch the fray unfold.

"Oh, c'mon, let's talk about this."

I could see her face through the windshield. Kitty was pissed. She stepped on the gas pedal with all of the weight and force she could muster, and the car lurched forward.

I didn't get out of the way fast enough, and the front of the Mustang scooped me up onto the hood. For a moment, I replaced the Mustang pony.

She quickly turned into the gravel alleyway next to her neighbor's garage with me hanging on, then she suddenly slammed on the brakes. I flew like I had been jettisoned from a circus cannon into the alley. I felt the sting of gravel being ground into my knees and the palms of my hands as I landed. I scrambled to the side of the road as fast as I could as she gunned the Mustang again. This time, though, she wasn't aiming for me. As Kitty sped by, I collected myself and got to my feet.

Her neighbor, ever the master of understatement, sauntered out of his garage and said, "I suppose she's upset about something?"

"Yeah, something like that."

I walked back to her house, went inside to close the windows, and then left, pulling the door shut and locked behind me. I walked home.

A near miss with a Mustang can certainly tame your passion for a woman. I was really wondering if I wanted the same kind of relationship that I'd seen Mom and Dad live out.

That all happened the summer before Dad died.

Dad had met her.

Mom and I had been barbecuing in Mom's backyard when Dad stopped by. Even though they were divorced, Dad would pop in now and then. Kitty was there, too. Kitty was wearing a white T-shirt and a pair of denim short-shorts, leaning over the grill and looking at the hamburgers when Dad walked into the backyard. Her round cheeks were peeking out from her shorts. He had never met her, though he had certainly heard about her.

When he saw her, he asked me, "IS THAT THE CAT LADY?"

Kitty's Siamese caused me to break out with hives. She said she had the cat before she had me and was not going to get rid of it no matter what it did to me.

"Yes, that's Kitty," I answered.

"SHE'S GOT LEGS JUST LIKE I LIKE 'EM. THEY START ON EARTH AND GO ALL THE WAY TO HEAVEN. BUT SHE'S A SKINNY-LEGGED LITTLE THING, ISN'T SHE?" Then Dad said with a wink, "THE CLOSER TO THE BONE, THE SWEETER THE MEAT." Even though he was trying to make the comment in a discrete way, his voice was so loud and carried so far that she heard it clearly.

Kitty whipped around on one heel and said, "Wilbur, there are more important things than skinny legs!"

Dad looked at me and said, "OH, SHE'S FEISTY, TOO. I LIKE THAT." He laughed, but Kitty wasn't amused. He didn't care.

* * *

When Kitty and Brian pulled up, I was relieved. I was also glad to see Kitty behind the wheel instead of Brian. While Kitty could intentionally be a hazard to a pedestrian she had her Mustang's sights set on, Brian, a notoriously inattentive driver, was an unintentional hazard.

I was in a car with Brian in Omaha when he was merging into traffic. The car coming down the street wouldn't let Brian in, so he jumped the curb and drove on the sidewalk until the car passed and then veered into the traffic lane.

I was in a car with Brian when we drove down to Missouri Valley to pick up liquor for Mom's tavern from the state-owned liquor store. Brian hit the back of the building as we pulled up to the back door and scraped the back of the car against the building as we pulled away after we had loaded the boxes of liquor.

I was in a car with Brian as he pulled out from the parking lot behind Mom's bar, barely missing the back of truck but coming so close that it snapped the side mirror off our 1962 Impala.

Brian was a hazard behind the wheel.

Brian and Kitty stepped out of the car. They both gave me a hug.

Brain asked, "How are you doing?"

"I can't believe it. We just saw him Sunday," I said. I felt myself start to tear up. He was the first person I could talk to that day. Obviously my roommates had been no comfort. "He was supposed to get out today."

"I guess he did," Brian said, with sad irony in his voice.

Kitty had popped the trunk on the Mustang, and I threw my bag in.

"Do you want to drive?" she asked me.

"No, go ahead."

Kitty got behind the wheel.

Brian said he'd take the back seat and pushed the release that snapped the bucket seat forward. He climbed into the back seat of the car, and I sat down in the bucket seat on the passenger side.

The door slammed shut, and Kitty started the car. The first few blocks were tough. I wanted to talk, but I didn't know what to say. I was still in shock.

When I left the hospital ward on Sunday, I had felt like something was worse than we were being led to believe, but I couldn't put my finger on it. Two days later, I found out that gut feeling was right.

There was a long silence, which was broken by Brian's question, "Do you think Dad believed in God?"

"He certainly invoked His name a lot if he didn't," I said half-jokingly.

"No, seriously."

"Yes, I suppose he did in his own way. Though, I know he didn't particularly think God was doing a very good job of running things."

"What? What do you mean?" asked Brian.

"Don't you remember how Dad would say, 'IF THERE IS A GOD IN HEAVEN, I CAN DO A BETTER JOB'?" I turned around in my seat to look at Brian.

"No, I don't remember that."

"Oh, yeah, I remember the first time I heard him say that, I wanted to get under a lead shield before the lightning struck. He said, 'NO, REALLY, IF THERE'S A GOD IN HEAVEN, I CAN DO A BETTER JOB. FOR INSTANCE, WHY DOES IT FLOOD OUT PEOPLE IN ONE PLACE AND DROUGHT IN ANOTHER PLACE? WHY WOULD GOD LET PEOPLE STARVE TO DEATH? I COULD MAKE IT RAIN WHERE CROPS NEEDED IT. FOLKS COULD GROW FOOD; NO ONE WOULD GO HUNGRY.'"

Dad had felt that hunger. He knew the feeling of starvation firsthand, which was why he always made us eat whatever we put on our plates. He was a member of the clean plate club—and we were to be, too. When he would say, "THERE ARE PEOPLE STARVING IN THIS WORLD," he wasn't thinking of foreign places and faceless people. The person he pictured had a face he recognized—a little boy living along the foothills in Harrison County, Iowa. A little boy whose mother had left him alone and hungry to go off with another man.

Clyde and Ada Rife, wedding day, 1916

3

"I'd just as soon hear a dawg howl."

CLYDE AND ADA

"Do you think Dad loved us?" Brian asked me as we drove toward Logan.

Another question. Brian was really turning this all over in his head trying to make some sense of it.

"Yes, I do."

"Well, he sure didn't show it very often."

"I just think he didn't really know how to express it. After all, think about where he came from. Who would have taught him about love?"

"Yeah, I know. Grandma didn't know how to love anybody but herself," he said. It was said as fact because we all grew up knowing it.

Dad never really had a chance to learn about being loved—the long legacy of benign neglect and active abuse had been handed down several generations on his mother's side until he finally inherited its full wrath.

* * *

Dad's maternal grandfather was Amos Harrison Anderson. He went by Harry, a bastardization of Harrison, which seemed appropriate. It was said that he was just one step ahead of a posse most of his adult life. He was a ne'er-do-well itinerant farmer and sharecropper who was constantly on the move.

Harry was tall, thin, and often unshaven, with a long, drawn, gaunt face. His cheekbones were high and his chin strong, and his skin stretched thin across his face, leaving deep lines and giving him the appearance of a skeleton with gray stubble and a hat. Harry's blue eyes were deeply set into his skull. He wore glasses, the wire kind that held the lenses together with no frame. Most of the time he had a mustache streaked with as much gray hair as black. He wore denim overalls, then the uniform of farmers. It made him look the part. To dress up for dances, where he played his fiddle, he'd cover his overalls with a black suit jacket. Sometimes he'd wear a tie.

His wife, Sarah Caroline Harrow Anderson, known as Callie, was shorter than Harry and round. Her hair was always pulled into a bun with more strands out than in. It looked like she had a dust mop on her head. She wore a loose housedress with an apron, both of which were dirty.

Callie couldn't stand Harry or his fiddle playing.

About his music, she'd say, "I'd just as soon hear a dawg howl," drawing out the word *dog* almost as if it had two syllables. Harry, though, was reported to be good on the violin. He'd go to barn dances all around and play. When Ada, my dad's mom, was young, she would accompany Harry to the dances and chord on the organ.

Callie didn't like it, no, sir. More than likely, the fiddle playing wasn't really the source of her irritation. It probably had far more to do with what happened at the dances and who Harry came into contact with there. Women's fascination with musicians didn't start with rock 'n' rollers.

Callie's temper wasn't reserved for just Harry either. Callie slapped her children for no reason as they passed by her. She'd raise her fleshy arms and warn them, "Dodge. You know you need it!" as she swatted at them. She had an explosive temper and got so angry once she kicked the doors off the kitchen cupboards in a fit of madness.

Harry and Callie had a hard time making it. Harry had many jobs—he farmed, cut wood and sold it, supervised a streetcar crew in South Omaha, and worked on the railroad at odd jobs and as a laborer, a tenant farmer, or a sharecropper in the sugar beet fields.

The family was constantly on the move. Nearly every one of their eleven children was born in a different place—Emma and Nona were born in California Junction, Iowa; Albert "Buck" was born on Crow Island, Iowa; Orie somewhere in Missouri; Opa Pearl in Blair, Nebraska; Ada (my Grandma) in Arlington, Nebraska; Lorena "Bill," no one remembers where; Frederick "Ted" was born in South Omaha, Nebraska; Irvan "Boone" in Hershey, Nebraska; Myrtle in Little Sioux, Iowa; and Harriet Caroline was born in Blencoe, Iowa.

Sometimes they lived in abandoned farmhouses. Sometimes, when times were good, the family had enough money to pay for rent. When Harry worked as a tenant farmer, the family lived in the tenant house. Sometimes Harry fought with other squatters to take over a vacant house in Council Bluffs that the family returned to several winters in a row.

His most steady occupation was as a worker in the sugar beet fields of southern Minnesota. Harry was a beet man. He knew beets. He almost always worked the beet fields as a supervisor.

His brood did the backbreaking work of blocking and thinning the beets. When the kids turned five or six, according to Harry, they were old enough to work the beets. Harry would load his family up, and they'd leave Council Bluffs around the middle of March to go to the beet fields to plant the beets and work the fields until the beets were harvested.

The kids wrapped rags around their knees to pad them as they crawled up and down the beet fields. Even Myrtle, the baby of the family, was not exempted. She had bright red hair and the fair pale skin that usually comes with it. When she worked the fields, she had to cover her head to keep the sun from blistering her tender skin.

The beets were planted in close rows. As the beets came up, the kids worked as blockers. The blockers crawled along and thinned the beets. Then, there was a first and second hoeing. Slowly, painstakingly, the weeds had to be spotted and pulled. Harry's kids had clean fields or there would be hell to pay and it would be on somebody's ass!

Harry and his brood would work the beet fields until the season was over. Then they'd go back down to Council Bluffs and move right back in the house they'd left months earlier. Often they had to chase out squatters. They would get through the winter and then start the cycle all over again. Life mirrored the growing cycle of the sugar beet.

When the boys got older, Harry took them to Nebraska and Iowa for various jobs. Buck, the oldest boy, was farmed out to a sugar mill. Ted got a job wiping and greasing farm equipment engines at night. And the younger kids headed back to Minnesota with Harry and Callie.

Harry did not treat his children well. He whipped them and worked them hard. It had even been rumored that Harry had forced himself on his daughters. One of his daughters became pregnant, and the family left River Sioux quickly. The rumor, of course, was that Harry was the father of the child. When the kids thought back to their childhood, they weren't wistful about a wonderful time gone by.

* * *

Clyde, my dad's father, was the son of George and Annie Rife. Clyde was one of a pair of twins. His actual name was Claude, and his twin sister's name was Maude. Probably cute for 1886. Clyde was described as his mama's favorite—a gentle and happy boy who loved and teased his sisters. He was quick with a smile and a joke. He was good with horses, like most of the Rifes.

George had a whole passel of kids. He had three children with his first wife. She died in childbirth, as did her unborn third child. George remarried, and Clyde was part of this second family. Clyde was one of fourteen—Margaret "Maggie," Benjamin Franklin "Frank," Claude "Clyde," Maude, Mae, Forney, Blendena "Dena," Dora, Ada, Dewey, Irvin, Geraldine, Geneva, and Emmogene.

So, this farmer's son and this sharecropper's daughter found love. On Wednesday, January 12, 1916, Clyde and Ada drove up to Onawa to the courthouse to get married. They were married in the middle of the week. No one does that, but they did. It might have been an impetuous move on their part or the urgency of their circumstances. Clyde was thirty years old to Ada's seventeen years when they were married. She had been itching to get out of her parents' house, and Clyde was her ticket. She didn't want any more of the beet fields or playing chords on the pump organ for dances.

After the ceremony in the courthouse, the couple went to a photography studio in Onawa. At the time their photograph was taken, Ada was three months pregnant. There were rumors that the baby belonged to the janitor at the Rue School in Council Bluffs.

But then, Clyde hadn't been an angel either. He had fathered a daughter, named Myrna, with Rena Brunstedt. Clyde and Rena had been going together, but when she found out she was pregnant, she started dating another guy by the name of Smith.

* * *

Brian broke in. "How did you know that Grandpa had a baby with this woman?"

"Dad took me over to meet Uncle Dewey and Aunt Pearl at Sioux. Aunt Pearl told me the story. Reluctantly, too, I would say. Not the kind of stuff people from her generation like to or feel comfortable talking about."

I remembered the conversation all too well. Great Aunt Dora had added a few desperate details too.

Great Aunt Dora had begun, "Rena and Clyde dated quite a little while. But there was a guy in Little Sioux, his name was Smith. Rena thought because he was a town boy that she wanted to go with him awhile. So, her and Clyde had a date to go to *Uncle Tom's Cabin*."

Uncle Tom's Cabin was a theater production that played in Little Sioux every year where it wintered before the company took it on the road. The first shows would open in the spring, along about April every year.

"So," continued Great Aunt Dora, "Rena told Clyde she didn't want to go after all. Clyde decided to go to the play anyway and saw Rena. After Clyde saw Rena with Smith, that cooked it; she gave him the mitten!"

Great Aunt Pearl jumped in then, "She claimed that that's who got her pregnant. She had gone with him a couple of times. He didn't want to marry her. He knowed that baby wasn't his. But he did marry her. Ya know, she told him she'd make him marry her. So he married her and the day, the minute, the baby was born, why he left."

Kitty tapped her fingers on the wheel. "Do you think that the girl knew who her father was?" she asked.

"Well, a funny thing happened. Aunt Pearl told me that Rena got sick and decided that Myrna had a right to know who her real father was. So she called Myrna in and said, 'Myrna, I want to tell you something. Clyde Rife is really your daddy, and I want you to know that before I die, who your father really is.' So, the beans were out, and she lived quite a while after that."

"Ain't nothing wrong with our family, so why didn't she want to marry Grandpa Clyde?" Brian asked.

"According to Aunt Pearl, Rena didn't think he was good enough for her. And this other man had more—he owned a grocery store, little better educated, and all that."

* * *

Clyde grew up with farming in his veins. By all accounts, he was a good horseman and a hard worker, with the same clean and neat tendencies as his mother. Clyde farmed and worked as a section foreman for the Chicago and Northwestern Railroad. He often lived in bunk cars during the week while he worked on the railroad then went home on the weekends.

Clyde and Ada moved around quite a bit during their marriage. Lucy Mae Ruth, whom Clyde called "Sis," was their first child. She was born in a little house in River Sioux. Frederick Clyde, who Clyde called "Big Boy," was born in the section house on the road between Little Sioux and the

Little Sioux Cemetery. Wilbur Merle, "Little Boy," was born in a house at the base of the foothills on what was known as the Jardine Ranch.

Clyde was working as a tenant farmer for Gus Pearson at the time Little Boy was born, in the 1920s. Ada did some cooking for the family. Clyde and Ada lived in the tenant farmer's house, a big square house right alongside of a dike. It had a fountain in the backyard.

Also on the grounds was a cemetery. Surrounding the cemetery was a concrete wall over five feet high. Pilasters with pointed tops punctuated the walls every so often. It looked like a castle fortress. To the three kids, it represented hours of fun. A large tree grew just outside the wall. Lucy, Freddie, and Wilbur would climb all the way out on a limb and drop themselves into the cemetery on the other side of the wall, just as if they were storming the fortress walls.

The kids also played endless games of marbles. In those days, ten wooden marbles only cost a penny. Both boys were good marble players—even as a young'un Dad had strong fingers. Like most older brothers, Freddie would tease Wilbur when they were playing. Freddie would yell, "Grabbies!" Then he would scoop up all the marbles that were laid out in the big circle and run off with them. Wilbur would sit on the ground and cry. Freddie would take the snatched loot and hide the marbles up in a crawl space in the attic in a big glass jar where Wilbur couldn't reach them.

At the time, the family felt pretty prosperous. Clyde even had a car— he drove a 1914 Model T Ford. It was an early model that started by cranking it. To make the cranking easier, he would jack up the back end to start the thing. It was black, of course. Famously, Henry Ford said of his Model T, "You can have it in any color as long as it is black." Fifteen million Model Ts were sold—one of them to Clyde Rife.

The Rife family did a lot of things with the Pearsons. Sometimes, Wilma Pearson, their oldest daughter, would come over to watch the kids. She was quite a beautiful woman. The families were so close, in fact, that my dad—Wilbur—was named for Wilma Pearson.

One afternoon Wilma was at the house and everyone decided to go into Sioux for something or other. Clyde had jacked up the back end of the car and was cranking away.

Ada was sitting in the front of the car and was supposed to have turned on the switch. Clyde didn't get frustrated very often. But he had been cranking the car to get it started for quite some time when he realized Ada had not turned the switch over.

Sweat was pouring down his face as he let loose in disgust and frustration, "Oh, wouldn't that frost your balls!"

Just then, he looked up and saw Wilma sitting in the front seat next to Ada. He quickly added, "If ya had any."

Another site of great fun was nearby Smith Lake. Many hot days were spent there with the kids splashing around. The family often went there to swim, fish, picnic, and listen to oratory at the various Chautauquas that were put on.

Smith Lake was created when the Missouri River changed its path and left a lake standing that was fed by several springs. The lake was named for Solomon Smith, who owned the land that the lake occupied. Solomon Smith was surely named after the wise king in the Bible.

The Winnebago Indians believed that the lake was inhabited by evil spirits. Later, settlers believed that the lake was inhabited by the area's own version of the Loch Ness monster. Some even claimed to have had an exchange with the fifteen-foot, lizard-like creature and to even have killed it, though no evidence was ever produced to verify the claim.

The only verified spirits that could be found at the lake were the liquid kind, and those were found there on a regular basis.

Clyde and Ada often went to Smith Lake on Friday and Saturday nights to dance at the pavilion, a round wooden building built so part of it was cantilevered over the lake. The dance band was on an elevated platform in the middle of the building, and the couples danced around the band. On the part of the building that jutted out over the water were a couple of doors that led out to a balcony with a railing. Folks went out to get some fresh air, look over the water, and to grab a smoke during the band breaks. On a few occasions, fights broke out, and nearly every time, the loser went right over the railing into the lake. Truth be told, folks didn't think it was much of a fight if somebody didn't hit the water.

Just under the main part of the building were the bathrooms, which were hardly more than his and hers two-seater outhouses. They were constructed in such a slipshod way that the gaps in between the boards were big enough to look through. All the boys knew where the best gaps were, and they'd sneak down there and look all nonchalant until the girls went to pee, then they'd press their faces up to the boards to watch. With all of the extra material in the dresses in those days, most everything kept covered, but occasionally a boy would claim to see a flash of skin that made it all worthwhile.

All sorts of folks turned out for the dances. It actually became a problem for Clyde because Ada was constantly flirting with the men at the dances, and the mix of night air and large amounts of booze heightened his sense of jealousy and her sense of flirtation.

This place of dancing, gyrating, drinking, and malintent-ing was also the site of gospel revivals and spirits of a higher kind to illuminate and inspire the faithful.

The minister at one of the largest revivals at the lake was reputed to be charismatic. Ada was drawn to him. Maybe it was because she fought the battle of good and evil inside her, and she hoped to chase away a few of her own demons. Maybe it was so she could be swept away in the excitement of the revival, the thrilling sermon, the pulsating music, the energy of the crowd. Whatever it was, she was drawn in. Ada was always battling her baser impulses. This was to be a place of redemption. Ironic that it had also been a place of temptation.

The men and women and children flocked to the edge of Smith Lake where a canvas tent had been set up. Chairs filled the tent. In the front stood the preacher, and to the side was a choir.

"Have you received the Holy Spirit?" cried the minister. "Today you will receive the Holy Spirit!" Folks sat in folding chairs and fanned themselves. The feeling of excitement was in the air. It was mixed and mingled with the steam rising from the lake on the hot, sultry summer Iowa afternoon.

"The Bible says, 'Tarry ye here in Jerusalem 'til you're imbued with power from on high.' Jesus told when he was going to send them into the sky and so they tarried in the upper room and they was all in one accord a-praying and the Holy Ghost fell as living, as tongues of fire."

Ada had taken Wilbur to the Smith Lake revival. He was a small boy. He sat in his chair, wiggling around to get a better view of the minister.

The minister's booming voice wafted over the crowd, "They describe it that way as tongues of fire. They all talk in different languages. But without the baptism of the Holy Spirit, you won't have very many gifts. The gifts come after the baptism of the Holy Spirit. You have the gift of help and the gift of discernment and the gift of knowledge and wisdom and all kinds of things you have." The preacher walked in front of the assembled people under the tent with his Bible held high in the air. He spoke loudly so all of the folks could hear him.

"The Holy Spirit never embarrasses anybody," he said. "There are some here who are one thing in the church and something else outside of church. I say to you—get out! The journey starts in the House of God. God wants you to be more perfect. And God, God talks to us ever' Sunday. He talks to us." It was as if the minister was talking directly to Ada, who had secretly been rendezvousing with Charlie Gillett. Charlie was a tall, thin, ruggedly handsome man who had come to town looking for work. It started innocently enough—a conversation about who was hiring, places that needed a hand. Then it changed; there was a spark. After Clyde took off on Monday mornings in the bunk cars to work the week with the section crew, the two would meet up.

One young lady wearing a white linen dress raised her hand up in the air and received the spirit of the Holy Ghost. She twirled around and fell to the ground.

Several young men sprang to their feet to help the young woman get up and back into the chair. But the preacher said, "Stand back. She's okay! It don't hurt you when you fall on the floor when the Lord knocks you down. It don't hurt ya!"

Moved by the preaching and the events and feelings around them, several men and women started to dance in the spirit under the canvas tent. There was a great movement of God.

The minister led the faithful into the water to baptize the believers. Ada and Wilbur walked into the lake to receive the Holy Spirit for themselves and to be baptized. They were baptized that day in the waters of the oxbow lake created by the turn of the river. For Wilbur, it was a moment of wonder. Here he was in Smith Lake, surrounded by people of all shapes and sizes, being dunked under water in the name of the Lord.

It was not transformational enough for Ada.

Clyde sensed that things were different. He and Ada bickered. Accusations were traded. Ada denied that she was doing anything wrong but she continued to sneak off with Charlie as soon as Clyde took off for the week to work on the railroad. Ada would load the kids up into a buckboard and drive it to a nearby field where she would meet Charlie.

Charlie was a smooth talker. He would be standing in among the rows of corn waiting for Ada to show up. She would pack a few things for the kids to play with in the buckboard and then would wander off into the corn field. The kids would see the corn rattle and hear faint thrashing noises and muffled sounds coming from their mother, but they weren't sure exactly what was going on.

These were bad times for the kids. Their parents were constantly arguing. Ada would get pissed off, pull the kids out of school, and pack up the car. Before she left, though, she would rifle through Clyde's bib overalls. He had a habit of leaving a stash of money in the watch pocket. She'd take it all, not leaving anything for him. She'd load the kids in the car and away she'd go. Always to Council Bluffs down to her sister's house. Charlie was always close behind.

Clyde started drinking quite a bit, though he never missed a day of work and was always gentle and loving toward the kids.

Ada, though, wanted to be with Charlie.

Ada finally moved out for good in 1928. She moved down to Council Bluffs and filed for divorce. She claimed that she had moved to Council Bluffs as a measure of good faith and not for the express purpose of obtaining a divorce. The truth was that she was living with her sister, but she was also free to cavort with Charlie whenever she pleased and there wasn't anything that Clyde could do about it. The big question was what would happen to the children. Lucy was eleven years old, Fred was just nine, and Wilbur was four.

The divorce was contentious. Ada had made some pretty ugly charges, telling the judge that Clyde had been guilty of cruel and inhuman treatment and had threatened her life. She claimed that Clyde had beaten her and cussed at her using profane, vile, and obscene epithets.

He countered with the fact that she had been screwing around with other men.

She countered with his drinking. Ada claimed Clyde had become a drunkard since their marriage. Divorce was inevitable at that point. It seemed natural, really.

Our family was what you would call early adopters—early adopters of divorce, way before it was fashionable.

Ada pleaded with the court through her attorney to be divorced from Clyde. She was given sole care of their daughter, Lucy May, and all of the household furniture. Clyde was given custody of his two boys, Freddie and Wilbur. Each had "reasonable" visitation rights.

Seems odd that a mother concerned about the harm being done to her children because of the drunken abuse of their father would then agree to leave two of her children in her drunken husband's custody, but that is exactly what she did. She didn't want to be burdened with three children, especially two small rambunctious boys. Ada essentially abandoned her sons.

The divorce was granted and over. The bonds of matrimony existing between them were set aside by the judge, who also restored to Ada all rights, privileges, and responsibilities of a single and unmarried person, except the right to remarry. She had to wait one year from the date of the decree to get remarried.

Grandma didn't wait, of course. She not only had hot pants for someone else, but she was carrying his baby. On September 17, just a month after her divorce was made final and eleven months before she could legally remarry, she married Charlie Gillett.

George and Annie Rife with their twins, Claude and Maude, 1886

4

"She was no bigger than a pint of soap after two weeks of washin'."

LIVING WITH ANNIE RIFE

We were driving Highway 30 when I asked Brian, "Has anyone got hold of Uncle Ron to tell him Dad died?"

"I think Deke was going to try to get word to him through Jack Peterson. I guess they stay in touch."

"Really? The barber in Missouri Valley Deke goes to?"

"Yeah," Brian replied, "I guess they have been friends for decades, and Jack usually knows how to get in touch with Uncle Ron. I know whenever he needs a little loan, Jack has always been there to help him out."

"He must pay Jack back, or he wouldn't be too quick to let Uncle Ron keep borrowing!"

Brian laughed.

Jack was originally from Sioux, and even though Ron didn't grow up there, he went often enough to visit Ada's family to build friendships.

Dad, though, he grew up in and around River Sioux.

* * *

When Ada moved out, Clyde, Fred, and Wilbur moved in with Annie. Annie Rife, Clyde's mother, was just freshly widowed.

The house was not big, but it was orderly and immaculate. When you entered the front door, there was an enclosed staircase leading directly up to two small bedrooms. Doors were on each side of the staircase. To the left was the kitchen. The kitchen was small, and right off that was a small porch on the north side covered in pine paneling. Even the ceiling. To the right of the staircase was an elegant parlor with a bay window facing the street. It, too, was paneled but with knotty pine. It was the nicest room in the house. The parlor opened up to the family room, or in those days what they called the back parlor. This room, too, had a door to a small open porch on the south side of the house.

The tiny house that Annie lived in had been in the family for quite some time before Clyde, Fred, and Wilbur moved in. The first members of the family to own the house were Dave and Serena Herring. Serena was one of George's four sisters.

Serena was fun loving and ornery. The story often told of her was how she had a hired man to do odd jobs. He was somewhat dimwitted. She liked him very much but also liked to play tricks on him. One night, Serena sat him down to give him strict instructions. She said, "Now, I don't want you to let the windmill run all night. Do you understand me?" He looked up to her and pledged that he would not. He said, "Oh, I don't let it run. I shut off the windmill every night."

That night, she waited until well after dark. She got up, put her robe on, and sneaked down to the windmill. Sure enough, the hired man had dutifully shut the windmill off. Serena turned the windmill on. The next morning, Serena called the hired man into the kitchen. She told him that she had checked the windmill as soon as she got up, and it was on. She accused him of leaving the windmill on. Serena acted angry just so she could watch the expression on his face before finally letting the cat out of the bag and revealing her trick.

Serena loved kids. She talked Clyde and Maude into going out with her and stealing watermelons from the neighboring farmer's melon patch. She let the kids snoop around in her front room and look at the pretty things. She always had a jar full of fresh-baked cookies in the basement for when her nieces and nephews came around. She'd say, "Go down in the basement and get you some cookies." Serena and Dave never had any of their own, but they did raise a niece and nephew.

When Dave and Serena decided to move to California in 1914, they sold the house to one of George's other sisters, Mary, and her husband, Jimmie Harmon.

Mary, who went mostly by Molly, was not Serena; in fact, she was the polar opposite. Molly was an old crank. She didn't have a fun, spirited disposition like her sister. In fact, she could be downright mean and nasty. So much so that she had a reputation for it all around the little town of Sioux. She used to say, "If you don't want your kids, I'll take them to the Sioux River and hold them under."

Molly was a heavy woman like the older Rife women. She was dark and round, and her stature was often described as five by five. Dad had said, "IT WAS EASIER TO JUMP OVER HER THAN TO WALK AROUND HER."

Maude took her kids, Billie and Vivian, to visit Molly. Molly had a parrot that was a natural attraction for curious kids. But Molly was touchy and shooed the kids away from the parrot's cage. Molly also had a little colt. Colts are notorious for kicking without warning. Naturally, Maude was concerned and didn't want her kids around the colt. Like most kids, they wanted to anyway.

"Please, please, please," begged Billie.

Molly said, "Let little Billie go out and pet the little colt," knowing full well the possible danger.

Maude stopped Billie and said, "Billie, you might get kicked."

Molly popped back, "Oh, I don't care if it kicks his head off."

Disgusted, Maude said, "If my children aren't welcome, then I'm not welcome either." At that, Maude, Billie, and Vivian left.

Another peculiarity of Molly's was her decked-out toilet. Molly had her outside toilet all fixed up with carpet to give it a rich, plush, comfortable feel. If the kids were out there too long, she'd start hollering, "Get out of there! What are you doing in there?"

Molly was married to James Harman, whom everyone called Uncle Jimmie. Jimmie had fought in the Civil War and came to Harrison County afterward to set up shop as a carpenter and handyman. He was nice, jolly.

But poor ol' Jimmie couldn't say a word because Molly would throw it back in his face. She would look at him and tell him what to do all the time. But he didn't pay much attention to her. If he had, he couldn't have lived with her. Mostly he listened and then went on and did what he was going to do anyway.

The young kids in the town liked to tease Molly because she was so excitable. They rode their bicycles through her yard so many times they wore a path in it. Molly was determined to stop them from racing around her place. Chasing after them and yelling had not worked, so she put a little white picket fence up around her yard. Since the bike path had been blocked, the kids started riding along her fence, banging sticks along it as they rode by. They knew the clatter bothered her.

Molly fumed.

Uncle Jimmie tried to get her to forget it. He tried to reason with her not to pick a fight with a bunch of kids having a little innocent fun. But Molly would have none of it. She hollered at them, which only inflamed the feud.

Eventually, she decided that she would get even and stop the kids from going along her fence once and for all. Molly spread carpet tacks on the bicycle path.

But the plan didn't quite work out the way she wanted it to. The afternoon she spread the tacks out on the path was the same afternoon

Uncle Jimmie decided to cross the street to have a beer. It was a hot day, and since the tavern was only a few steps away, Uncle Jimmie lit out in his stocking feet. When his feet hit those tacks, you could hear him cussing and yelling all over town!

*　*　*

Uncle Jimmie died at the age of seventy-three, shortly after he had eaten supper. He had suffered from heart trouble, and before Molly could call a doctor, he was gone. Alone and distraught, and hobbling on a cane, Molly decided she didn't want to live in the house by herself, so she asked her brother George to move in with her, along with his wife, Annie.

George had so many kids and grandchildren that Molly had a hard time avoiding children altogether, which is exactly what she wanted to do. She was laid up in bed a lot, and her only weapon was her cane, which she used and misused. When my dad's sister Lucy visited, she would sneak into the front parlor to tease Molly. Since the dislike was mutual, the game was elevated by Molly's desire to wrap the round part of her cane around Lucy's ankle. With a sharp jerk, Lucy would spill to the floor and cry. Off little Lucy would go, crying to her dad. "Now, Sis," Clyde would say, giving her a gentle rebuke, "I told you not to go in there with Aunt Molly."

The morning Molly died, George, Annie, and Emmogene, their teenage daughter, were in the kitchen. Annie was rattling around the kitchen making breakfast—eggs, bacon, toast, and coffee—and the house filled up with the warm smell of Annie's cooking. Usually Molly would have joined them by that point, but she was still in bed. Since Molly had been having trouble walking, George and Annie had set her bed up in the front parlor. Next to the bed was a nightstand. Her cane leaned up against the nightstand so she would have easy access to it when she awoke.

George asked, "Isn't Molly up yet?"

Annie said, "I don't think she's moved since I looked in there last."

George walked from the kitchen to the parlor to check on Molly. She was still in bed with the covers drawn up on her, facing the wall. George couldn't see her face. He also could not see her body heave up and down from the deep breathing of sleep. When he went to touch her shoulder, it was ice cold. She was dead. She had lain there so long that the side of her face against the pillow was turning color. Molly's cane was no longer a danger to any unsuspecting child who might wander into her path.

* * *

George was a short, stocky hardworking man. His full name was George Washington Henry Rife, but he just went by George. Robust, he was about five-foot-two with a large, barrel-shaped chest. He had a large, pronounced nose with a thick bushy mustache underneath. And he was loud. When he drove his horses into town from working them in the field, everyone in Sioux could hear him shouting instructions to them. He was a good horseman and farmer. It was said around Sioux that if George Rife couldn't raise a crop, nobody could.

By the time he had grandchildren, he was tired and didn't have much to do with them. I suppose he was just tired of kids since he'd had so many of his own.

To relax, he used to sit on the porch and whittle peach pits into things—little baskets and stuff like that. George would sit on that front porch with his pipe, smoking and whittling. Most of the time, he'd sit there, and if any of the kids came around to watch him, he'd run them off.

George liked to have a drink. Nearly all of the Rifes liked to drink. His problem was that he would not quit drinking until the barrel was empty. He worked hard and he played hard. George would always come home drunk after selling his grain. You could count on that. Sometimes he got mean after a bout of drinking, and sometimes the kids would have to hide until he slept it off.

George didn't drink beer so much as he drank whiskey. Often, though, it came down to what was available.

Annie didn't like drinking, and she would lock the door when he got liquored up. She hated the stuff. Sometimes, in the harvest fields, he'd get a barrel of beer. It wouldn't be in cans or in bottles, but in a barrel. Annie always said if he wouldn't hog it down like that, she wouldn't mind him having a beer or two. But George always stayed at the barrel until it was gone.

Sometimes after a good bender, George would fall asleep in the yard. Fred and Wilbur and sometimes their cousin, Gladys, would sit around and count the flies that would go in and out of his mouth.

One day, George was riding a load of straw over railroad tracks. The dirt had washed away from the ties, and when he went across the tracks, he was jostled off and fell on a post that struck him in the middle of the chest. For a while after, it was bothering his stomach, and he couldn't keep food down, so he went to see a doctor in Council Bluffs who said he had a growth where he fell on the post. Although it was not diagnosed as cancerous, the doctor was determined to operate to remove the growth. George took his clothes and left. He wouldn't let them touch him.

George finally agreed to go up to Onawa to have surgery because it was closer, but the same thing happened. When the time came for the surgery, he put his clothes on and went home.

Having lost quite a bit of weight and much of his strength because he hadn't been eating, George finally consented to surgery if the doctors would perform it at his home. They reluctantly agreed. They decided to put an opening in his stomach so Annie and Emmogene could feed him directly. George was laid out on the kitchen table, and the doctors did the surgery. Despite Annie's efforts to keep the wound clean, gangrene set in.

A few months later, Annie, Geneva, and Emmogene watched as he lay there in his bed, breathing deep and struggling. His eyes rolled back, and he exhaled. Geneva said, "He's gone." George Rife died in 1928, ten days shy of being seventy-seven years old. Annie, always stoic, held back her tears, but it was the first time in her married life that she was alone.

*　*　*

Clyde worked for the railroad as a section foreman—ten hours a day for three dollars and forty cents—a good job in those days. But it meant traveling most of the week, living in a boxcar, and getting home late on Friday nights. So, it made sense that Clyde and the boys, Wilbur and Freddie, would move in with Annie.

The boys had initially started at Kaufman School, a one-room schoolhouse that had all eight grades. Clyde asked the teacher if his two boys could both go to school there even though Wilbur was only four or five—not really of school age yet. The teacher said, "All right, Clyde, send him on, and I'll watch him." She just kinda babysat him at first. He sat on her lap, and she'd hold him because he was just a little guy.

When they moved to Annie's house in River Sioux, they switched schools and started going to the two-room schoolhouse in town. Even though they had two rooms of equal size, one room was called the little room and the other the big room. The little room had first through fourth grades, and the big room had fifth through eighth grades.

So, when Clyde, Fred, and Wilbur moved in, it was a mixed blessing. Clyde's sister Dora had always said that Clyde, a gentle man, was Annie's favorite. She said it in a way that wasn't resentful but rather showed that she understood. Clyde liked to tease and play tricks, and he had always babied and taken care of his mother. Dora said, "Lots of time, boys won't pay no attention to their mother very much."

Clyde always paid his way, too. He gave his mother room and board and extra money. He always got after his sisters if he walked in the house and his mama was working in the kitchen, puttering around, and the girls were sitting. He would give them a mild scolding, "Now here, you girls are settin' around, and Mama here is doin' the work. I just don't know about this."

He had a good sense of humor, and he was honest and hardworking—he had the railroad job and on weekends he cut wood. He could get seventy-five cents a cord. And even though Annie was happy to have her son home again, she didn't want to take care of Fred and Wilbur. She loved them, but she had already raised her own fourteen children. Now was supposed to be her time to rest some, not have children underfoot to look after and fuss over. All she thought about was her house, keeping it clean and fixing it up.

Adjusting to their new life proved difficult for the boys. Being the older brother, Fred was trying to put on a brave face, but his heart was breaking. He missed his mother very much. He tried not to show it at the new school, but at his Grandma Annie's house, he would sit wedged between the wall and the heating stove in the kitchen and cry silently, unnoticed.

Wilbur settled in with his dad, his brother, and Grandma Annie. Dad later said Annie was a little bitty thing, "NO BIGGER THAN A PINT OF SOAP AFTER TWO WEEKS OF WASHIN'." She probably never weighed more than a hundred pounds in her life. She had a little pinched face and was clean as a pin—legendarily clean. You never saw anything like it. You could not find one speck of dirt anywhere in that house or on her children. It was said that she starched her aprons so much, they rattled when she walked. And she would stay up late into the night to keep cleaning.

When her children were still at home, she'd get the kids, give them baths, put them to bed, and then stay up to scrub the floors. She would go over everything thoroughly. There was a place for everything, and it better be put there. Sometimes she didn't get to bed until after midnight. If she saw a speck of dirt anywhere, she got it. Annie had an old cookstove, one that you feed corn cobs and wood into. Her cookstove was a testament to her ability to clean. It was just a cookstove, but the top of it glistened. You could see your face in its polished surfaces. And you could lift the lids and give them a swipe with white gloves and not soil the starched white cotton fabric with a speck of grease. Annie Rife was so clean, in fact, that folks around Sioux talked about it. Mrs. Anderson, the section foreman's wife, said, "You could eat offin' her floor anytime."

Annie had come from a large family. She had seven brothers and sisters. Jane, her sister, was the only one who lived in Sioux. When Annie's mother, Annie Fowler, was sick, Annie would go over to help Jane, who lived with their mother. Often Annie would take one of her daughters along as company while she helped Jane take care of their mother, who was a tiny little woman, bedridden. Annie would fret and worry about her mother. As soon as she was in Jane's house, she was changing the bedding, getting her tiny mother's frail little body into dry clothes, and cleaning everything around her mother's bed. Then, on the way home, Annie would fret some more.

"Aunt Jane isn't doing enough," she'd lean over and say. "She isn't keeping Mama dry enough. It ain't very clean when I take my babies there with white stockings on and put them on the floor. Their stockings get dirty."

Annie was also a good cook. She'd bake pies and cake and bread, and, of course, clean a little in between times. What's more was that she was quite precise. After years of cooking for a great tribe of husband and children, she had learned just how much to cook for each meal. She made what she anticipated would be eaten by each person coming to the table and no more. What she put on the table was for that meal, and you needn't ask for anything more.

In spite of Annie's reluctance to have Clyde's two boys in her house, she treated them with tenderness and affection. They ate good meals, had clean sheets and pillowcases, and slept in a nice bed. And once in a while, she'd even give them spending money.

But Annie was strict. She shared the Victorian belief that children should be like pictures, seen and not heard. She didn't countenance silly chatter. And she had strict house rules—one of which was that the doors were locked at 9:00 p.m. sharp and not unlocked until the next morning. Many times, Wilbur wouldn't make it back to the house by the appointed time and the door would be locked. No amount of pleading or banging on the door could move Annie to make an exception. As far as she was concerned, he knew the rules. So he'd stay just wherever he could find a place to. Sometimes he slept on the open porch on the south side of the house. When the weather got colder, he slept under a box at Walker's Store, which was just across the street from Annie's house. The first morning after it happened, Miss Walker arrived to open the store and saw a little lock of hair hanging out of a great big bread box that Wilbur had turned over on himself. Looking closer to inspect it, she muttered to herself, "What in the world is that . . . is that a dead body or what?" Opening it up, there was Wilbur, sound asleep. It was frosty that morning, but the box had helped give him cover and keep him warm.

* * *

Clyde was tenderhearted, unable or unwilling to administer any kind of firm discipline.

Often Fred and Wilbur would be ornery or get into some kind of trouble. Most of the time, the mischief was fairly innocent. For instance, Annie used to make whipped cream and set it out on the porch to cool.

Fred and Wilbur would sneak out to the porch and take a spoonful. When she'd come out at dinnertime, she would scold them and threaten, "I'm going to tell your dad." But when Clyde heard his mother recount the story of what they had done, he would grin while he told them not to do it again.

Fred and Wilbur also played with an old whip, and when it came up missing, they were blamed for losing it. The whip was a family heirloom. After Serena and Molly went out to their father's funeral back in Pennsylvania in 1909, they brought a few trinkets back—shawls, a watch, and a bone-handled whip with a whistle in it. The whip had belonged to their father, David; he had used it when farming in Virginia before the Civil War had commenced. The keepsakes were distributed to the kids, and the whip had been given to George. Generations later, several family members laid claim to the whip, and they naturally were suspicious of the boys. Clyde didn't press either of his boys about the whip, however, even though it was never found.

Despite Clyde's lack of reaction, Annie continued to relay the boys' misdeeds to him when he came home from his week's work on the section crew. By then, he was working on buildings and bridges. He'd listen sympathetically and say, "Well, I'm going to whip them boys." And then when he saw them, he couldn't. He'd say, "Come here, Big Boy, and you too, Little Boy. Now you listen to Grandma Annie when she tells you to do something." That would be it.

Sometimes Wilbur would stay down at his aunt Pearl and uncle Dewey's place. He loved to go there. Pearl would often fix him goulash and cornbread, which were two of his favorites.

Wilbur lived off and on with Annie and Clyde. That home life would be disturbed when his mother, Ada, would show up and take the boys off with her. It wasn't that she missed them—it was more a way to torment and torture Clyde. Quite often, she just stuck them in a boys' school or orphanage.

Clyde would get home on a Friday night and ask his mother, "Where are the boys?"

"Ada was here this week and took them along with her."

There was no explanation and no telling where they were.

Ada's mean spirit knew no bounds.

Clyde would drive down to Council Bluffs and start calling on the homes and orphanages until he found his boys, then he'd drive back up to Sioux.

To make extra money, Annie had a garden and sold fresh garden vegetables. She also sold the berries that grew in her yard. From time to time, she would take in boarders.

Fred and Wilbur were fairly enterprising, too. There were two elderly brothers and a sister—Jim, Dave, and Mildred Herring—who lived in town and had quite a bit of money from an inheritance. Even in the heart of the depression, they had money. They owned all the farmland right around where the schoolhouse sat.

So, Fred and Wilbur knew that there was money at the Herring house. They started calling on Millie to see if they could get any of that generosity bestowed upon them. Just about once a week, they'd make a trip up there. They'd either get an apple or a nickel. They always wanted the nickel. Millie would welcome the little boys into her front parlor. Then she'd waddle to the pantry to fetch a gift. It was better if it was your birthday—sometimes you'd get a dime. Millie must have thought the kids were fifty years old because they each had about four birthdays a year and shiny dimes!

Clyde should have discouraged the trips to the Herring household, but he just laughed about it—another reason that Clyde was remembered by his children as a loving father.

Even though he worked and lived in bunk cars during the week, both boys loved the time they spent with him on the weekends.

Once, though, Clyde heard, while working away from River Sioux, that a vaccine had been discovered for diphtheria and whooping cough. Both were scourges that killed thousands of children. He surprised Fred and Wilbur by driving through the night to get to River Sioux, where he woke ol' Doc Cutler to administer the shot to two sleepy boys.

They never forgot that act of love and told and retold the story many times. It was an act of love that any parent would have done for his children, but these acts must have been few and far between for it to stand out so singularly in their memories. There was no such similar story they could share about their mother.

Wilbur Rife on a pair of skates

5

"Gramma fried them taters offin' that grease from Howard Bly and Lish McQueen."

Harry Hatheway

"I can't imagine growing up in River Sioux, can you?" Brian asked.

"There must not have been much to do," Kitty said in agreement.

"Well, they did live close to the river and could go fishing. Dad had a trap line, too. But a lot of the entertainment was supplied in a most unexpected place—Harry Hatheway's Funeral Parlor."

* * *

Annie Rife's neighbors were Harry and Hortense Hatheway. The couple was the living embodiment of Jack Sprat and his wife. Harry Hatheway was a tall, thin, lanky fellow. Hortense, on the other hand, was a great big heavy woman who listed from side to side as she moved. She was also one of the kindest people you'd ever meet. She had a good sense of humor and enjoyed gentle and good-natured teasing. When someone was getting married, she teased, "You'd better get two rings, ya know, a wedding ring and a teething ring."

The stories about Harry's drinking were as legendary in River Sioux as Annie Rife's house cleaning. Harry liked to drink. He used to drink a lot, and then he quit drinking for about five years. But, he eventually got started again. Some thought what got him started again was his wife's brother. Hortense's brother came to live with them, and Harry couldn't stand his brother-in-law.

One of the favorite stories that my uncle Fred used to tell was when Harry bought a brand-new car. Harry had gotten a snoot full of liquor before he headed home to River Sioux.

"Some way or another," Uncle Fred recalled, "he run that goddarn thing off the road somewhere between River Sioux and Little Sioux into a stand of trees. Harry wasn't far from home, so he got out and walked the rest of the way. There that car sat in the middle of the trees. The next morning, Harry went back to fetch his car. He was expecting the worst, of course, but low and behold, there was that brand-new car sitting in the middle of that stand of trees with not even a scratch on it!

"Harry got in it and revved it up. He inched it forward, turned the wheel a bit, and inched it backward like that for the good part of an hour. No matter what he tried, he could not seem to find a way to get that car out of that stand of trees."

At this point in the story, Uncle Fred would just scratch his head. No one could figure out how in the world the car got in between those trees. Finally, some of the neighborhood men came to lend Harry a hand. Dad and Uncle Fred were right in the middle of the men, watching everything.

"When they tried to get the car out of those trees, they tried every which way but couldn't do any better than Harry. They finally had to cut some of the trees down to get it outta there. Nobody knew how in the hell he ever got it in there in the first place. That car didn't have a scratch on it, I'll tell ya!"

Harry's drinking wouldn't have been so bad except that it affected his two main jobs—preaching and undertaking. It was bad enough that he was preaching, but he preached in one of those churches that railed against the "Demon Rum." The members of the church were very displeased with his intemperate behavior and finally confronted him.

They said, "Harry, if you don't quit drinking so much, we gonna get a new preacher." The main problem with that was that Harry had built the church.

"You can't do that," he said. "I'll just take my church home." So, he kept on preaching.

The drinking affected his thinking when it came to his undertaking business too, of course. There were two buildings to the east of Annie's house. The front building had been Hatheway's Store. They used to sell dry goods there, but by the time Fred and Wilbur had come to live with their grandmother, there hadn't been anything in the store in years.

Harry did all his undertaking business out in the building behind their house and the old store. He had all of the coffins stored in that building. Folks came there to pick out the coffins, and that's also where Harry laid out those who had departed. Because he was just an undertaker—not a coroner—he wasn't licensed to embalm anybody. He could only pick them up, wash them, and dress them. In those days, you only got embalmed if you died of some contagion or something.

Harry didn't seem to care much for convention when it came to his preaching or his undertaking. He didn't care much about propriety either. He once picked up a dead woman to take back to his funeral parlor. Only he didn't take his horse-drawn hearse to pick her up; he drove his car. When he picked her up, Harry just propped her up in the front seat of the car and drove her back to River Sioux. But he stopped at Ab's place for a drink. Ab's was a local watering hole in River Sioux. It was during prohibition, but he sold spirits anyway. It was an open secret—even the county law enforcement folks knew. People just closed one eye.

Anyway, Harry went into Ab's. In a big voice, he said, "Hey, Ab, my lady friend out in the car wants a drink of water. Get me a drink, and would you take her out a glass of water, while you're at it, too?" When Ab got out there, he found out she was dead. The joke was on Ab.

Harry evidently liked that practical joke because he repeated it at least once in Missouri Valley. Harry had just loaded a dead man into the front seat of his car and was driving back to River Sioux when he stopped at a bar. Somebody said, "Why didn't you bring your friend in?" He repeated his joke and requested a glass of water for his friend who was thirsty. Sure enough, the man in the front seat was stone-cold dead, leaning against the car window.

Once Harry picked up a body with his horse-drawn hearse, but he was so drunk that he ran the hearse off the side of the road. Somehow, he got the hearse stuck and just left it sitting there. He unhitched his horse, left the hearse, and went home. He slept it off and went back up the next morning to retrieve the hearse and the dead man. The story got around Sioux, and people were really raising Cain about it. Harry replied, "He wasn't hurtin' nobody; he wasn't goin' to leave." Some folks put up with it; others had another undertaker take over for him.

There was only a fence between Annie's yard and that back building. And whenever a story got out that someone had died, especially in some sort of horrendous way, those two boys, Fred and Wilbur, were hanging on that fence to catch a glimpse of the corpse. Harry would oblige.

Right up there in Little Sioux, a guy hanged himself in his barn. Harry went and got him and just hauled him to the funeral parlor in the front seat of his car. As Harry opened his car door and stepped out, he could see those little boys peering over the fence. Harry hollered over to them, "Looky here!" They scampered over the fence. Harry opened the door, and they could see the dead man slumped over in the front seat. Harry took the man by the hair and shook his head back and forth. "See, his neck is broken." The boys stood frozen in amazement and horror.

Another time, Harry had been called to pick up a woman who had been killed in a train accident. Her husband was a thin, agile man who was driving a tin lizzie. They were driving across railroad tracks when the car stalled. They could see the train coming toward them. The little man jumped out of the car and tried to push the car off the tracks. When he realized he was not going to be able to, he ran to the passenger side of the car to help his wife escape. She was an enormous woman who was struggling to extricate herself from the car.

This was no easy task. The little man grabbed her arm and tugged as hard as he could, trying to pry her out of the car. But her nervousness and girth kept him from succeeding. The train was blowing its whistle. Try as he might, he could not get her out soon enough and realized that if he did not jump back from the tracks, the oncoming train would hit him, too. Just as he jumped back, the train hit the car, killing the woman inside.

This was a big news story in River Sioux. Sure enough, the boys were on the fence the next morning. Harry spotted the two and asked them if they wanted to come have a look-see.

Over the fence they went.

Harry had the woman laid out in the back room. She was a large, fleshy woman dressed in a big tent-like housedress.

Fred and Wilbur were standing at eye level with her body. Her arm had been torn off by the impact. The tendons and dried and bloody skin hung up toward her shoulder, but no arm was to be seen.

Fred asked Harry, "Where is her arm?"

"Under here," said Harry. Then he lifted her housedress. After he had lifted her to the table the night before, he had just thrown her arm up under her dress. Her fingers were at her knees. It looked like her arm was growing out of her crotch. At least they hadn't been exposed to the torn part of the arm.

The most gruesome, though, was when Lish McQueen and Howard Bly burned to death. Elisha—everybody knew him as Lish—McQueen was seventy-six, and Howard Bly was seventy-four. They were two old men who were batching it together in a shack by the river.

It was about nine o'clock on a Saturday evening and someone noticed an unusual light coming from that little house. It was a tar paper shack, really, down by the Little Sioux River, close to the bridge and the railroad tracks—about three-quarters of a mile north of Annie's place.

Black smoke began to billow from the shack. Clyde saw the fire and smoke.

"Put on your shoes," he said, and he started up there with Fred and Wilbur racing behind him. They took off as fast as they could, running all the way to see the fire. The two boys stood there watching as men grabbed buckets and tried to put the fire out.

Clyde called out to the boys, "Little Boy and Big Boy, stay back."

As the *Little Sioux Hustler* paper later reported, "It was impossible to get in the building, hardly near it for the heat and black smoke from the tar paper used in the building. It burned so that spectators were horrified to observe the bodies of two in the fire, which proved to be Howard Bly and Elisha W. McQueen, both of whom were trapped in the building."

There was a collective horror felt through the crowd when they realized the two old men could not be saved. All they could do was stand helplessly by and watch this tragedy.

Fred and Wilbur crowded as close to the cabin as they could. They watched men throw bucket after bucket of water on the fire. Through the window in the shack, they could see the inside of the cabin engulfed in fire. The fire illuminated the interior. The slumped figures inside were an eerie image.

When the fire was put out, they finally walked the three-quarters of a mile back to Annie's house.

That night, all that filled the boys' minds were the gruesome images of those two men in the fire. Wilbur was scared and clung to Fred. It was hours before he could fall asleep, as every little noise seemed to be magnified. Every time they could see the car lights go down the highway, the strange shadows cast on their bedroom walls reminded Wilbur of the fiery death of Lish McQueen and Howard Bly. He closed his eyes tighter.

Early the next morning, Annie was frying bacon and eggs when the two boys came down the steps. The smell of the bacon had wafted up the stairs and woken them up. Clyde was at the breakfast table talking to his mom.

"What do you suppose caused that fire last night up Howard Bly's place?" Annie wondered out loud.

"Folks were talking last night thought maybe Lish and Howard were drinking and tipped over a kerosene lantern," replied Clyde.

Annie set down four plates on the kitchen table. Each plate had one egg, two pieces of bacon, and a piece of toast, except Clyde's plate, which had twice that. The boys sat right up to the table and lit into breakfast. Fred finished his breakfast first and grabbed a piece of bacon from Wilbur's plate.

"Land sakes, no good use comes of drinking," Annie said as she sat down to eat. She sipped her coffee.

"It looked like the fire got away from Howard and old Lish before they could get out," Clyde speculated. "They musta stumbled toward the door after trying to put the fire out. I guess they were overcome by the smoke."

"You know, old Lish was a nice man," Annie said. "It sure is a shame that such a thing would happen to him like that. Horrible."

"They're fixin' to have the funeral today, just as soon as Harry can get the bodies laid out."

They finished breakfast. Annie cleared the table and immediately began washing the dishes. Her apron rustled as she went between the table and the sink. The clatter of the dishes signaled the boys to scoot outside. Clyde sat at the table, still sipping coffee and thinking about the horror of the night before.

Fred and Wilbur headed out the kitchen door. Neither of them wanted to be in the house. Annie found too much for them to do if they were inside. Besides, it was September and there weren't going to be all that many warm days before winter hit.

From the backyard, the boys saw Harry Hatheway going in and out of his funeral parlor.

"DO YOU S'POSE THEY'RE IN THERE?" Wilbur asked.

"Of course, they is. They was took in there last night when the fire cooled off enough for as to go in and git them out."

"YEP. S'POSE HARRY'LL LET US SEE 'EM?"

They gathered at the fence to peek through the open door. Howard Bly and Lish McQueen *had* been carried to his funeral parlor late the night before. Harry had their bodies in his building and was fixing them for burial. Because of the way the two men died, they were to be buried quickly, closed casket. There was to be a double funeral that afternoon in the Little Sioux Cemetery. Harry caught the boys looking over the fence in his direction as he was walking to the back parlor.

"Do you want to have a look?" Harry asked them.

"Sure, we do," Fred quickly said. There was no hesitation in his voice. There wasn't a kid in Sioux who wouldn't have jumped at that invitation.

They were about to see, close-up, what everybody in Sioux was talking about. Only a handful of people in that little town were going to see those two dead men. They were going to be in the same company as the grownups, the coroner, the sheriff, and the undertaker. They were going to see what no ten- and five-year-old ought to see. Wilbur was less sure of himself, but if his older brother was going, so would he. He figured it must be okay if Fred wanted to see it. They shimmied over the fence as quickly as they could.

Harry was a little ahead of them, his long legs taking what seemed to be giant strides. He got to the door first and put his hand on the knob. "Now are you boys sure you want to see this?" he teased them. Harry knew full well that they were dying to go inside.

He turned the white china knob and pushed the door open. The sound of his boot hitting the dry wooden floor startled Wilbur. He stepped back.

"C'mon, Wibbie," Fred said, coaxing Wilbur in behind him.

They stepped up to the threshold and looked in.

Fred and Wilbur caught a whiff of the pungent smell of burnt flesh even before they went into the building.

"Git in here now and shut the door. We don't want to draw any more flies in here."

The boys scooted in, Fred first with Wilbur practically clinging to his pant leg. Their eyes stung from the putrid odor, but they stepped clear inside and shut the door behind them. Wilbur had pushed the door so hard on his way in that the windowpane in the door rattled.

Harry had laid each man's charred body out on planks. The planks were laid across sawhorses raised up off the floor. The two men had not yet been stripped and cleaned. Their shoes and clothing were still on them, some of the clothing melted to their bodies, some burnt clear off. Their blackened bodies were dripping fluids.

Harry had a series of jar lids under the sawhorses to catch the "grease" dripping from Lish McQueen and Howard Bly.

Plop. Plop. Plop.

The sound of droplets of fluids from Howard's body into the jar lid, nearly full, was startling to Fred and Wilbur as they watched the liquid splatter onto the floor from the jar lid. They were scared and horrified to see these neighbor men stretched out. Yet, they slowly, almost at a crawl, walked into the funeral parlor to see the most bone-chilling sight they would ever see in their lives.

"It sure is an awful sight, these two men all burned the way they are," Harry said in a matter-of-fact way.

"Yep, it sure is," Fred responded in a sort of mechanical way, slowly moving further into the room, Wilbur as close behind him as he could be.

Fred's little blue eyes and Wilbur's little gray eyes were wide open, big as saucers. There in front of them lay the charred bodies from the shack on fire the night before. Howard Bly was stretched out, one arm dangling down. Their eyes followed the arm to the wrist and then quickly turned away. His hand burned off in the fire. All that was left was a mangle of blackened flesh oozing liquid that slowly dripped into a waiting jar lid below.

Plop. Plop. Plop.

"About the best I can do is wash them up and put clean clothes on them. There's not going to be an open casket. No one is going to want to see these two looking this way." Harry took a look at the two boys. "I reckon you've seen enough. You'd better run along now."

They had both seen plenty and quickly left the funeral parlor. Wilbur felt sick to his stomach.

That night, Annie was busy. She'd fried up chicken and fried potatoes for supper with green beans, fresh bread, and apple pie. Usually Sunday dinner was the biggest and the best. When Clyde was gone for the week working with the section crew on the Chicago and Northwestern Railroad, Annie tended to cook a little less. But she liked to prepare a nice big Sunday dinner.

The table was set for four. Each plate had its fare loaded onto it, the most food on Clyde's plate—a chicken breast and a drumstick, a big mess of fried potatoes, and a heap of green beans.

Wilbur was feeling a little queasy from all of the sights he'd seen during the day, but he was hungry. Annie was a good cook. Fred could see Wilbur waver a bit. Fred certainly was hungry, and he saw an opening with Wilbur pushing his food around his plate.

"Wibbie," Fred whispered.

"YEP?" Wilbur whispered back.

"Gramma fried them taters offin' that grease from Howard Bly and Lish McQueen," Fred whispered into Wilbur's ear.

Wilbur looked down at the fried potatoes and pushed them to the edge of his plate.

"Aren't you going to eat your taters, Wibbie?" Annie asked.

"NOPE."

"Well, I'll sure eat 'em up for ya," Fred said. And with that, he scooped Wilbur's fried potatoes off his plate and ate them right down. He had just unlocked the secret of how to get more of Annie's cooking.

Freddie, Lucy, and Wilbur Rife

6

"He's a gritty little guy."

Dead Cat

"That must have been a pretty rough time for your dad," Kitty said offhandedly.

"Well, it was rough. His mom had gone off with some other man. His sister, Lucy, was gone. His dad was gone most of the week working on the railroad. And Dad and Uncle Fred were living with a woman who really didn't want to be tending to children anymore. She was emotionally detached," I said.

"Yeah, she'd already had her fourteen and raised them," Brian chimed in.

"Not only that, but Grandma Annie wasn't too keen on raising kids who weren't hers. After all, she farmed Dave Rife, George's son from his first marriage, to the Ruffcorns to raise."

"You've got to be kidding," Kitty said.

"On top of that, the stories I've heard about Grandma Annie Rife were that she was Victorian in her beliefs about children."

"Not exactly warm and fuzzy," Brian added.

"Like ours was? When I think back on our childhood, I remember crawling up on Dad's lap. Like all kids, I would look up and say, 'Love you, Dad.' His response wasn't 'LOVE YA, TOO.' It was 'GODDAMN GLAD SOMEBODY DOES.'"

"That's pretty harsh," Kitty remarked.

"I think it's like a milk pitcher; if somebody pours milk into the pitcher, you can pour milk out of the pitcher. If it hasn't been filled up with milk, it can't pour milk out. Same with love; if you pour love into someone, they can pour love out to someone else. Who was pouring love into Dad when he was a kid? His mother who abandoned him? His dad who was working away? His grandma who was tired and distant? I'm not sure he had much of a chance."

We decided to pull into a gas station to get gas before we got onto the highway.

"You know, Aunt Pearl told me a funny story about Dad when he was about five or six years old," I said as we got back into the car. "Dad didn't spend all of his time at Grandma Annie's. He actually spent quite a bit of time with Uncle Dewey and Aunt Pearl. Aunt Pearl thought he was just about the cutest little boy she had ever seen."

***

When Dewey and Pearl were first married, they lived in a little house just across the way from where they lived nearly all of their married lives. It wasn't a great house, but it was their first one. Pearl kept it fixed up nice and fine enough, but it wasn't much of a house. It was tiny, old, and worn out.

A dog or a possum had dug a hole under their house. It wasn't until Dewey started smelling something that he noticed the hole.

Pearl was just as clean as Annie. But she too smelled something. She couldn't locate the smell even though she searched the house high and low. She went from room to room trying to figure out just what could be making the foul odor.

"Dewey," she said, "there's a horrible smell in here, and I don't know just where it is coming from. I've looked the whole house over, and there is nothing in here that smells. It's gotta be coming from somewhere else."

It was summertime, and the smell kept getting worse and worse day by day. Pearl figured out that it was strongest in the bedroom.

"Dewey," she said, taking him into their bedroom, "I think it is something under the house."

"Well, it is possible," he said. "A dog or something has dug a hole out there, and there is a place where something could get under the house if it wanted to."

"Then there is something dead under the house. How to get it out, that's the next thing. Dewey, I can't stand it here. I've got to go over and live with the folks. I just cannot stand it here. I can't stand to sleep in that bedroom one more night," she insisted. "That smell is so strong, it's just coming right up through the floor. Oh, it is awful."

"Now, Pearl," Dewey said, trying to calm her down, "I'll take care of it."

"I just gotta get out of here. That is all there is to it."

"I know. I know," Dewey said. "We've got to get it out from under here somehow. But I don't know really how." There was a crawl space under the house that had been burrowed out by animals, but it was so tight only a small child could fit.

Their daughter Betty was little at the time, but she wouldn't have gone under the house for anything.

Then Dewey got an idea. "I wonder if Wibbie would go under there."

"I don't know, but I'd hate to ask that little kid to go under our house. It is dark and full of cobwebs, and there is something awful smelling and *dead* under there, Dewey."

"Oh, I don't think he'd care. He's a gritty little guy."

So, Dewey got in his pickup truck and drove up to Annie's, got Wilbur, and brought him back down to their house. They lived all of five minutes apart, so Dewey and Wilbur were back in no time at all.

"Wibbie," Dewey asked, "would you go under the house?"

Wilbur stood there. He was wearing a pair of bib overalls, a pair of work boots, and a blue shirt. He looked at the crawl space.

"Take this flashlight, and find out what is under the house. If you find something under there, bring it out. Do you think you can do that?" asked Dewey.

"SURE," Wilbur said confidently, "I'LL GO UNDER THERE." He grabbed the flashlight, got down onto the ground on his belly, and shimmied into the hole.

Dewey and Pearl stood by the opening, calling to Wilbur to make sure he was okay.

"You okay under there, Wibbie?" Pearl yelled out.

"YEP, I'M FINE."

"Oh, I wish there was another way to do this, Dewey. I am worried about that little guy."

"I FOUND HIM, UNCLE DEWEY, IT'S A CAT! IT'S ALL SWOLLED UP!" Wilbur hollered.

"Bring him on out!" Dewey hollered back.

Wilbur had the cat by the tail and shimmied around to head back out. As he crawled under the house on his belly, dragging the cat behind him, dust filled the top of his bib overalls. When he got back to the opening, out poked Wilbur's head as he shimmied out the same way he went in. When he stood up, the dust that had collected in the top of his overalls sifted down his pant legs and the grimy powder emerged from the bottom. Wilbur was standing in a swirl of dust, proud, and happy to help—grinning ear to ear. He had a flashlight in one hand and a dead cat by the tail in the other. He held the cat out like he'd captured big game.

Dewey took the dead cat out of Wilbur's hand while Pearl dusted Wilbur off and combed the cobwebs out of his hair with her hand.

"Well, how much do I owe you, Wibbie?" Dewey asked.

"OH, YOU DON'T OWE ME NOTHING. THAT WAS NOTHING TO GO UNDER THERE AND GET THAT OL' DEAD CAT."

"Well, I'll tell you what I'll do, Wibbie. I'll just give you a dollar." Dewey pulled a silver dollar out of his pocket and handed it to Wilbur.

Wilbur looked down at the dollar like he'd never seen one before. "OH, UNCLE DEWEY, THAT'S TOO MUCH!" he muttered.

"No, Wibbie, it's worth more than that." Pearl said, "I've got some pennies in the house. I'll give 'em all to you, too."

Wilbur was overwhelmed with the money.

There were quite a few ways to spend money around River Sioux. Various forms of entertainment blew into town. There was the play, *Uncle Tom's Cabin*. There was also the Chautauquas, which were very popular, but by the time they ended in Sioux in 1930, admission was a whopping $3.00 per person to attend.

There were also traveling tent shows. Many of them came to River Sioux. The crew put up poles. Then they hung canvas on the poles to create four fabric walls. The stage would be built on one end with the entrance on the other. Then the crew set up wooden chairs for the audience.

The shows were a mixture of magic, singing, joke-telling—a little bit of vaudeville.

These shows only cost a quarter to get in. The company would set up and vary the shows every night so people would come again and again. The company would hold up for four or five nights and then move on to the next town.

Wilbur wanted to get into these shows in the worst way. Sometimes he had the quarter and sometimes he didn't. But that didn't stop him from thinking of ways to get in.

Once, Pearl looked for Wilbur in the audience, and he wasn't anywhere to be found. But when she looked up at the stage, he was standing there with snakes wrapped around him. He had made a deal with the tent show crew to let him in for free if he'd be part of the show.

Another night, Pearl and Dewey were at the show and again they couldn't spot Wilbur anywhere. As Pearl sat there, a leaf fell on top of her head. Then another one. When she looked up, she saw the branch of a tree that stretched up over the canvas into the middle of the tent. On the branch was Wilbur, laid out watching the show—*for free.*

That night, Wilbur spent the night with Dewey and Pearl. Wilbur's favorite dish there was Pearl's goulash. He could sit at the table and eat one bowlful after another.

The house they lived in had a tiny little room in the attic with a small bed in it. So when Wilbur stayed the night, he slept there. One night,

Wilbur was struggling to fall asleep. Earlier that day, Pearl had cleaned house, including the attic bedroom. There was an old eight-day wind-up clock that had a loud chime on the hour. Pearl had lifted the clock to dust under it, which started the clock to ticking. It seemed all Wilbur could hear was the tick, tick, tick of the clock. The more he tried to ignore it, the louder it seemed to get.

Tick. Tick. Tick.

On top of that, Wilbur had been having nightmares for the week or two after he'd been in Harry Hatheway's back room and seen Lish and Howard. Wilbur would wake up in the middle of the night, raise up in bed, circle his head, and say, "THERE'S OLD LISH MCQUEEN AND HOWARD BLY." Clyde would say to comfort him, "No, they're gone; they're not here." But the whole experience and sight of it all had made him a nervous wreck.

So, nightmare-stricken Wilbur lay in the attic bedroom, all alone, staring at the ceiling, listening to the clock tick, unable to fall asleep, when all of a sudden the clock began to bong. The noise startled him and down the stairs he ran as fast as he could run.

He shot into Dewey and Pearl's bedroom, catapulted himself into their bed, and landed right on top of them. It scared them almost to death. Dewey and Pearl snuggled him in between them and let him sleep in their bed for the rest of the night.

Lucy, Wilbur, Freddie, and Rolland "Ronnie"

7

"I hope he grows up to be a cop."

In Search of a Home

Charlie Gillett and Ada were traveling around looking for work—taking jobs here and there—and moving from one place to another, most often ending up back in a house somewhere in Council Bluffs. Wilbur and Fred were still living in River Sioux with their dad and Annie. But those little boys missed their mother terribly.

***

"Grandma Ada didn't help matters any. She stirred up the boys emotionally. It was cruel," I said.

"Really?" Brian asked.

"Well, she was sending those two boys postcards, saying things like, 'I miss you. Come visit me sometime. I miss you so much that I meet every bus that comes to Council Bluffs hoping that you will be on it.'"

* * *

Those kinds of cards made the boys that much lonelier for their mother. It also stirred things up for Clyde, and ultimately that was always Ada's goal. She was down in Council Bluffs with Charlie, Lucy, and their baby, who was always referred to as "Little Charles."

Ada was already pregnant again.

Fred and Wilbur were busy trying to make some money. And Fred was secretly squirreling his money away to buy a bus ticket to Council Bluffs. He believed that his mother was actually at the bus depot waiting for the buses and that if he took the bus to Council Bluffs, she would be there—after all, her postcard had said so.

"Hey, Big Boy, you did a good job with those chores." Clyde handed Fred the change in his pocket—seventy-six cents. That was enough to buy a bus ticket to Council Bluffs so he could go see his mom.

The bus for Council Bluffs stopped across the street. The eleven-year-old knew when it stopped and had asked how much the ticket cost. The fare was seventy cents. Fred had six cents to spare.

When the bus came the next day, Fred got on it. He was scared but slowly climbed the steps onto the bus and found a seat next to a window. As the bus lumbered away from River Sioux and the safety of his grandma Annie's house toward Council Bluffs, Fred got excited to see his mom. It took nearly two hours to make the forty-mile trip, but the whole time he was filled with thoughts about her and his half-brother Little Charles.

When the bus pulled up to the bus station in Council Bluffs, Fred bolted out of the bus, expecting to see Ada. He ran into the waiting room and quickly looked from one side of the big cavernous room to the other. She wasn't there. His mother wasn't there. How could she not be here? he thought. Her postcard had said she missed him and she met every bus waiting for him to visit. He didn't know what to do. He looked all around the depot, but she was not to be found. He found a bench and sat there, expectantly, watching every door, hoping that at any moment, Ada would walk in. But she didn't come. He was alone. He sat there for hours.

From time to time, Fred would walk to the bathroom and then walk around the bus depot, looking in every corner. He also looked at the lunch counter, but he didn't have enough money for a drink or anything to eat—his leftover six cents wasn't going to go very far. He was standing in the middle of the bus station when a newsboy asked him if he was lost. Fred explained that he'd taken the bus to join up with his mother but she wasn't there. He didn't know what to do or how to find her.

The newsboy told Fred, "The best thing to do is to go to the police headquarters; they'll help find your mama."

The newsboy offered to take Fred the few blocks to the police headquarters, and Fred willingly went along, not knowing what else to do. When they walked into the station, a uniformed officer asked if he could help the two boys. The newsboy piped up and said, "Officer, I found this boy in the bus depot. He is looking for his mother but can't find her."

The police officer leaned over and asked, "What's your name?"

"Fred Rife."

"Where are you from?"

"I'm from River Sioux, Iowa, and I come down here on the bus to see my mom only she ain't at the bus station and I don't know where she is," Fred said meekly.

"Did she know you were coming?"

"No, I didn't tell nobody. I just saved up my money and hopped on the bus to come down here and see her. She told me she met all of the buses waiting for me to come visit."

"What about your pa? Does he know where you are?"

"No," Fred replied as he looked down at the floor. He knew he shouldn't have gone off and not told anyone.

"I did some chores for my pa, and he paid me. I took my money and hopped on the bus. He don't know I come down here."

"Well, Freddie, we'll help you find your ma. But first, we probably oughta get you something to eat."

A couple of the newspaper men who covered the police beat for the Council Bluffs *Nonpareil* said they'd take Fred to supper with them and get him something to eat. After supper, they brought him back to the station, where the police gave him a bunk in a cell for the night. They promised to find Ada the next morning.

The next morning was Saturday, and after a few calls, Ada had been located at Jennie Edmundson Hospital. The police drove Fred over to the hospital where Ada had just given birth to her fifth child, Rolland Keith Gillett, days earlier. Ada named her newborn baby after the handsome, urbane, and debonair English actor Roland Coleman, only she misspelled it and gave Rolland two *l*'s.

The police walked into the room with Fred leading the way. Ada was in bed holding her newborn infant, who was swaddled up pretty tight with only his face protruding from his flannel swaddle.

Ada looked surprised to see Fred, especially with the contingent of cops trailing in after him.

"My goodness, Freddie, how did you get here?" Ada asked.

Fred walked over to the bed to see his mother and explain how he ended up in her hospital room and the adventure of spending a night in the Pottawattamie County Jail.

He then pulled back the light blue flannel baby blanket to peek at this new brother. He looked up at the policemen who had been so kind to him and said, "I hope he grows up to be a cop."

The irony of Fred's words would not be realized for decades.

Wilbur Rife, bill turned up, typical defiant stance

8

"She could eat watermelon through a picket fence."

Shanty Town

Lucy, Clyde's oldest, was living with Ada and Charlie Gillett in Council Bluffs. Lucy was fifteen and becoming a striking young woman. She was slender with fiery red hair and noticeably buxom. Her stepfather, Charlie, was starting to notice his stepdaughter a little too much. That was when Ada made a decision. True to her nature, she decided to eliminate the competition and sent her daughter to the

Chillicothe Industrial Home for Girls instead of throwing Charlie's ass out. The home was specifically charged by the state of Missouri for the development and treatment of juvenile offenders. The "home" was set in the small town of Chillicothe on a campus-like facility, though it was surrounded by a tall fence, presumably to keep the wayward girls in and wayward boys out. Lucy was in the Chillicothe Industrial Home for Girls for six long years, from 1931 to 1937.

With Lucy out of the way, it was just Ada, Charlie, and their two sons, Little Charles the love child and Ron. It was around this time that something happened to Little Charles. Charlie and Ada had a stint in Missouri while hopping around looking for work, when Little Charles died.

The stories about what happened vary wildly. One rumor was that Little Charles died of malnutrition. Ada told a different story—more fanciful. She said that Little Charles was playing in the yard and caught a small bug, put it in his mouth as all children do at that age, and swallowed it. Ada claimed that the bug ate the lining of his stomach and he died. They buried him in a dresser drawer somewhere in Missouri—no one remembers exactly where. Whether it was the stress of the loss of their child or the relationship just played out, Charlie and Ada split up.

Around the same time, the living arrangement that Annie, Clyde, and the boys had split up, too. Annie sold the little house in River Sioux and moved to Des Moines to be closer to her daughters—Dora, Geneva, and Geraldine—in 1935. Annie ended up marrying one of her son-in-law's relatives, Lyman Miller.

Clyde bought a tiny trailer and they moved to Blencoe, a small town in southwest Monona County, just eleven miles north of River Sioux. He parked his trailer on Main Street between the Shay's Grocery Store and the blacksmith shop. His trailer, about twelve feet by fourteen feet, was tiny with barely the necessities. It didn't have a toilet. They had to use the facilities at the grocery store. As the old joke goes, it was so small he had to go outside to change his mind.

At this point, Fred was in high school. He asked his dad for book money, and when Clyde gave it to him, Fred skipped out on school and took off to work as a jockey—that left Wilbur and Clyde to batch it together in the trailer.

There wasn't room for one person, much less two. So Wilbur started spending his time in different places. For a while, he had a place made up for himself in an abandoned icehouse in River Sioux. It had a small cot and bedding and a few essentials, like a chamber pot and some candles. He took one of his first girlfriends there—a little redheaded freckled-face girl who was bucktoothed. "SHE COULD EAT WATERMELON THROUGH A PICKET FENCE." But that didn't keep Wilbur away.

He also spent time in Council Bluffs, living off and on with his mother and his half-brother, Ron. Ada and Ron were moving from house to house in Council Bluffs. They lived in several places. One was a little yellow house that was close to the newly opened Dodge Riverside Golf Park, which they referred to as the "Cold House." It got the name for an obvious and uncomfortable reason—it was always cold. The neighborhood was only a few blocks long and was a shanty town—small square clapboard houses built on a flood plain that had been drained. Nothing fancy.

By June 1936, Wilbur was living in the Cold House with Ada and Ron. Ron was a typical little brother. He wanted to follow Wilbur around and be wherever he was. Though Wilbur loved his little brother, Ronnie irritated the shit out of him.

For one thing, not long after Wilbur moved in, Ron learned a new poem:

> Gene, Gene, made a machine
> Frank, Frank made a crank
> Joe, Joe made it go
> Art, Art, let a fart and blew it all apart!

Ron recited it over and over and over and would laugh—*every* time. He said it so many times, that Wilbur started calling him "Art." And it stuck.

Ron knew that Wilbur admired his cousin Walter Anderson. Wilbur talked about him with admiration and maybe a little envy. Ron started calling Wilbur "Walt"—and that stuck.

It was the same year boxers Joe Louis and Max Schmeling fought in what was deemed "the fight of the year." Wilbur and Ron huddled around the radio to hear the fight. Ada had a WPA job as a practical nurse. She was taking care of several people, as well as cleaning their houses. She was making twelve dollars a month.

Wilbur was hustling to make money of his own to help out. However, he often didn't get any money for the work he did—instead he'd get some groceries, maybe a can of beans, a pound of bacon, or a can of peaches. He started weeding people's gardens almost like a sharecropper for a share of the vegetables in the gardens he tended and weeded. And about once a month, Ada got commodities. When times were tough, the county would give Ada a little crate with some oranges and a couple of grapefruits and a big box of oatmeal or cornmeal. Most mornings started with a meager breakfast from the county oatmeal. Oatmeal day after day. Sometimes they got sugar, too.

Using the sugar would get Wilbur into trouble. Because the three of them had so little sugar—it was like white gold—they had to use it sparingly. But Wilbur had a sweet tooth and so did Ron. So while Ada was off working and the boys were on their own, Wilbur attempted to make fudge. It never set up. What he made was a gelatinous mess they had to dip out and eat with a spoon, so they dubbed it "spoon candy." Wilbur would try to make fudge again and again but never could get it so he could cut it into little bars—it just wouldn't harden. It would always end up being the consistency of pudding.

Ron would beg, "Walt, would you make some spoon candy?"

"SHIT NO. YOU'LL TELL ON ME JUST AS SOON AS MOM WALKS IN THE DOOR."

"No, I won't. I promise, Walt, I won't tell. I really want us to have some of that spoon candy you make. It tastes so good."

Wilbur almost always gave in and would whip up his chocolaty confection.

"Oh, this is good, Walt."

"NOW, GODDAMMIT, ART, DON'T TELL MOM, OR I AIN'T GOING TO MAKE IT NO MORE. YOU HEAR ME?"

"I won't tell. I promise."

"'CAUSE WE AIN'T BARELY GOT ANY SUGAR LEFT."

No sooner would Ada walk in the house than Ron would blurt out, "Momma, Walt made a big batch of spoon candy today, and we ate it all up!"

There were all sorts of ways to get a little taste of food here or there. The woman who lived across the street made hot rolls and sold them to folks in town. Her son had to take these rolls and deliver them around. That was his job. Wilbur and Ron thought it was a good idea to befriend the boy. They got in good with him. The smell of the fresh-baked hot rolls would waft into the neighborhood. Wilbur and Ron would saunter across the street to each get one. The boy's mom would offer each of the boys a hot roll slathered with butter. She knew they didn't have any money. They would sit on the curb and just tear off pieces of the hot roll, which melted in their mouths.

Since their neighborhood was next to the golf course, Wilbur and Ron would scour the course for errant golf balls and amass bucketfuls. They also managed to "find" a few golf clubs with which they practiced hitting balls at dusk after the golfers packed up and left the course.

The marble tournaments were Wilbur's favorite, though. He'd win oodles of marbles. According to Ron, Wilbur was the best marble player in Council Bluffs. When they would square off and have the marble championships, often the prize was a popsicle and some coveted marbles. Wilbur would square off against an opponent—serious play—while Ron would lean up against a tree and sleep. Some of the games took a long time to play. Wilbur could shoot so hard, he'd break marbles that he hit. He always used an agate that wouldn't break. But the agate would shatter the glass marbles. As soon as the competition was over, Wilbur would give Ron a nudge to wake him up.

"HEY, WAKE UP, ART—IT'S OVER AND I WON. WANT HALF OF THIS HERE POPSICLE?"

Sleepy-eyed, Ron would stretch a little. "You bet I do." Then he would take his half.

Wilbur kept his marbles in the attic. They were his treasure for sure. They were all his, earned fair and square. To keep Ron out of his stash of marbles, he told him a whopper of a story.

"NOW, LOOK, ART, YOU CAN'T GO UP INTO THAT ATTIC, SEE? THERE WAS A MAN WHO DIED IN THIS HOUSE, AND WHEN THE COPS CAME, THEY FOUND HIS BODY BUT NOT HIS HEAD. THEY LOOKED AROUND ALL OVER FOR IT, BUT THEY COULDN'T FIND IT."

"Really?" Ron's eyes got really big. He swallowed hard.

"I WENT UP THERE TO SEE WHAT WAS UP THERE, AND I FOUND HIS HEAD. YOU DON'T WANT TO SEE THAT. IT IS PRETTY BAD."

There was a house behind the Cold House that had caught fire and the family burned up inside. A man, a woman, and four little kids. The shell of the house was left standing for many years with the bottom floor windows blown out. The attic windows were still intact. It was rumored that the house was haunted by the family who had lived and died there. People reported hearing noises that sounded like screams at all hours of the night. People swore they saw a light go on from inside the house at the same time every night. Many of the neighbors claimed they personally saw it—their eyes would get real big when they talked about it in hushed tones. They always whispered, like talking about it in a regular voice would somehow summon the spirits.

"There is a light that comes on in the attic. It comes on, and it goes on down the stairs at the same time as the fire that lit and burned 'em all up," they said in whispers.

Kids even took to running by the house as they went by, too scared to slow down and look.

So, the kids in the neighborhood had heard that Wilbur was pretty tough. He had made it clear he wasn't really afraid of anything, so they pooled their marbles together to make a prize of fifty marbles if Wilbur could sleep in that house all night long.

And so they put up a prize for one of the kids to hold until morning. Wilbur and Ron checked out the marbles and wanted them because there were some really good ones in the mix.

"OKAY, WE'LL DOER. WE WILL STAY FOR THE WHOLE NIGHT. IFF'N WE DO, WE GET ALL THEM MARBLES."

The kids all agreed.

Wilbur and Ron took an old blanket and a couple of pillows and headed up to the house. They walked in and could still smell the fire that had consumed and gutted much of the downstairs before it was put out.

Well, Ron fell asleep. Wilbur sneaked off during the middle of the night to do something else, and it was actually Ron who slept there all night. He didn't even know Wilbur was gone.

"ART, GET UP. IT'S DAYLIGHT. WE GET THEM MARBLES."

Wilbur and Ron came out of the front of the house, and the other boys were standing there.

"WE STAYED ALL NIGHT. WE WANT OUR MARBLES. THAT WAS THE DEAL."

One of the kids asked what they saw or what they heard. And Ron piped up, "Yeah, we was in there all night, but I didn't see no light or nothing." His chest was a little puffed up because he was feeling pretty tough. He never bothered to tell anyone that he fell asleep and slept clear through the night. This escapade made him tough. He was already famous in the neighborhood because, even at his small size, he could piss over the clothesline. He had the arc of a pro!

Wilbur would say to the other kids who lived across the street, "OH, THAT'S MY LITTLE BROTHER. HE CAN PISS OVER THE CLOTHESLINE."

Now Ron had one more notch in his belt—bravery.

Wilbur and Ron got their loot from the bet. As they were walking home, Wilbur asked Ron, "HEY, WERE YOU SCARED IN THERE, ART?"

"When you first woke me up and I wiped the sleep away and figured where I was and 'bout shit my britches."

Wilbur laughed.

* * *

Most of the houses in Shanty Town were small, no more than a bedroom or two, a kitchen, a tiny living room, and a porch. Most of these homes still had an outhouse. These houses were built before insulation was in wide use and were usually heated with a small stove in the center of the kitchen, close to the living room door. Families kept bedroom doors open at night to receive a little of the heat from the coal stoves as the fires died out. No one had enough coal to keep a fire going all night long.

At the south end of the golf course was a set of railroad tracks for the Union Pacific Railroad. Wilbur and Ron often walked the tracks. Wilbur would get up as soon as the sun came up to pull a little coaster wagon along the rails looking for coal. As trains went through poor neighborhoods, hobos riding the trains would lift up coal from the cars and throw it out on to the side of the tracks. One morning as Wilbur and Ron were walking the tracks, they spotted an enormous piece of coal.

"GOD, THAT MUST WEIGH FIVE HUNDRED POUNDS. THAT'LL KEEP US WARM FOR YEARS!" exclaimed Wilbur. "PUSH ON THAT END. LET'S TIP IT INTO THE WAGON."

They both put their shoulders up against the massive chunk of coal, but no matter how hard they tried, it could not be budged. They certainly could not lift it into the wagon, and if they could've, the wagon would have gone bust.

"YOU WAIT HERE AND GUARD THIS!" Wilbur ordered. "I'LL GO AND GIT UNCLE BOON TO HELP US."

Ron, all of six or seven years old, stood straight as an arrow guarding their found fortune.

Uncle Boon, properly named Irvan Des Moines Anderson, was Ada's brother. He didn't live far off, so Wilbur ran off to fetch him while Ron stood next to the largest piece of coal they had ever seen.

"COME QUICK," Wilbur said, panting and out of breath, as he dashed up onto the porch. "WE GOT COAL, A BIG PIECE, AND WE NEED HELP BREAKING IT UP."

"Wibbie, how big is it?" Uncle Boon asked.

"NEARLY AS TALL AS ME."

Off they went to the railroad tracks, Uncle Boon carrying a pick.

"Goodness, Wibbie, you found enough coal for all of us to share."

It was as if Wilbur had come across a lump of gold!

After quite a bit of time of hacking and chopping, Uncle Boon had the enormous lump of coal into bits small enough for Wilbur to cart it back to their house and enough to heat the Cold House for the rest of the winter.

*　*　*

Even with the coal, it was a gloomy, sad, and depressing winter. One of the neighbors had called in a complaint about their dog, Freckles. They told the sheriff that the dog was foaming at the mouth and went around barking and, worst of all, biting people.

On Christmas Day, a sheriff's deputy pulled up. The deputy knocked on the door and Freckles ran out into the yard.

Ada asked what the problem was and the deputy said one of the neighbors had complained about the dog. He told Ada he would have to take care of the situation and that it would be best to take the kids inside. But before they all filed into the house, the deputy took out his revolver and shot Freckles—in front of the two boys. Ron burst into tears. Wilbur, trying to tough it out, clamped his teeth.

"Jesus Christ, what in the hell did you do that for?" Ada asked. Ron was clinging to her apron.

The deputy said that because of the complaint, it was his duty.

Ada said they would bury the dog as the deputy drove away.

The boys ran out to Freckles's limp body.

"LET'S MAKE CHRISTMAS TREE ORNAMENTS. GO GRAB SOME COTTON BALLS."

Wilbur and Ron tied string to cotton balls and dipped them in Freckles's blood and hung the homemade ornaments on the tree.

Then they buried Freckles.

* * *

In the middle of May 1938, the boys were out weeding their garden plot in the backyard. Wilbur was wearing a cap that had a bulldog on it to keep the sun out of his eyes. He always wore that cap with the bill turned up. They had walked in the house to get a little sip of water and headed back out when they heard a plane flying overhead. They also heard a shrill whistling noise coming from the sky. When they looked up, they saw a man falling.

"Look, Walt!" Ron yelled.

A few seconds later, the man hit and hit hard. He hit close by their house, right in Carl Addington's garden in the neighborhood. Carl was outside at the time. Another one of their neighbors, Mr. Park, was out in his garden, too, setting out tomato plants.

The body hit Addington's garden with such an impact that it then bounced up into the air and then fell back into the dirt—a cloud of dust wafting up around him. The impact made a loud noise that sounded like a car crash.

Wilbur raced out to where the body had fallen. Ron was close behind him. A few of the neighbors were already gathering around, but none of them paid any attention to the boys.

"What do you see?" Ron asked, as he stood peering around Wilbur.

"DON'T GO OVER THERE RIGHT NOW. DON'T GO OVER THERE. STAY THERE." Then Wilbur walked closer to the scene.

"What's the matter with him, Walt?"

"HE'S DEAD."

"He's dead? Holy smokes."

He was dead, but it didn't look like he was. His face was straight up and his legs were straight out. He'd sunk into the ground about a foot or two. In a way, he looked peaceful.

He was a young man about five-foot-ten tall with sandy-colored hair. He was wearing a light pair of pants, a white shirt, and a sweater with an Omaha Technical High School pin. His whole body had a light dusting from the freshly tilled garden spot. He hit the ground so hard the heels snapped off the bottom of his shoes.

One of the neighbor boys, cried out, "Hey, I think I found his watch." It was about four feet from the man's body. The watch had stopped at 7:30 p.m., the moment he hit the ground. The watch was engraved with one word, "Babbs."

After Mr. Addington saw the dead man sprawled out for himself, he ran back to his house to call the police and then came back outside to wait.

For a couple of hours that evening, the boys watched from their backyard as the police came to investigate. Eventually an ambulance lifted the man's body to load it onto a gurney and into an ambulance. His clothes had ripped apart in the back from the impact. They watched as the authorities took the man's body away.

The next day after the dust settled and the commotion was over, Wilbur and Ron set out their carrots, tomatoes, and radishes. Life went on.

The newspaper gave details of what happened the night before and reported the man's name and age. Ward Fritz, twenty-two, a dancer from Omaha, paid two dollars to Alvin Knudsen, the local weatherman, to go up in his open-cockpit two-seater plane for a ride. The plane was flying at an elevation of about two thousand feet when Knudsen looked down to check the instrument panel. When he looked up, he saw that Fritz had undone his seat belt and stepped out onto the wing. Just as the pilot looked over, Fritz jumped. The pilot tipped his wing to circle around to see where his passenger fell then headed back to the airport.

The headline, "Motive for Death Plunge Is Mystery," told the readers that no one was able to come to a conclusion about why Fritz jumped to his death. His sixteen-year-old dancing partner, Betty Wetenkamp, the "Babbs" engraved on the watch, told reporters that he seemed perfectly normal during their dance practice only an hour before he went up in the plane that Sunday evening.

* * *

For a while after they moved out of the Cold House, Ada started taking other jobs. When one would run out or she could make a little more somewhere else, she'd move on. She had learned how to take care of old people. She'd take jobs out on farms where she had to take care of invalids. Sometimes they were right in Council Bluffs, and sometimes they were out in the country.

Ada got a job at this farmhouse just outside Macedonia, which was a small town about twenty-five miles south and east of Council Bluffs. The farmer was named Ernie, a great big huge guy, who listed from side to side when he walked. And even though he was a large hulking figure who would have struck fear in any kid he talked to, he was a gentle man. Mild mannered. Ada was there to take care of his mother. And, as it turned out, Ada had figured out how to wrangle a few more benefits from the job by sleeping with him. That last perk gave Wilbur and Ron the run of the farm.

One day, Wilbur and Ron were leaning over the rails of the hog pen. Wilbur picked up a stick and just chucked it at one of the hogs in the pen. Somehow that stick hit that hog just right and down it went. The boys both gasped and waited for the hog to shake it off and stand up. But he just lay there.

"JESUS CHRIST, ART, I THINK I JUST KILLED THAT GOD-DAM HOG."

"Walt, you hit it right behind the ears, just, boy, right there."

Ron and Wilbur were scared.

They walked up to the house, hoping Ernie was in the house having coffee and sitting at the kitchen table, but they found Ada by herself and timidly told her what had happened.

"Oh, my god, you know a big sow like that is a whole winter's meat, and it is gone." She shook her head.

"MOM, WHAT CAN I DO?" Wilbur asked.

"Now, Wib, you gotta go out and tell him."

Wilbur went out to look for Ernie on the farm. By the time he found him, it was dusk. Wilbur looked at the ground and began telling Ernie what happened.

Ernie looked down at Wilbur and said, "Well, what'll you suppose we'll have to do with the sow now? She's been laid out there in the hot sun for most of the afternoon so we can't butcher her. Come morning, we gotta bury it. That's all there is to it. It's just been dead too long. Laid there in the hot sun."

The whole time Ernie was talking to Wilbur, he never raised his voice, never got angry about it—not then, not later.

It was a great place for the boys to live. They had lots of fresh air and plenty of space to roam around. It sort of felt like they were all a family. Sunday mornings, Ernie liked to sleep in. The boys would pile into bed with Ada and Ernie. Ernie made the boys rubber guns. He'd cut a rubber inner tube that was pulled over the end of the gun-shaped piece of wood Ernie had fashioned with a whittling knife. Then the end had a clothespin you'd hook the inner tube into. You'd load the projectile, and when you wanted to let the rubber go, you just squeezed the clothespin to let it release.

The old farmhouse needed a little tender loving care. The ceiling wallpaper was loose. A few pieces of it had ripped, and short strips of it were hanging down like stalactites in a cave. Ernie usually got up at four o'clock every morning except on Sundays. That was when they all lay in the same bed and took turns shooting at the paper peeling off the ceiling with the rubber guns. When the rubber hit, bits of papers would rain down like confetti on the bed, and they would all holler in delight.

After about half a year, Ernie's mother passed and the job was over. Ada and the boys moved back to the Cold House, which was still vacant and still cold.

* * *

Somewhere, Wilbur got a hold of a .22 single shot pistol. Ron found the gun. Chuck Betts, a cousin, had come over to hunt for golf balls. Ron wanted to show off the gun. He was waving the gun around when it discharged. It scared Ron practically to death. What he didn't know was that the bullet grazed Chuck's britches.

It scared the piss out of Chuck, too, and he was dancing around because it was burning where he got shot. He fell over in pain.

"You shot me, you little sonofabitch!" Chuck screamed at Ron.

"Oh, god, did I just kill you?" Ron took a look at Chuck's leg. It looked like a lit, red-hot cigarette had been rubbed down all along his leg.

Wilbur heard the gun and ran into the backyard to see what happened.

"WHAT THE HELL IS GOING ON?" he bellowed.

Ron said in a shaky voice that he'd accidentally shot Chuckie. Wilbur took the gun away and said, "LISTEN, YOU ARE TOO LITTLE TO BE FUCKING AROUND WITH GUNS. YOU'D BETTER STICK TO PLAYING WITH MARBLES." Wilbur knew that Ron wasn't worth a shit playing marbles, but he couldn't kill anybody with one of them, not even if he used an agate.

Fred Rife on "Nat Bragg" at Epsom Downs, March 8, 1937

9

"Give me a nickel, or I'll pee in your beer—again."

BEER AT UNCLE DAVE'S

Out of the blue, Kitty asked, "Were all of the Rifes big drinkers?"
"All of 'em I know!" Brian chimed in.

"Well, during prohibition and a good deal afterward, nearly everybody brewed or distilled something—beer, bathtub gin, homemade whiskey, wine. The Rifes were no exception.

"In fact, Great Aunt Dora, George Rife's sister, said George was one heck of a farmer. If he couldn't grow a crop, nobody could."

He worked hard, and when the work was done, he liked to have a drink. Dora said her father would stay by the barrel of whatever had been tapped until it was dry. Many of the kids adopted his view of the drink.

* * *

One of the annual family events was a big picnic on the Fourth of July held on Forney's farm up around Blencoe. Forney was born on the fourth. Everybody brought a little something to eat and a lot something to drink.

Forney's wife, Joy, would lay out the food on picnic tables. There would always be a big spread of fried chicken, ham, potato salad, coleslaw, beets, green beans, peas, corn, and a slew of desserts—apple pie, peach cobbler, rhubarb surprise, and brown betty.

In those days, ice was in blocks and usually each town had an icehouse. Ice trucks delivered ice to people's homes. The running joke was that the ice man got his pick—a joke always sure to get a grin and a giggle. Some of the deliveries of ice were delivered from as far away as Sioux City.

In Blencoe and Sioux, though, neighbors would gather in the wintertime and head to Blue Lake with teams and wagons. The men would cut ice in big blocks with massive saws, lift the ice up with iron tongs, and haul the blocks of ice home. Nearly everyone had an icehouse or one shared by the men who were cutting the ice together.

The icehouse where Forney got his ice had been built for shared use by the families who pitched in and did the winter work. Part of the building was dug down in the ground. The men unloaded the ice, which was packed in layers in the subterranean "ice box." Each layer of ice was covered with a thick layer of sawdust, which kept the ice from melting. Forney usually had ice all year long and could go to the icehouse and use an ice pick to break off the size of ice block for whatever he needed. The Fourth of July picnic at Forney's was one of those events where they shaved off some ice to pack around the beer kegs down in the cellar to keep the beer cold and refreshing.

Everyone would pitch in some money, and Forney, who had made arrangements to get the beer kegs to his place for the picnic, would travel to a tavern in Blencoe to fetch the kegs. He'd haul them back, get them down to the cellar, lower them into big tubs, and fill the tubs with ice. The kegs, of course, had a pump on top to draw the beer, and Joy laid out a collection of mismatched glasses alongside the kegs to draw the beer in.

The first year that Wilbur got into the beer at Forney's was in 1937. Wilbur and his cousin Bill had decided to give it a try. Wilbur was fourteen; Bill was eleven.

That was an exciting year at the picnic. Alongside the usual commotion of all of the family getting together was the added excitement of Fred showing up. He had gone off to become a jockey and was having great success. He was racing at Longacres and different racetracks, and that he year he showed up at the picnic driving a shiny, new, red Terraplane convertible with a sharp-looking brunette in the seat next to him.

Back in those days, only a few of the most expensive cars had color. Most of the cars were black in keeping with Henry Ford's edict to his Model T customers that they could have "any color they wanted, so long as it was black." All of the aunts and uncles and cousins huddled around the Terraplane to gape at its luscious interior—including the brunette. Fred stepped out of that car like he was a sultan—so proud—and surrounded by adulation, admiration, and attention.

In addition to the excitement of Fred's new car and girlfriend was also the usual events that took place. Joy would get drunk and pick a fight with Forney. Forney and Joy fought all the time and were well practiced. When he was yoked for milking and carrying a pail on each end, he could dodge everything she threw at him; the family, describing his skill, would say, "He would never spill even a drop of milk!" Every year, Joy would climb to the top of the windmill and threaten to jump when their argument erupted. The activity with Joy was coming to a crescendo with all eyes on Joy as she teetered atop the windmill. Again, she yelled at Forney, "I'll jump!" Even with much encouragement, she never did. Eventually she climbed down and everyone went back to eating, drinking, and talking.

But it was while all of this was going on that Bill and Wilbur decided to go down to the cellar to give the beer a try. At first, neither of the boys thought much of the taste, but it was cold, and it was wet, so they continued to slake their thirst. One led to another and another until Wilbur's thirst was quenched. He was evidently not new to beer, but Bill was. Bill had to crawl to the weeds where he threw up. Bill's dad, Irvin, was mad as hell when he found out.

* * *

Clyde's half-brother, Dave, was no exception to family brewing. He brewed beer in a washhouse on his place in Mondamin. Home-brewed beer.

Once when Clyde was down at Dave's place, one of Dave's little kids bounded out of the house, nearly breathless. The little guy tugged on Dave's shirt to get his attention. Like most parents who learn the art of ignoring children, especially their own, he tuned the little guy out.

But the kid was not going to be dissuaded. Finally, he popped off with what he wanted at a pitch that couldn't be ignored.

"Dad, I want a nickel to go to Dale Alton's store!"

Dave looked at the little boy and said, "Now shoo, I ain't going to give you a nickel. Run along and play."

Discouraged, he walked away, but it wasn't long before he got his nerve up and came back.

"Dad, give me a nickel to go over to Dale Alton's store!" he said, even more insistent than before.

"Now, I told you, you ain't gettin' a nickel," Dave said. "If I give you a nickel for candy, I'll have to give each and every one of you a nickel, and I don't have that kind of money. Now run along."

Dave and Clyde sat on the back porch step, talking and drinking a little beer in between the conversations.

Dave always wore overalls turned up to the middle of his calf.

The little kid came out again and asked Dave for a nickel. He really wanted to go to Alton's store and get a handful of candy. In those days, a nickel could go pretty far.

Dave said to him again, "Git outta here, son, I'm talkin' to your Uncle Clyde."

This time the little boy was pissed off. He stomped his little foot and said, "If you don't give me a nickel, I'll pee in your beer—again."

There wasn't any part of that sentence that was as bad as the last word—*again*. That *again* echoed like it had been broadcast from a microphone directly into their ears.

Clyde had just raised the glass of beer to his lips when he heard that.

Oh, boy, now Clyde was clean as a whistle. He came by that honestly, since his mother, Annie, attacked every piece of lint and crud that ever made it into her house. Even with fourteen children, her linoleum had a high gloss free from dirt and grime, and when he heard *again*, he took that beer away from his mouth, leaned over to Fred, and said, "Let's go, son."

That was the last time Clyde ever drank beer at Dave's. Many people describe weak beer as piss water. Clyde didn't want it to literally be true.

Wilbur Rife, Fort Robinson Nebraska, about 1943

10

"I joined for three hots and a cot."

The Army

"Mom called Jack to tell him that Dad died."
"I'll bet it hit Jack pretty hard."
"Who is Jack?" Kitty asked.
"Jack—Jack Hampton, Dad's best friend," Brian answered.
"Yeah, they met in the army out at Fort Robinson. Two hapless kids who both joined the army because they needed three square meals a day, a job, and a sense of belonging," I added.
"We grew up around Jack and Leona and their kids, Jeff and Susan. Dad and Jack were really close—like brothers," Brian explained.

"Dad lied about his age to get in. He was tired of being on the constant search for food. Dad always said about joining the army, 'I JOINED FOR THREE HOTS AND A COT.'"

* * *

Annie Rife was a great cook but not an abundant one. At Fort Robinson, Wilbur finally had good food and lots of it. The pain and emptiness in his stomach was gone. Wilbur had suffered through the Depression like most other Americans, and hunger had always haunted him. At Fort Robinson, Thanksgiving dinner was so formal each place setting had a small printed program describing the holiday feast that was served to the soldiers.

Wilbur met his best friend in the army in this barren outpost in the Sand Hills in the panhandle of Nebraska. Fort Robinson had started as a camp, and later it became a fort. It was named for Lieutenant Robinson, who was killed in the Indian wars.

Jack Mansel Hampton was a scrappy kid. He was born in 1923 in Neligh, Nebraska, just a couple of months before Wilbur. Jack had, for all practical purposes, been orphaned. His parents weren't dead per se, but they could no longer take care of him. His father, Roy Hampton, had killed his best friend in a drunken dispute over a card game and was sentenced to a prison term. Since it was his best buddy that Roy killed, the court gave him a reduced sentence—one year and one day—as there wasn't premeditation or malice involved.

His mother, Blanche, couldn't see how she would take care of four children by herself, so she placed an ad in the newspaper: "Boy will work for room and board." He was seven years old when he was first farmed out to the different families in search of a home. He lived with seven different families in about as many years working farms, tending to cattle, sometimes cows, sometimes sheep.

Jack and Wilbur both arrived at Fort Robinson. Jack got there a month or two before Wilbur in late 1940. Jack had decided that he had had enough of moving from family to family and working for his keep. While none of the people he lived with were exactly cruel to him, they didn't provide much of a real home either. Jack always knew he was to earn his keep. He decided that he was going to join the army and asked if he could have enough money to take a bus to the army station in Omaha, Nebraska. When the last folks he was living with refused to spot him any money, he took to the road. Jack hitchhiked to Omaha. When he got there, he found the army recruiting station and asked the recruiter if they had something where he could continue to work with animals. He had always liked working with cattle and horses, even chickens and sheep.

Jack was assigned to Fort Robinson, a former Indian fort turned horse and mule outfit. Fort Robinson was often referred to as the Outpost on the Plains. And a barren outpost it was, stuck out in the Sand Hills—desolate, windswept, and teeming with soldiers training horses, mules, and K-9s. There were about three hundred guys in four barracks. There were also a number of outbuildings, such as horse barns, a veterinarian building, and a command post. All commanded by Colonel Jumpin' Jimmie.

After Jack signed up for the army in Omaha, the army put him on a train headed back to the area he had just come from, the Nebraska Panhandle.

Jack arrived at Fort Robinson and was set to clean out box stalls and take care of horses. About a month later, Wilbur was shipped to Fort Robinson, too.

Wilbur was assigned the same job. Jack had four stallions to take care of, and Wilbur had four stallions to take care of. Each horse had to be fed, curried, rubbed down, and exercised. Each horse had to be kept clean, as did their box stalls. The hay had to be changed and kept fresh.

Since Wilbur was new to the base, Jack decided to have a little fun at his expense and take it a bit easier. Jack thought, Hey, I'm smarter than this fresh recruit and country boy from Iowa. Jack convinced Wilbur that he was supposed to clean out the stalls that Jack had been assigned to clean. Jack was going to supervise the work.

After about two weeks, one of the other privates walked up to Wilbur and asked, "What in the hell are you doing? Why are you doing Hampton's work?"

Wilbur cocked his head and asked, "WHAT ARE YOU TALKING ABOUT?"

The private said, "He's tricked you; he's supposed to clean that box stall."

"THAT SON OF A BITCH!" Wilbur said to no one as he walked over to Jack.

"HOW COME I'M CLEANIN' YOUR BOX STALLS?" Wilbur yelled, moving closer to Jack.

"If you don't like it, let's go in this box stall and we'll just take care of this right here, right now," Jack retorted.

Jack and Wilbur stepped into the box stall to continue the argument. A couple of guys came over after hearing the exchange to watch what was unfolding.

Jack turned around to lean his pitchfork up against the box stall wall. When he turned back around, Wilbur hit him square in the jaw.

Down Jack went. Out. Wilbur landed his punch so hard that he coldcocked Jack. He wasn't moving, and he looked pale. He was out for nearly twenty minutes.

"SHIT, I KILLED HIM." Wilbur said nervously.

When Jack came to, Wilbur was standing over him fanning his face. Wilbur was afraid at this point that he was going to get in trouble on the base for fighting. But when Jack opened his eyes, he started laughing and so did the other guys who'd come over to watch the action.

Wilbur and a couple of the other guys grabbed Jack and carried him out of the box stall so he could get some fresh air.

Jack knew that he had it coming, so he didn't report Wilbur to the commanding officer. From that point on, they worked side by side in those box stalls and began to talk and struck up a lifelong friendship.

They were very much alike—farm boys who were, for the most part, on their own. They were together all the time. When Jack went to town, Wilbur went to town; when Wilbur went to town, Jack went to town. They just clicked.

Sometimes neither of them had much money. They were only paid twenty-one dollars a month, which didn't seem to go very far, especially in Crawford, the nearest town to the fort, where soldiers went to dance, drink, and chase women.

One of the local taverns had a basement. They'd cover up the holes in the pool tables and let the men throw dice. Wilbur liked to shoot craps, so he'd take Jack's money and shoot craps. Sometimes Wilbur would have a bad run and Jack and Wilbur wouldn't have any money for a whole month. Sometimes Wilbur would literally be on a "roll," and they'd have all kinds of money.

The year that Jack and Wilbur arrived at Fort Robinson was a busy year. It was announced that the fort would be taking on foreign prisoners of war. In the first year, nearly seven hundred Italian and German POWs were quartered at the post. K-9s were trained on the grounds—over three thousand were sent to the fort that year. And the animal population grew to its largest number by June of '43—over eleven thousand horses and mules were at the Fort Robinson Remount.

Some of the barns had studs, and some had horses that were about ready to kick the bucket. Wilbur and Jack both took care of the horses. Wilbur also jumped horses. If you had a good horse that would jump, you were all right. If you didn't have a horse that would jump, you couldn't do a good job, of course. Jack once jumped a horse that was wind broke. He would get up to the last jump and he would be out of wind. Jack went over the jump, and the horse stayed on the other side.

Along with the horses, Wilbur and Jack trained mules. There wasn't much to training the mules, though. They would mount the mules and ride them through the buttes—the soldiers rode them to add weight. They had to be trained to carry weight and get used to it as they walked through the trail. The mules were led by an old bell horse. Each team of twenty or so mules would follow that bell horse up through the buttes and down. It was a slow slog but not too taxing.

* * *

Clyde died in 1943 of a heart attack in the Onawa Hospital, Monona County, Iowa. Clyde was still living in his trailer on a vacant lot in Blencoe at the time. The night before Clyde died, he had been having chest pains. He thought it was indigestion, but the pain became more severe through the night. Clyde did not want to wake up anyone in the night so he waited until morning to get some help—by then it was too late. He was fifty-six years old.

A man named N. C. Gray took care of the arrangements for Clyde's funeral. On the morning that Clyde died, N. C. Gray wrote the following letter to Ada Jansen, Clyde's sister:

Dear Ada:

Your brother Clyde took sick early this morning and was taken to the hospital at Onawa. He passed away about seven o'clock this morning. His son, Private Wilbur Rife, is coming tonight from the army camp to take charge of the funeral. The body is at my place. Forney was here a few minutes ago and wanted to know if a grave site on your lot in the Little Sioux Cemetery could be used for his resting place. If this is satisfactory with you, you can write me. The funeral will be Wednesday afternoon at two o'clock here in Blencoe.

Very truly yours, N. C. Gray.

To get to the funeral, Wilbur took a bus.

Clyde's *Little Sioux Hustler* obituary inaccurately read, listing his age as fifty-five instead of fifty-six: "*Clyde Rife, 55, of Blencoe, maintenance worker for the Northwestern railroad, passed away in the Deering Hospital early Sunday morning after a few hours illness with heart trouble. Services are being held this Wednesday afternoon at the Congregational Church in Blencoe, and interment at the Little Sioux Cemetery. Clyde was the son of Mr. and Mrs. George Rife, now deceased. He is survived by two sons, Pvt. Freddie Rife now in Africa and Wilbur Rife at Ft. Robinson near Crawford, Nebraska, and a daughter, Lucy, in St. Louis; and also four brothers and eight sisters; and other relatives.*"

The paper didn't really speak to the kind of person Clyde was. His sister-in-law, Myrtle, Ada's sister, offered some comfort to Wilbur. "Ya know, Mama just loved him. He was a good guy, Clyde was. Oh, Mama thought Clyde was just, well, he was nice. Clyde was a good guy."

After the funeral, there wasn't much left to do but head back to Fort Robinson. Wilbur drove Clyde's beat-up four-cylinder Ford back to the Remount. The Ford, which didn't even have a back seat, only lasted about a few months and was torn to hell when Wilbur got it, but it was a set of wheels, such as they were.

Wilbur had gone into Crawford to do some drinking—one of the few times Jack wasn't with him. In those days, the cops wouldn't arrest soldiers headed back to camp drunk. They would just make the least drunk person in the car get behind the wheel. It was sort of a "point them in the right direction and let them take off" gesture. That particular night, it happened to be Wilbur who was the least drunk—most likely a rare occurrence. Unfortunately, though, on his way back to the fort, Wilbur swerved to miss something he saw or thought he saw in the road, and the car headed into a road ditch and straight into a pasture, barreling through a fence on the way. The old Ford rolled three times and landed sitting upright, tangled in barbed wire.

The guys all shook it off, bruised and battered. When they got their wits about them, they cut their way out of the barbed wire. The car was in really bad shape. Some bales of straw, which were being used as seats, exploded in the rollover. They pulled the straw out of their hair as Wilbur drove back to the base.

The next day, Jack and Wilbur picked up some sacks of straw as replacement seats for the back. The car was practically good as new!

Only a few weeks later, Jack drove the Ford into town. He got drunk and got most of the way back to the base, but when he rounded a turn, he lost control and drove the car into the ditch. He couldn't get the car started, so he left it and walked the rest of the way back to the base.

When Jack got back to the barracks, he woke Wilbur up.

"Hey, Wib, I wrecked your car," Jack said, as he stood there swerving back and forth.

"DON'T WORRY ABOUT IT. GET YOUR ASS TO BED, AND WE'LL TAKE CARE OF IT IN THE MORNING."

The next morning after an inspection, which didn't take long, Wilbur determined the car couldn't be fixed. The Ford was done.

* * *

The army was a good place for Wilbur. It gave him a sense of family and a sense of belonging. He had made friends in his unit, with Jack

Hampton nearly always at his side. They were inseparable—which did cause a few troubles for Wilbur. For one thing, Jack lipped off to other guys rather freely. Jack was always getting Wilbur into fights. Jack held Wilbur's coat many times while they were at Fort Robinson. Wilbur liked to fight, so he wasn't altogether mad at Jack for egging on a bit of the fighting.

One fight got started when a big staff sergeant barked at Wilbur, "Hey, soldier, put your hat on."

They were off base, and it irritated Wilbur, who shot back, "I DON'T REALLY LIKE HOW YOU SAID THAT."

The sergeant came back, "If you don't like it, why don't you do something about it?"

The fight was on. Wilbur won. After that, others wanted to give it a try to see if they could whip Wilbur.

On the heels of the fight with the sergeant was another argument that started in one of the local bars in Crawford—off base. Wilbur and Jack were standing at the bar quaffing a tall cold one, when a soldier of Italian descent came in. Everyone called him Dago.

Dago said to Wilbur, "I heard you been fighting a few guys, and you think you are some sort of tough guy."

Wilbur turned around. "HEY, WE ARE JUST HAVING A COUPLE OF BEERS."

"Well, I guess maybe you ain't as tough as maybe you think you are."

"I DON'T WANT ANY TROUBLE. JUST LEAVE US ALONE."

"That's what I thought."

"OKAY, THEN, DAGO, LET'S GET IT OVER WITH."

The two of them walked out the back door with Jack trailing. It was raining pretty hard, but the two squared off anyway in the empty lot behind the beer joint. There was some construction work going on, with dirt piled up about waist high in the middle of the lot.

Dago put his hands up in a fighting position, his feet planted firmly on the edge of the pile of dirt. Wilbur punched him in the jaw. Dago fell backward into the pile of what was now mud because of the rain. Wilbur turned around and walked back into the bar. Wilbur and Dago never had another problem after that.

* * *

Wilbur and Jack lived in the barracks on base. It was a large two-story wooden building. On the first and second floors were large rooms lined with single bunks where they slept.

One summer, Jack had been out the night before and got in after Wilbur had gone to sleep. They were getting ready for morning mess.

"Wilbur, I think I am in a shitload of trouble."

"WHAT DID YOU DO?"

"Well, last night I got to talking to Susan."

"THE SERGEANT'S DAUGHTER?"

"Yep."

"ARE YOU SHITTIN' ME? YOU SILLY SON OF A BITCH. YOU OUGHT TO KNOW BETTER."

"Anyway, we was just sittin' in the backseat of my car when her mama came out looking for her and spotted us. She comes over to the car, and I rolled down the window and she asks, 'What are you kids doing?'"

"HAMPTON, YOU ARE IN DEEP SHIT."

"I told her we was just talkin'. But her mama wasn't having it. I'm pretty sure she thought we were necking. She told Sue to get into the house, and she marched her right in."

Jack should have known better, but the allure of a young and beautiful girl turned Jack's head and got the better of him. All of the soldiers knew better than to approach the daughters living on post, but that night, emotions got the better of Jack.

"Goddamn, here comes the sergeant."

"You son of a bitch," the sergeant said, "if I catch you with Sue again, I'll kick the hell out of you."

Two weeks later, Jack was history, headed for Texas. He shipped out with the Thirtieth Division, 119th Regiment, headed for the European Theater.

"That bastard is sending me out on account of Sue. He doesn't trust me on the base with his daughter," Jack said. "I just got shanghaied."

* * *

About a month or so later, Wilbur and his other buddies headed to India, Burma, and China.

It was September 1943 when the Fighting 54 Plus 2 Plus 2, which they called themselves, were shipped by train to Pittsburg, California. From there, they boarded the SS *Peter Silvester*, packed with soldiers, supplies, mules, and horses. By November, the Remount and all of the animals they were transporting with them landed in Hobart, Tasmania. The crew members went ashore and celebrated. Then they were off to Karachi, India.

Shirley Rasmussen (Rife)

11

"The first one can come anytime; the rest take nine months."

Marriage

We were driving past the frozen, frost-covered corn stubble. The clouds were low in the sky, and the day was gray and bleak and mirrored the cold, desperate feelings of loss I was struggling with.

After a long silence, Brian asked, "Do you know the story of how Mom and Dad met?"

"Yeah, I do," I said, as we rode along the Lincoln Highway.

***

Shirley had been anxious to get out on her own.

Her folks were hardworking farm people. They had started their marriage in the far northwest corner of Nebraska.

Though the panhandle of Nebraska was not the most productive farm ground, Hans and Carrie Rasmussen, Shirley's parents, were able to start a family on the income produced by ranching in the sand hills. Their first two children, Leona and Lavane, were born in western Nebraska. By the time Crofford, their third child, was born, Hans and Carrie were farming outside of the little town of Custer, South Dakota.

The rest of their children—six more, making the brood total a whopping nine—were born in Custer: Claudia, Earl, Laura, Wilber, Shirley, and Perry.

Farm life in South Dakota was hard. As one farmer put it, "farmin' in the Black Hills was slim pickins." The farm in Custer was relatively small at 160 acres, with a 60-acre plot off to one side and a 40-acre plot on the other, as well as land leased from the US government for grazing. Since Hans was not a progressive farmer, he would not allow the government to bring electricity across his land nor telephone lines. Kerosene lamps lit the farm, even up into the 1930s and 1940s after the REC had wired most of the farms around the countryside. Though Hans had an old tractor or two from time to time, he was far more comfortable working his land with horses. Hans knew horses. He raised horses that he sold to the Remount during World War II.

Hans also raised cattle and hogs and made ends meet by mining mica from a small mine on the farm. The mica was used in the manufacture of aircraft during the war.

They did all sorts of different things to raise a little money here and there. One year, Hans and Carrie had so many potatoes that they allowed people to come out and dig up their own potatoes for so much as a bushel basket.

Life was hard for a woman on the farm. Carrie had been a schoolteacher after she received her Normal Training, with a passion for reading poetry and Shakespeare. Most of the reading, though, was laid aside when she began having children of her own.

Carrie was a hardworking woman—she had to be. She canned over a thousand quarts a year. She was the kind of woman who took care to put up everything that was in season—corn, beans, tomatoes, peas, carrots, and pickles, which she literally made by the barrel. She canned milk. She made butter, cottage cheese, homemade cheese, sauerkraut, and canned meat. Even ketchup. Sometimes the meat was packed in lard and stored in the cellar; sometimes it was canned and put up in brine. She made jams and jellies from the strawberries, raspberries, and wild berries around the farm. She also made delicious apple butter.

She raised chickens. Every spring, Carrie bought between 1,000 and 1,500 chicks and raised them to lay eggs and to butcher. She always singed them and then put them in a pan of water and scrubbed them in soap and water, then rinsed them. She butchered them and then took the dressed chickens to town to sell for extra money. She could kill and dress a hundred chickens in a day. She also raised and butchered turkeys. Along with making assorted canned goods for the family, she also made her own soap.

From all descriptions, she was a great cook and baker. She even made great fruitcakes. She baked her fruitcakes in September for Christmas. After they were baked, she poured brandy over the top of them, wrapped them in cloth, and packed them into round tins. When her sons were overseas during World War II, she packed the tins with extra care and shipped them.

As hard as life was on the farm, there was time for house dances. The men would move the furniture out of the main rooms of the house where the dancing took place and the women would cook and put on a meal. Neighbors for miles would come and dance until the wee hours of the morning. There was no liquor. No one drank, nor was it allowed in their home except for cooking purposes and peach brandy for use in a hot toddy for the odd cold.

The farmhouse was big and spacious. The upstairs was sort of split into two barracks or dorms. On one side was the girls' room and the other was the boys'. In the boys' room there were two double beds and a single bed. The girls' room had two double beds. One of the walls in the hallway had floor-to-ceiling books; there was never any shortage of things to read. Hans and Carrie were sort of opposites. Hans was strong-minded, stubborn, and quick-tempered. Carrie was a gentle, easy going, and kind woman.

While there was a break in the work from time to time, it was still drudgery, never-ending drudgery.

Shirley wanted to get out of the house and out of school. She was shy, quiet, and awkward. She didn't have but two sweaters and two skirts for school, and she had cut off bib overalls to wear in PE class instead of the standard white one-piece gym suit. Some of the other girls made fun of her. She hated school because she didn't feel like she fit in. So, in 1947, at the tender age of sixteen, she quit high school, hoping to escape from the farm drudgery and the girls in school who teased her.

Shirley first started working as a dishwasher at the Black Hills Café, the best café in Custer she always said. Later she moved to Hot Springs, where she got an apartment and started waitressing at a café there.

The restaurant was long and narrow. So narrow, in fact, that it only had counters running down the length of the building with no booths. Shirley was working as a waitress, taking orders and delivering the food up and down the long counter.

At sixteen, she was five-foot-six, thin, with curly dark brown hair, and big brown eyes.

* * *

In July of '45, when the war ended, Jack came back to the United States, and the first thing he did was go out looking for Wilbur. He sought out Don Hall, or "Hall D" as he was called, at Fort Robinson to find him.

A few months later, in October, Wilbur left Karachi and landed at Pier 88 in New York. He was sent to Camp Kilmer, New Jersey, and ate a big meal—probably plenty happy to be off the rations. He was discharged at Fort Leavenworth, Kansas, and hitchhiked to Dallas, Texas, where his mother was living at the time. A few days of that was enough, so he made his way to River Sioux, Iowa, which he considered his hometown—such as it was. Then he headed out to the fort to see it again and see if he could reconnect with any of his old buddies.

Needing work, Wilbur eventually landed in Omaha pounding the pavement, answering ads looking for a job. While he was looking, Hall D got word to Wilbur that Jack was looking for him. The two best friends finally reconnected. Jack had an apartment and Wilbur moved in—saying that he'd start paying his share as soon as he found work.

Wilbur was eager but not having any luck when the old gal from the employment office noticed that he was serious about working. She put Wilbur in touch with a plastering contractor. He signed up and started learning the trade at a whopping seventy-five cents an hour. Wasn't much, but he was glad to have it, and he stayed with it for about eight months. When the plastering work dried up, he went back up to River Sioux for the season and worked as a bartender.

The next several seasons were erratic. The following spring, he went to work as a railroad and bridge carpenter but was laid off after seven months. Again, he set up in River Sioux for the winter. In the spring of 1947, Wilbur went to Lake Andes, South Dakota, to work on the Fort Randall Dam as a heavy equipment operator. In the fall, though, the weather was bad and he was only working one day a week, so several of the crew members loaded up into a car and headed south to look for work that was steadier. One of the guys had a brother-in-law who was a superintendent for Peter Kewitt at Hot Springs. Three of the five got jobs. One of them was Wilbur.

* * *

In early spring, after getting this gig, Wilbur went into the Black Hills Café for breakfast. He noticed Shirley straight away. She was wearing a light blue uniform that was a knee-length dress with a bright white starched apron, stockings, and white shoes. Wilbur said of this first encounter with her, "SHE WAS ALL LEGS AND TITS."

He struck up a conversation with her and asked her to a dance. They both enjoyed dancing, and they hit it off pretty quickly. The first time they met to dance, it was in a bar. They had fun and agreed to go out the next night to the auditorium in Hot Springs, where a live band was performing. A big band.

Wilbur wasn't looking for a long-term relationship. He was only twenty-four and just wanting to have fun. Shirley was a good dancer, and that seemed enough for him right then. He and Shirley even fooled around the Saturday night after the dance.

The very next morning, she was anxious to talk with him. When they got together, Wilbur could tell that something was wrong.

"Wilbur, I'm pregnant."

He cocked his head and looked at her in disbelief. "JESUS, SHIRLEY, YOU CAN'T KNOW THAT YOU ARE PREGNANT THE NEXT DAY."

"Well, I can tell," she said. "I just know that I am."

Wilbur wasn't sure if it was the guilt talking or remorse. In those days, when you got a girl in trouble, you married her. But all Wilbur knew was that he wasn't going to do that.

The next day, he took off.

Nine months later, Wilbur Michael "Mike" was born on the Rasmussen farm. Carrie served as the midwife, which she had done for many others in their neighborhood and farm community. There was a snowstorm, and the doctor had a hard time getting there, but he made it. Shirley was now back on the farm and not where she hoped she'd be.

Wilbur did not jump at doing the right thing. He ignored the letter he received from Carrie Rasmussen telling him that he had a little boy he should come see. Long about three months later, Shirley heard that Wilbur was working at Lake Andes and sent word to him that she'd had the baby. The plea spurred Wilbur to go to Hot Springs to see baby Michael.

Shirley had named him Wilbur Michael—she said years later that Mike was named after her brother, Wilber, but that he spelled it differently. Maybe it was to shame Wilbur, maybe not. Anyway, Wilbur was pretty hard to shame. He looked at his hands and said, "YEAH, THIS IS MY KID." Even as an infant, Mike had very square hands—the palm shaped just like Wilbur's.

Wilbur was working on a construction project on the Fall River at the time—a truck driver during the winter months and heavy equipment operator at the Fort Randall Dam in Pickstown during the summer and fall months.

After a brief, unromantic courtship, Shirley and Wilbur married. The Custer newspaper society pages reported their wedding in a fairly brief paragraph:

RASMUSSEN-RIFE NUPTIALS AT CUSTER LAST THURSDAY, Miss Shirley Rasmussen of Custer, and Wilbur Rife of Lake Andes, were married at Custer April 14 at 4:30 p.m. with Judge Webster Davis officiating. The single ring service was used. The bride chose for her wedding, a powder blue suit and white accessories with which she wore a corsage of red carnations. Her attendant, Miss Margaret Wilhelm, of Hot Springs, was attired in an aqua dress and white accessories. She wore a corsage of pink baby roses. Andy Thorn of Murdo, attended the groom. A reception was held at the home of the bride's parents [Hans and Carrie Rasmussen]. Mr. and Mrs. Rife left Friday for Lake Andes, where they will make their home. Rife, who formerly was employed by Peter T. Kiewit and Sons on the Fall River project, is now employed on the Garrison Dam project. Mrs. Rife, until recently, was employed as a waitress at the Cave Café here.

At first the happy couple lived at Lake Andes in a dinky little trailer house on the outskirts of town. They didn't stay there too long before they moved into a one-room cabin right out on the lake. A one-room cabin with just the bare necessities. A bed, a stove, an ice box. That's it.

They hopped around a bit. From there, they moved into town into a small trailer house. It had a bunk bed on one end of it, and on the other end, there was a little stove, a refrigerator, and a table that made down into a bed. They put Michael on that table at night. There wasn't much room at all. Shirley was nearly stir-crazy sitting in that little trailer all day with a baby. Wilbur went off to work every day, and Shirley sat in that little trailer taking care of their baby. Wilbur made it clear that he was not going to be one of those fathers who was active in the care and feeding of his children. All of those duties were going to be hers and hers alone. Shirley was in a slump and felt trapped in a life she'd not planned for.

At this point, Wilbur was a seasonal worker going from place to place for a job—any job. By that fall, Wilbur and Ron worked for Billie Welsh as farmhands in Harrison County, Iowa. Ronnie's wife at the time, Norma Rae Capehart, and Shirley did laundry and cooking. Norma Rae didn't much do her share. She was a layabout. Shirley told Wilbur she was sick and tired of carrying Norma's weight with the chores and taking care of her son at the same time.

"Why the hell do I have to do all of her work, for god's sake?"

"DON'T ROCK THE BOAT, SHIRLEY. TRY TO GET ALONG."

"I don't know why she can't get off her ass and do something. Anything. I am doing it all and taking care of Michael. All she does is lay around!" Shirley started having long bouts with depression. She picked up smoking—unfiltered Chesterfield Kings.

In early '51, Shirley and Wilbur moved to Sioux City, and Wilbur drove a truck for Bob Smith and his wife, Zeta. Bob Smith had served overseas with Wilbur in the Fighting 54 Plus 2 Plus 2. They trucked eggs mostly.

By June, Shirley and Wilbur were on the move again. That year, they moved to Norfolk, Virginia. They rented a room in a boarding house from Neda Bea Custis. Her husband was said to be the last surviving descendant of Martha Dandridge Custis Washington. According to Shirley, Neda Bea carried herself like a proper lady. She wasn't very excited about Wilbur's cussing and remarked to Shirley, "That man of yours is the cussingest man I have ever met." It was true, Wilbur peppered even average sentences with swear words—and he could string them together creatively.

Later that year, Wilbur shipped out to Thule Air Force Base in Greenland. He was to work on heavy equipment building the air base there. A base of sorts already existed at Thule, but under a secret and special arrangement between the United States government and the Danish government, a new agreement was reached to update and modernize the base at Thule. The building began in secret under the code name Operation Blue Jay in 1951. Wilbur was given a series of immunity shots and worked on the base from 1951 to 1953, and from 1956 to 1958. Each of those years, Wilbur had to be given typ-para and tetanus shots before he flew to Greenland. Wilbur shipped out in April or May after the first year and then would come back in the fall after the short construction season. The first armada of men and supplies arrived in Thule in July 1951. Twelve thousand men and some three hundred thousand tons of cargo were shipped to Greenland from the Norfolk Naval Station. That first season, the men lived on the ships until they could get accommodations built on the base—then the ships returned to the Naval Station.

Again, Shirley was all alone with the sole responsibility of taking care of an infant without any help from Wilbur—he was gone. It was all up to her and in a place where she did not know anyone or have any family or friends nearby. So, in the spring of 1952, Shirley picked up and moved to Laytonville, California, to be close to two of her sisters, Laura and Claudia.

Wilbur returned to Greenland for another season of operating heavy equipment at the air base at Thule. He spent a total of six seasons in Greenland on construction. Clyde Mansel (Deke) Rife was born in Willits, Mendocino County, California, in July 1952. Wilbur was in charge of naming this baby. Clyde after his father. Mansel after Jack Mansel Hampton. Clyde was a sick baby who cried night and day. He was born with a double hernia and was in pain much of the time. Everyone knew he was in pain, too, by the way he screamed. One of Shirley's brothers looked in on the little baby was who screaming his head off and made the comment that the baby looked like a little old church deacon. The name Deacon stuck and eventually got shortened to Deke.

In 1954, Shirley gave birth to stillborn twin daughters. She spun into a long depression. She badly wanted a girl. She had planned on naming Michael, then Deke, Michelle if either had been born a girl. Now she had lost twin girls. She was hurled into a depression and grieved for her lost daughters.

It was the same year that the family moved to Omaha, Nebraska. Shirley and Wilbur bought a small stucco house with a front porch that led to the living room and dining room area. A stairway led to a two-room second floor, one finished, the other unfinished.

Off one side of the dining room area was a door that led to a bedroom and a little plywood door with a silver knob that went down to the dirt basement. The basement would often get infested with rats. The dining room also had a doorway that opened to a long narrow kitchen. On one side of the kitchen was a small porch that had just enough room for a washer and dryer and a door that led outside.

Just to the side of the house and back was a little one-car garage that was in bad shape. It had rafters and storage over the rafters. On the other side of the house was a chicken coop.

Wilbur went to work for Howard Johnson as a plasterer.

The last two of their sons were born in Omaha, Nebraska. Brian Mark was born in September 1955, in the University Hospital. He was named for a golf buddy of Wilbur's.

I was born October 16, 1956, in the Doctor's Hospital. The nurse brought in this new little moon-faced bundle of joy, and Shirley was just about to name me Douglas *Montgomery* Rife. Then she looked down at her newborn baby boy and thought to herself, He'll never be able to spell all of that. So, there on the spot she changed her mind and named me Douglas *Marlin* Rife. That decision didn't demonstrate a lot of faith in her newborn but was practical. Incidentally, *Marlin* was the name of a boy who had tormented Shirley when she was a young girl by putting frogs down her bloomers. She couldn't pull her pants down to release the frogs squirming around in her pants, so she had to walk out of sight before she could get the frogs out.

Wilbur went for a vasectomy. He didn't want any more children and said that I would be the tailender of the W. M. Rife family. There would not be another chance at a daughter.

With four boys, they needed more money to pay the bills. Shirley first went to work at the Wander Inn Café. We spent many nights sleeping on potato sacks in the kitchen waiting for her shift to end. The pay was bad and the hours worse. So, contrary to her teetotaling upbringing, Shirley took a job as a bartender for Bus Triplett at the Wander Inn Bar, which neighbored the café of the same name.

* * *

Wilbur didn't go to Greenland the spring of 1957, which turned out to be a good thing.

One Wednesday, just a little after noon, Deke began a search for one of his toys—a little red Indian doll.

He went to the stove, turned on the gas jet, and waited for it to ignite. Click, click, click, and then poof, the blue flame twinkled. He lit a candle, so he could look for it in all of the dark places.

Deke began by looking under a bed and couldn't see anything, so he moved on. He opened the closet door in his parents' bedroom. There was a dry-cleaning bag hanging in the closet. Deke got the flame too close to the bag, and it just went *whoosh*.

"Oh, no!" Panicked, he ran to the kitchen to get a bucket of water.

The drain pipe underneath the kitchen sink wasn't hooked up. The water drained from the sink directly into a bucket, and then we would throw the water out, either out the back door or down the bathtub drain. Deke, at five years old, couldn't lift the bucket, so he ran to the living room. Shirley had put Brian and me down in the living room on a sofa sleeper for our afternoon nap. She lay down with us to settle us down and fell asleep herself.

"Mom, Mom, there's a fire!"

After that announcement to a groggy mother, Deke ran out the back door and into the garage to hide. Shirley raised her head and smelled smoke. She got up and headed to the bedroom door, and when she opened it, smoke billowed out. She bolted for the sofa sleeper and scooped Brian and me up and dashed outside. It had snowed the day before—she laid us down in a snow bank by the driveway and headed back into the house to look for Deke.

"Deke!" she called out, but no answer. "Deke!" still no answer.

The flames were climbing the living room walls. Shirley backed out of the living room coughing. She picked us up from the snow drift and ran to the neighbor's house.

"Quick, call the fire department; our house is on fire!"

Shirley left the boys at the neighbor's house and ran back to her house. She kept calling for Deke but couldn't get into the house. She was frantic.

At least Mike was at school and safe.

Wilbur heard the news through a coworker, who said, "I'm not sure but from my wife talking to your wife, I think your house burned down. I think you should go home."

Wilbur responded, "YEAH, I THINK I PROBABLY SHOULD."

The fire crew arrived and began spraying the house to douse the flames. Deke sheepishly emerged from the garage, safe but terrified.

Douglas, Mike, Brian, and Deke Rife

12

"If there weren't two kinds of luck, we wouldn't have any."

Luck

The house was nearly totaled. Much of the interior was gutted, and windows on the bedroom side and front of the house were blown out. It was not livable.

The family moved into an apartment in Omaha. Owned by a city engineer, it was a big old white frame house. The family we rented from lived upstairs with their six kids. We lived in two rooms on the bottom floor and shared a bathroom on that floor.

Over the next two or three months, the crew Wilbur worked with at Howard Johnson's came to help at the burned house. They tore the plaster down to the studs in the living room, dining room, kitchen, and Shirley and Wilbur's bedroom, and they put up new lath and plastered it. They also installed new windows and put down linoleum tile in the entire bottom floor. They painted—the dining room and living room were gray, the bedroom green, and the kitchen was a bright yellow, which Shirley never really liked. It was just too sunny for her disposition. Sunny she was not. She was the living embodiment of the Eeyore character. The two rooms in the upstairs were mostly spared, but the room on the north side was repainted. The room on the south side was literally carpeted floor to ceiling, the entire ceiling—a neutral beige color with no personality. A bare light bulb hung down in the center of the room.

Wilbur hired a guy to start building the cabinets in the kitchen. While he was installing the frame and the white-with-gold-flecked Formica countertops, he was essentially using Mike as his helper.

"Hey, kid, grab my saw." "Hey, kid, run and get me another box of finish nails out of my truck." "Hey, kid, go get me a piece of wood about this size out of the back end of my truck."

Mike was getting tired of being bossed around by this guy and told the guy to go to hell. The cabinetmaker was pissed off enough that he walked off the job and never came back. The frame of the cabinets was up but with no doors, no drawers. It was left undone—just a wooden frame with a countertop.

Once they moved back in, things got back to a sort of normalcy. Shirley and Wilbur bought a sectional for the living room. They had a blonde Philco television set—the kind that looked like a piece of furniture. It had a small round screen. Wilbur had a big, gray easy chair planted directly in front of the television that backed up to the staircase leading upstairs. Right around the corner was the metal dining room table and chairs. The top of the table was red. Up against one wall was a china cabinet. On the wall facing that was a telephone with a long cord. The basement door was in the dining room, too. The stairs were precarious leading to the dirt basement. The water heater and furnace were set on concrete slabs, but the floors and walls were dirt—stale dirt, parts of which were covered with a white film. The basement smelled old and musty.

Shirley told Wilbur that as long as he was fixing up the house, he should do something to rid the basement of rats. "Jesus, Wilbur, they are scratching at the basement door. I can hear them at night, and sometimes I can see their paws coming up from underneath the damn door!"

"I CAN GET A BULL SNAKE DOWN THERE. THAT'LL TAKE CARE OF IT." Wilbur thought that was just the right solution.

"If you bring a goddamn snake into this house, I am moving out," Shirley answered.

So, from time to time, Wilbur would go down to the basement and corner the rats, stomp them to death, pick them up by their tails, and throw them up on the railroad tracks behind our house.

* * *

In April of '58, Wilbur headed back to Greenland to the Thule Airforce Base to work heavy equipment. Things seemed like they were getting back to normal. But, on Wednesday, July 9 of that year, all of that was to change, and change for the worse.

That afternoon, some of the neighbor boys had come over to play—a boy Mike's age, nine, and one about Deke's age, five. Deke and his friend were wrestling out in the front yard. In the scrimmage, I got pushed forward and fell on the front step face forward. When I hit the cement step, I bit through my lip, cutting open a gash about an inch and a half or so long. Blood started dripping down my face. I ran crying to Shirley, who held a washrag against the cut to stop the bleeding.

Shirley loaded me into the front seat of our black and yellow Catalina Pontiac and headed to see the doctor to get the wound stitched up. Shirley left Mike in charge.

Mike and his friend kept playing. One of them had crawled up in the loft of the old garage and got a gas can down. They built a little fire out in the backyard, but it didn't flame up like they thought it was going to. So they dumped gasoline on it. They stood back and struck matches and pitched them at their stack of twigs and paper scraps to see who could get a match to light it up—sort of a flaming basket.

Mike had just turned to go inside the house to fix something for everyone to eat when the other boy struck a match, but he didn't think it lit. He flicked the match behind him to discard it, not paying attention to either the gas can that was there or Brian who had walked up to see what was going on.

What was thought to be an unlit match landed right in the gas can. Brian stumbled and fell toward the gas can just as the match flew in, and it exploded. Gas shot out of the mouth of the gas can onto Brian's face, setting his face aflame.

Deke was sitting on top of the chicken coop, which he called his fort, with his friend. He heard the poof of the gas pouring up out of the can and looked in Brian's direction to see what had happened.

A jar Deke had up on the fort rolled off the chicken coop and broke. When Brian cried out, Deke jumped off the chicken coup to see what he could do to help and landed on the broken jar, cutting open his foot.

"Oh, god," Mike screamed. "Go tell the Rayburns we need help." Off Deke went, hobbling as quick as he could, his foot bleeding all the way over to the Rayburns', which was directly across the gravel road from the house. The Rayburns called the rescue unit.

Mike ran into the house to call Jack and Leona Hampton's house. Leona answered, and Mike panted out the news that there had been a terrible accident and to come quick to help. On the race out of the house, Mike grabbed a stick of butter. He had heard that was what would make a burn feel better. By the time Mike got back outside, Brian had fallen. Mike lifted him to his feet and began patting out the fire on Brian's face and applying the butter as pieces of Brian's skin came off into Mike's hands.

After what seemed like a lifetime, Shirley's car pulled up. Shirley could instantly see that something was wrong. A wave of panic washed over her. From her neck down, she started to feel hot. Brian was standing in the doorway, and she could see his face looked different. Shirley got out of the car and ran over. Mike said, "Brian's been burned. Brian's been burned." Mike, standing next to Brian, looked down.

By that time, Shirley could see there was no skin on his face, which was scarlet. Brian looked like a ghost. He was standing somehow, but his body felt limp.

Mike blurted out, "I'm sorry. It was my fault."

Frantically Shirley asked, "What happened? Michael! What in the hell happened?"

Mike was in a state of shock himself. His hands were burnt from putting out the fire on Brian's face, and he was scared. He was already awash in guilt.

"It was my fault," he repeated. "We was playing with the gas trying to make an explosion. I turned my back to go inside to make some food to eat. Just for a minute. But, when I turned around, the gas can blew up on Brian."

"Jesus Christ, Michael!"

Leona Hampton's car pulled into the gravel road that led to the house. Within seconds, the ambulance that had barreled into the neighborhood—siren screaming—had thrown open the back door with EMTs emerging.

"Michael, go in the house." Shirley's voice was stern. She was mad and overwhelmed by despair.

"Lee, can you watch Mike and Dougie? Oh, and take the neighbor kids home?"

Leona nodded yes as Deke and Brian were loaded into the back of the ambulance, which took off heading to Immanuel Hospital.

When Jack got home from work, Leona went to the hospital to see how Brian and Deke were doing. The emergency doctors had bandaged Brian's face and Deke's foot. As Leona got there, the doctors were releasing both of them. Shirley and Wilbur didn't have insurance, and the costs were racking up without a way for them to pay.

Wilbur's sister, Lucy, had come to get Mike, Deke, and me for the night.

Shirley packed up and carried Brian to the car and drove to stay the night at Jack and Leona's. Brian lay there like a tiny, still mummy. Only his eyes, nose holes, and a slit for his mouth weren't covered.

Through the night, Brian just kept getting worse and worse. It was as if she could feel the life leaving his frail body. Occasionally, Shirley would put her face next his mouth to check for his breath.

"Jesus, Shirley," Jack said, "I was in the army. I knew guys that was in shock, and he is in shock."

Brian was motionless.

"Shirley, you better take that baby to the hospital right now. If you don't, I'm going to take him myself."

Jack continued, "He's in shock, that's what it is, you know. I've seen them in that. Goddamn it, he has got to go to the hospital right now."

Shirley called the doctor and told him what had happened and the condition Brian seemed to be in. Her voice trembled.

The doctor said, "Get him in here right away. He should never have been released from the hospital. Bring him in now."

Shirley said faintly, "Okay, I'll bring him back."

So, at around two in the morning, Leona drove Brian and Shirley to the hospital.

Brian was in bad shape and was barely hanging on.

As soon as they laid Brian down on a gurney, the nurses surrounded him and started rubbing him all over and getting the blood circulating. They were bringing him back from the brink of death, and none too soon.

Shirley and Leona watched the gurney trail off down the corridor, and all that was left for them to do was wait, hope, and pray.

It had been a horrendous day. Brian was burnt beyond recognition, Mike's hands were burnt, Deke's foot was cut open, and it all started with my lip getting stitched up.

Shirley sat next to Leona in the hospital waiting room. She was ashen and broken from the day. She could barely lift her cigarette.

"What a horrible day," Leona said.

Shirley thought for a while about everything she and her four boys had gone through in that one afternoon. She turned and looked at Leona and said, "If there weren't two kinds of luck, we wouldn't have any."

"Shirley, it will get better," Leona said.

Shirley, who could be prone to hyperbolic expression, said, "This has been the worst day of my life." And it was not at all overstated.

Deke

13

"For your information, it starts with a w."

Ashes

When Wilbur came back from Greenland for the last time, he went back to work for Howard Johnson's in Omaha as a plasterer. Things then got into a routine of sorts. Wilbur and some of his co-workers from Howard Johnson's had fixed up the house on Craig Street so it was livable.

He worked during the day. He was an early riser, getting up every morning at 5:00. He would shave and head to work well before any of us stirred from our beds. Shirley worked at night at the Wander Inn Bar, so she was in no position to get up the next morning and get us ready for school. Most mornings, Shirley slept in and we got ourselves ready.

If we ate breakfast, it was a bowl of cereal or oatmeal. Sometimes we would see her after school as she was dashing out to work. She'd say, "You little curtain climbers better be good!" or "I don't want you crumb snatchers to get into any trouble!" Then off she would go. She left the house at 4:00 in the afternoon and usually didn't get home until after closing time.

Wilbur would take care of us at night—sorta. And he became the primary disciplinarian. He would often leave us instructions on things we were to get done before he got home from work—pick up the house, empty the ashtrays, wash the dishes, sweep—general household cleaning.

If he walked in from a hard day's work and the chores weren't taken care of, there was hell to pay.

"WHY DIDN'T YOU DO WHAT I ASKED?" he would yell—the volume at a higher decibel level than usual.

Meekly, one of us would respond, "We was gonna do it."

"GONNA. GONNA? WHAT IF I WAS GONNA GO TO WORK AND THEN DIDN'T?"

He would stand there waiting for an answer, though knowing we weren't going to give him one.

"IF I WAS GONNA GO TO WORK AND DIDN'T, ALL OF YOUR ASSES WOULD BE HOMELESS WITH NO FOOD TO EAT!"

Once, Brian and I were up in a tree sitting on a limb. We had taken a can of Nestle's Quick up with us and were eating it with a spoon when Wilbur pulled into the driveway. We knew we were in trouble because none of us had done any of the chores he'd said better be done when he got home.

Wilbur got out of his truck and spotted us. He walked into the house and then right back out with Mike and Deke in tow. He looked up at us in the tree—"GET YOUR ASSES DOWN HERE."

We knew we were in trouble.

"WHY DIDN'T ANY OF YOU LITTLE SONS OF BITCHES DO WHAT I TOLD YOU TO DO? DON'T GIVE ME ANY OF THAT SHIT ABOUT HOW YOU WERE GONNA DO IT, EITHER."

Silence.

"ALL RIGHT, WHO WANTS TO GIT THEIR ASSES WHIPPED FIRST?"

You half wanted to jump up and yell, "Oh, I want to go first, I do, I do," but it was no time to be a smart aleck. No sense making the situation worse. I did think, though, if I went last that Wilbur would wear down some and I would get it a little easier. Everybody else just wanted to get it over with. We ended up lining up oldest to youngest while he broke off a switch from the mulberry tree and peeled the bark in the front yard.

"LINE UP, YOU LITTLE BASTARDS."

Mike was first. The anticipation was excruciating. One by one, he switched us. We all knew that if we put our hands behind us to shield our backsides, he would whip us harder, so we fought to urge to be in a protective mode.

His last admonition to all of us as he finished whipping me, "NOW THE NEXT TIME I TELL YOU TO DO SOMETHING GODDAMIT, MAYBE YOU'LL DO IT."

* * *

Sometimes there would be an hour or two between when Shirley left for work and when Wilbur came home from work. During that time, we had a succession of babysitters we did not like. They came and went for a variety of reasons—the inconvenience, the pay, the timing, us—whatever. The last babysitter we had, we absolutely hated. I remember her as a large, dark, hulking figure. I see her more as a specter of evil than a person. She barked at us, and Brian and I especially did not like her.

One time, she told us to do something that we were bound not to do, and we leapt up the stairs to get away from her wrath. She was close behind. There was an old door at the top of the stairs. When we got to the top of the stairs, the old door wobbled and we pushed it just enough that the hinges, already loose, gave way. The door fell and landed squarely on top of the babysitter, pinning her to the stairs. We bounced over the top of the door, and her, and out of the house to hide until Wilbur came home. That was the end of the babysitters. Mike watched us from that point on.

I was taken to River Sioux successive summers after Brian's accident to stay with Fred and Amy. Wilbur was working during the day, and Shirley was spending nearly all of her free time at the hospital to be with Brian for his multiple operations and procedures.

Fred worked on the Illinois Central Railroad after his jockey days were over. Amy was an elementary school teacher. Their son, Rick, and their four daughters, Rhonda, Robin, Rochelle, and Reynie Shawn, were like my other siblings. We were all very close. And during those summers after Brian's accident when he was going through skin grafting, it was like my home away from home. In fact, I was left behind so often I started to develop a complex about it. I had a little gray coat with brown buttons shaped like barrels. It seemed to me that when people put on their coats they got to leave. I became convinced that if I had my coat on, even if I didn't have on pants, socks, or shoes, that my parents wouldn't forget me. I was ready, I'd get to go.

Fred was sort of ornery. He liked to tease, and at times, he probably went too far, at least for the sensibilities of a frightened and homesick three-year-old. But he really didn't mean any harm as he would threaten to wrestle off my coat. As he would tug, I would pee my pants out of fear. That would unleash belly laughter from him. His job was done—I was wet.

Sometimes when Shirley and Wilbur came up to visit Fred and Amy's place, they would bring Brian along after one of his skin grafts. He would be bandaged like a mummy. He would hop out of the car, and I would yell, "Let's play mummy." Brian would put his arms straight out stiff and make chase. Obviously, Brian was destined to always play the mummy. It was type casting, or in the case of a low-budget theatrical group, he had the costume, so he always got the part.

Though just a tiny little wide spot in the road, the town of River Sioux, if it could be called that, had so many things to do and see, starting with Fred and Amy's place. For starters, they had a cellar. Sometimes if we ate too many green apples, Amy would make us go down to the cellar and she would put car tires on the door so we couldn't get out. That was punishment—a cold, dank, spider-webbed, and dark cellar, with no way out.

And the apple trees were so tempting—always full of green mouth-watering apples. Sometimes they were slightly out of reach, and I had to crawl a little further on the branch to get the one that looked best—like the time I got too far out on the limb and fell out of the tree onto a barbed wire fence. The barbs tore open the top of my foot, and I ran screaming to get help. Amy's common refrain in situations like that, like most parents at the time, was "it is too far from your heart to kill you." As she laid on the medical advice regarding my heart, she stuck my foot in a bucket and pumped ice-cold well water over my bleeding and gaping wound. Her prognosis had been correct, of course: I lived.

Amy not only dispensed needed medicine when necessary but also told great stories. I can remember those nights they put us to bed before they all went drinking in River Sioux. She would get us all tucked into bunk beds. Usually the stories would start in a whispered tone, "I was a cub reporter and had just been assigned to cover the recluse who lived in a large foreboding house high on a hill." She would always have to walk up the lane to get to the house, usually as night was falling—in that in-between time, between daylight and night, right at dusk when your hands start to disappear in front of your eyes because of the darkness. She would walk slowly up the tree-lined lane to the front door and knock on the door. The door would slowly creak open, and then there was a pregnant pause. We knew something grotesque was about to happen. We would be on the edge of the beds in anticipation. At this point, Amy would let out a bloodcurdling scream, and we would jump halfway off the beds—there was a mass levitation! Amy would howl laughing. We would beg her to tell the rest of the story, but there was no ending. The story would haunt us all night long as we lay in our beds trying to get it out of our heads. There was always the decision about whether or not to go to the outhouse in the middle of the night to relieve yourself. Fortunately, if all you had to do was pee, you could use the thunder mug under the bed.

The stories Amy told us were just to get us to settle down so she, Fred, Wilbur, and Shirley could head off to the bar. The night in the bar usually led to the four of them coming back drunk and in an argumentative mood. Wilbur and Shirley were natural-born fighters but were pikers compared to Amy and Fred. In one of their epic rants, Amy stabbed Fred in the back, and the knife blade broke.

Amy was also prone to telling huge lies, which is why she was such a good storyteller. Well, to be honest, some were really more about parenting than telling a lie. For instance, she said that kids who played with matches wet the bed. Clearly the message there was don't play with matches, and that warning came with some sort of medical ailment that if you did, you would find yourself lying in a puddle of your own urine. As a kid I believed her, but even still, I couldn't understand the connection between my urinary tract and the act of striking a match.

She used the same methodology when it came to her warning about the ills of lying and what could befall someone who did. Going north on old Highway 75 there was a little white frame house on the left-hand side of the road. The house was downhill a bit but close to the highway. It had a little white picket fence. In front of the picket fence was a wooden sculpture of a little boy by the front gate. The sculpture was painted and looked lifelike, especially if you were buzzing by in a car going sixty miles an hour. We would be packed up in the backseat of Amy and Fred's '58 Ford, dubbed the Green Diamond, watching the scenery go by when Amy would point out the statue. "See that? Did you see that little boy standing by the fence? Do you know he was a real boy? And guess what happened to him . . ."

Wow, there he was standing straight and still *forever*. Whatever could have gone wrong? All sorts of things coursed through my head.

"He lied, that's what he did. He told a lie. And, that's what will happen to you, too, if you lie. You will turn to wood just like he did," she said. She said it with so much conviction and confidence it had to be true. Plus, Amy went to Dana College to get her degree and her teaching certification. She was a teacher. She was a mother of five kids. She was a grownup. She knew. I had to believe her, and that little wooden boy by the gate scared the bejeebers out of me. Every time I would get ready to go to Fred's house, I would think of that boy as I packed my bag. It wasn't a bag, really—more of a brown paper grocery sack with my clothes in it. Still, I had my luggage in hand ready to go. I would think of that little boy and would make sure I looked out of the car window to catch a glimpse of him as we buzzed by—*Don't lie*, he called out to me.

River Sioux had so many wonders to keep a child entertained. We would always walk up to Granny's house when we went to Sioux. Granny was Amy's mother, and everybody in town called her Granny. She was one of the sweetest people I ever knew. She was a tiny little woman who had owned a grocery store in River Sioux. She had carried boxes balanced on her hip so long that her body was bent and misshapen because of it. She had false teeth that were so loose that when she talked, they clacked. They were also too big for her mouth, so her lips wouldn't actually close—lip to lip. You could always see a circle of teeth, and when she kissed you, you got more teeth than lips. She was an incredible cook and baker, so we always stopped by for a treat. It might be cookies or a peach pie or a piece of a cobbler. We would get our energy stocked up on some sugary confection that she had baked in the early morning hours before we explored the apple trees, the creek bottoms, or her neighbor's basement.

When Wilbur was a kid, he had gone to Hatheway's Funeral Parlor for fun. Up in Sioux, we had Floyd Smith, who was Granny's neighbor. Floyd was a strange old man—harmless really, but one of those characters that you find in a small town. He had a door on the outside of his house that led down to his basement. He would stand behind a tree, and as you walked by, Floyd would come out and motion you to come toward him. Then in a low mysterious voice that had a slight lilt at the end of the sentence, he would ask, "Do you want to see Raw Head and Bloody Bones?" His eyes would get bigger and his eyebrows would arch as he pointed to the basement door. A great sense of curiosity would well up inside. Who wouldn't want to see Raw Head and Bloody Bones? But the competing sensation of "Oh my god, I am going to shit my pants" would overwhelm you and wash over your body in a shiver. Then we ran to the basement door, which he had already flung open. We would stand at the top step—at the precipice of mystery—engulfed in fear. No one wanted to chicken out, so our collective fear was overcome by collective peer pressure. No one wanted to be a chicken.

"Go ahead, walk on down there." Floyd beckoned us to venture down into the unlit basement.

Slowly we walked down, moving closer to the doorway into the basement at the bottom of the steps. As we took each step, we were scared of the unknown—our imaginations conjuring images of what this monster might look like. Floyd closely followed us down the steps. Each step increased our fear factor by some exponential measure. Closer to the monster—closer to each other. We were nearly walking as one in lock step. I could feel breath on the back of my neck. We emptied into the basement, our eyes squinting to see into the blackness of the room pierced by slivers of light coming in from a couple of the small basement windows. We heard a crack and a pop as a skeleton jerked up into our view.

"Holy crap!"

We shoved each other as we turned around and scurried toward the door and ran up the stairs, adrenaline pumping, panting. Once we got out into the open and started to gather ourselves, we could hear Floyd's laughter. His trick had worked. He had rigged up an old skeleton to a rope system that was activated by a foot peddle that yanked the skeleton into view when he stomped on it. Floyd's basement contraption was a hit.

The neighborhood in Sioux was not the only place populated by scary things. Our house on Craig Street was, too. Cousin Rick assured me that if I misbehaved, Tilly Witch and Miss Rat, who lived in our attic, would eat me up. To torment Brian and me, Rick would lure us into the attic room, screw out the one bare bulb that lighted it, and slam the door shut behind him, leaving us in total darkness waiting for the moment when we would be eaten by Tilly Witch and Miss Rat. We heard muffled sounds outside the door, which turned out to be shrieks of laughter, but to us, it sounded like Tilly Witch and Miss Rat were closing in on us. The natural reaction, of course, was to pee one's pants.

If Floyd's Raw Head and Bloody Bones and Rick's Tilly Witch and Miss Rat weren't enough, Brian's trauma from the burn and skin grafts gave him nightmares. Often in the middle of the night, he would wake up screaming. I was the lucky recipient of the middle-of-the-night-wake-up scream since we shared a bedroom and a bed. If I had forgotten to kick any clothes under our bed before we got in, Brian might wake up in the middle of night and look at the floor and imagine that giant poisonous turtles were slowly crawling toward the bed to eat us.

His fallback was to scream. I would have to get up and kick the giant poisonous turtles under the bed so he couldn't see them. And God forbid we would leave the closet door open with clothes hanging on the hangers. He would see Dracula in our closet slowly moving toward the bed to eat us. Again, it meant hopping out of bed to shut the closet door—no more Dracula.

***

One night after the Wander Inn had closed, Wilbur and Shirley came home drunk—which really wasn't unusual for either of them. They were arguing as they came in the house. The door slammed behind them.

On this particular night, the arguing reached a fever pitch, and the decibel level woke everyone in the house. We all filed out of our rooms to watch the drama unfold. The anxiety level was too high to sleep. Besides, we were always afraid that they were going to kill each other. I guess we all wanted to make sure that we had front row seats for the action. Usually we would only go as far as the kitchen door and peer around the corner to watch. On this particular night, Shirley was more drunk than Wilbur. She was weaving quite a bit and her speech was slurred.

"You son of a bitch!" she yelled as she struck him.

"CALM DOWN, SHIRLEY," Wilbur said, trying to get her to get herself under control. As she tried to hit him again, he raised his arm, which she struck. When she did, she lost her balance a little and lurched backward. She fell into the china closet door and the front panel of glass broke. As she straightened herself out and stood up, the glass clinging to the back of her dress fell to the floor and splinters of glass shot across the room like glitter.

"Now look what you did!"

"HEY, I AM SITTING AT THE TABLE. I DIDN'T HAVE ANYTHING TO DO WITH YOU BREAKING THAT DOOR."

"You think you can get away with that shit? I am calling the police."

Shirley weaved her way across the room to the telephone on the wall and picked up the receiver to dial.

"DON'T CALL THE POLICE, SHIRLEY. THEY ARE GOING TO COME AND HAUL YOUR ASS TO JAIL!" At that point, Shirley must have realized that Wilbur was right, because she took the receiver and beat the phone off the wall in her anger.

She started toward the front door to make some sort of escape. Wilbur wasn't about to let her drive anywhere as drunk as she was. He hopped up and blocked the door.

"Goddamn you." She went to the kitchen and came back with a butcher knife.

"PUT THE FUCKING KNIFE DOWN, SHIRLEY. YOU ARE GOING TO HURT SOMEBODY—AND THAT SOMEBODY MIGHT BE YOU!"

Whenever they had these flare-ups, we each coped differently. Brian had a hysterical scream. Mike often found a corner and a book to read. I had the misfortune to have a nervous laugh, which really irritated Deke. He would look at me laughing like some sort of loon and say rhetorically, "So, you think it's funny?" I didn't, of course, but still couldn't stop my reaction. "You won't think it is funny when I get done with you." Then he would lay into me. Shirley and Wilbur were in the middle of their own drama and had little or no idea of what was going on around them.

By this point, Shirley was brandishing the knife, waving it in the air. The blade of the knife flashed the light around the room.

Mike had receded to a corner of the dining room—close enough to see what was going on but far enough away to not become part of it. His head was down, staring at the book like he was actually reading it. I doubt, in retrospect, if he actually read the book; he probably just used the book to shield his eyes. At any rate, he seemed deeply interested in the latest adventure in the Louis L'Amour paperback in front of him. Brian had begun his high-pitched, ear-piercing, unrelenting scream. He leaned forward and began slapping the fronts of his legs as he rocked back and forth in a steady rhythm. By this time, I was on the floor, and Deke was kicking me. I was facing Shirley and Wilbur by the door. I was the only kid still watching them in between receiving blows.

Shirley released the knife and hurled it at Wilbur, who was standing with his back facing the front hollow-core door. From my vantage point, it looked like the knife had hit him in the chest. We all heard a noise as it hit. We stopped what we were doing and looked toward the sound.

Wilbur, in a very theatrical way, slammed his back against the front door and grabbed the knife. He yelped, "UOOHM!" and slid down the door like one of those cartoon characters that gets hit by an anvil and turns flat and slides down the wall, flat as a pancake.

On his way down, he looked my way and winked. I was relieved but still scared. I couldn't hold back my hysterical laugh.

"Really?" Deke asked. Then he punched me in the stomach and knocked the air out of me.

Wilbur tipped over when he hit bottom, and the knife spilled out onto the tile floor.

Shirley looked at Wilbur. She ran up to him like a lightning bolt and kicked him three times in the side.

"Take that, you son of a bitch."

In a flash, she realized that she had probably just killed the father of her four sons, and in front of them to boot.

She dropped to her knees to survey the damage close-up.

By this time, Deke was standing over me, I was gasping for air, Mike was still huddled in the corner with his book firmly planted in front of his eyes, and Brian was still practicing for the Olympic yodeling team. Pandemonium reigned.

Wilbur had not been knifed by Shirley after all. The knife had struck the door in between Wilbur's arm and chest and stuck. He pulled it out of the door on his way down to make it appear like Shirley had wounded him. That action had been a sobering agent for her. After she had kicked him, she realized what she had done and backed off. We all sort of limped to our own corners of the house. After that particular escapade, whenever we heard them get into it, we always made way to hide the knives as quickly as possible.

* * *

At first, I didn't know that we weren't supposed to talk about our parents' epic fights. But I found out a day or so after their big brawl with the knife.

I got a free lunch at school but had to work in the kitchen for it during my free period. I would go to the lunchroom and had to roll a spoon, fork, and knife into a paper napkin, laying in a straw. The lunch ladies nearly always rewarded me with an ice cream bar. I had lunch after my free period and would grab my tray and sit with my friends. That next day in school, I was telling the story of how Wilbur had faked dying, when Deke was going by my lunch table in the cafeteria. He came over and said he wanted to talk to me, and he quickly pulled me outside. Deke pushed me up against the school building and said, "You can't tell that story, you little dumbass."

"Why? I told the truth, I didn't lie."

"Cuz, the cops will come take us away, that's why. Do you want to be taken away and adopted out?"

"No."

"Then keep your fucking mouth shut."

That advice came in handy, since I needed to refer to it many times. There were many nights when our parents got into fights after the Wander Inn closed. It often happened at 3:00 in the morning when they got home. We would be woken up by the yelling and slurred name-calling.

Shirley would say to us, "Who do you want to go with? I am leaving your father—do you want to go with me or stay with your father?"

She would make a slapdash effort to put some bedding in the car along with a few clothes, and we would be marched out to the car—usually just Brian and me—and take off. Shirley didn't have a plan or money, so we would pull up into a parking lot at a grocery store or behind a bar—something that had enough lights to feel relatively safe. Then she would fall asleep in the front seat and Brian and I would fall asleep on the heap of clothes in the backseat. She would get us home too late in the morning for us to go to school the next day.

My kindergarten teacher was especially interested in my absences. She even drove her VW Beetle to our house once to check on me. She asked me once if I missed school because I didn't have any clean clothes to wear. I lied and told her I had been sick the day before.

In the mornings before school, our house was pretty cold. We would stand next to the hot air vents and warm up. One morning, I got up and put my coat on instead of a shirt, thinking I would put the shirt on when I got ready for school. But when it came time to go, I forgot that I wasn't wearing a shirt, and when I got to school and started taking off my coat, I realized I hadn't put on the shirt. I was embarrassed. When the teacher asked me why I wasn't taking off my coat, I told her I was still cold. It wasn't long after that when her bug showed up at our house.

But I didn't tell any more stories of what went on in our house—I had learned my lesson.

* * *

When Deke was a teenager, he wasn't tall, maybe five-foot-six or -seven. But he was thin and muscular. He kept in shape and had longish hair that drove Wilbur crazy and the girls, too, only in a different way. Wilbur would ask Deke, "YA WANT ME TO PUT A BOW IN YOUR HAIR, SUSIE?" Deke didn't care—he liked it and so did the girls.

Deke was a wild kid. And he always had an eye for cute and shapely girls. Truth be told, he worked the eyes plenty. But the other parts of him were fully engaged in the appreciation of the girls, too. He started having sex at a young age. He sneaked girls into the house as soon as Shirley would leave for work in the afternoon.

Once he sneaked two girls into the house right after she left for work. But she forgot something and came back. Deke quickly pirated the girls away. As soon as Shirley got in the house, she could see he had a guilty look on his face. She sensed something was up and figured he had a girl in the house—she had no idea it was two. She went around the house looking, opening closet doors and peeking under beds, but never found either of them and left in frustration so she wouldn't be late for work. We had a large rolltop desk upstairs. One girl was snug under the roll, and the other was hidden inside the door of the desk. As soon as Shirley was out of sight, they popped out undetected!

One afternoon, when I was in fifth grade, I got home from school early. I walked into the house and couldn't see that anyone was home but thought I heard a noise when I walked in. I started looking from room to room. The closer I got to the back bedrooms, the more I realized that someone *was* already home. The bedroom on the left in the back was the room that Brian and I shared. I got close to the door and could hear some muffled sounds. Sorta like someone was trying to keep a dog from barking with a pillow.

I opened the door and peeked in. Strewn around the floor were panties, skirts, shirts, and pants. On my bed was Deke and a girl. Both were completely naked. On the floor was Skeeter, one of Deke's school friends, and another girl—both completely naked.

Collectively, I saw eight eyes in a sea of milky-white skin look my way.

The two girls grabbed for sheets, which they quickly pulled up to their chins.

"Oh, shit, he saw us," Deke blurted out.

I was too young to know exactly what the little naked fest meant, but I knew it wasn't good for me that I had discovered it. And by the tone of Deke's voice, I could tell that as soon as he could shimmy into some pants, he was going to beat the living shit out of me.

The fight or flight instinct took over. Even at a young age, it was my sworn policy not to fight until the race was over. If they could catch me, they could fight me. So, I took off out of the house as fast as I could.

I don't know how long it was, though it seemed like an eternity, until the girl who was with Deke bounded out of the house. She was by herself. I felt pretty brave, so I came out from behind the '57 two-tone Cadillac that was junked in our front yard and walked toward her.

She walked up to me, and we faced off.

"I know what you are, and it starts with an *h*," I said. I was defiant.

I knew I was really going to get it from Deke, but I knew what they were doing was bad. Why else would you have to scramble to hide? Plus, they were all naked. I knew Shirley was going to be furious if she found out. I decided to take my stand and say something.

I looked up at the girl. She was lean and pretty. Her long, straight, light brown hair (everybody had long straight hair then) was pulled back into a ponytail. Her green eyes narrowed as her eyes met mine.

"For your information," she said with loud authority, "it starts with a *w*."

With that spelling correction out of the way and to prove she was superior, if only in the realm of spelling, she slapped my face with her open hand so hard that it almost knocked me on the ground. Then she stormed off.

Fred Rife in Shirley's Northside Tavern, wearing pantyhose

14

*"I don't know how they make it so good
and sell it so cheap."*

The Farmer's Northside Tavern

"Was your dad from Logan?" Kitty asked.

"No, he was raised up by Sioux," Brian answered.

"It is a funny thing. I always thought that Dad's family had been in Harrison County longer than Mom's family. But a couple of years ago when Deke was going to college in Boone, this professor assigned the class to do a five-generation pedigree chart. Deke didn't have access to anything over there in Boone, so he called home and Mom and I said we would dig up as much as we could," I said.

"Is that what started your interest in family history?" Kitty asked.

"Yep. Funny how a class I didn't even take got me started on all of that. Anyway, I was trying to figure out how to get my great-grandfather Levi Smith's Civil War records when I figured out that his wife, Sarah, had remarried after Levi died to another Civil War vet named Similis Fowler. I knew if I sent away for Fowler's records that it was likely that Sarah had applied for a widow's pension, and it would tell where Levi had served."

"How did you figure that out?" Kitty asked.

"I don't know—I guess I had seen so many of those records that I had a hunch."

I had been at Mom's when the records came from the National Archives. I had them all spread over the floor and was reading through them when Dad came in. He looked down at the living room floor littered with paper and asked, "WHAT THE HELL ARE YOU A-LOOKIN' AT?"

When I told Dad how I had worked out how to get Levi's records, he looked down at me and said, "HEY, SON, YOU ARE KINDA LIKE COLUMBO, AREN'T YOU?" I felt pride not only because I figured it out and it was right, but because Dad admired me for figuring it out. He didn't pass out many compliments.

Kitty asked, "So, was it true?"

"Was what true?"

"Was your dad's family in Harrison County longer than your mom's?"

"Much to everyone's surprise, Mom's family actually settled in Harrison County about twenty years before Dad's. Mom's mom was born in Hay Springs, Nebraska. Her mom was born in Missouri Valley, Iowa, and her mom was born in a prairie schooner in Magnolia, Iowa—the first female child of European descent born in the county! Mom got to crow about that a bit—though Dad didn't really give a shit."

"When did you guys move to Logan?" Kitty asked.

"Douglas and I were just going into sixth grade." Brian said. "We moved that August just 'fore school started."

"Yeah, we moved into a little apartment above Doyle's Hardware Store."

"Mom, Deke, Douglas, and I moved up together. Dad kept our house in Omaha but came up to Logan on the weekends."

"What about Mike?"

"Mike shipped out to Vietnam in December of '67. He was in the 101st Airborne Division and went as a paratrooper, so he never lived in Logan with us," I explained.

Dad said to Mike at the time, "THE ARMY WILL KILL YOU OR MAKE A MAN OUT OF YOU—ONE OR THE OTHER—AND I DON'T CARE WHICH."

"Oh, and Fritzy, too." Fritzy was our feisty little toy Manchester dog.

* * *

Fred and Amy were the first to move to Logan. It was a small town—the county seat—in the county where Wilbur and Fred grew up. Harrison County was named after the ninth president of the United States, William Henry Harrison, who had the distinction of serving only thirty-one days after he was inaugurated, the result of pneumonia from standing in the rain to deliver the longest inaugural address in US history. Logan only had about 1400 people in it, and seven bars and seven churches. The sinners and the saints were about evenly distributed with an even spread of places to congregate.

Fred and Amy had started frequenting a bar that they liked—the Farmer's Northside Tavern—which had become their favorite watering hole. Shirley and Wilbur would go up to Logan once in a while, and they would all drink together. Fred loved to tell stories and make people laugh.

He would usually start by extolling the virtues of the beer he was drinking. He'd raise his beer glass up into the air and exclaim, "I don't know how they make it so good and sell it so cheap!" Once that got everyone's attention, he would launch into a story. For instance, when the speed limit in Iowa was reduced from seventy-five miles per hour to fifty-five on the highways to conserve gas, Fred strutted around the bar and said, "I don't mind that they changed the speed limit, but goddammit a combine passed me on the highway the other day." Then he would take a little sip of beer and pause in the story for effect. "That wouldn't be so bad, but he was pickin' corn on the way by!" Everyone in the bar laughed, but nobody laughed any harder than Fred.

Fred heard the tavern was up for sale and was convinced that Shirley and Wilbur could make a go of it. In August of 1968, Shirley purchased the Farmer's Northside Tavern, and we moved from Omaha. Wilbur kept the house we lived in on Craig Street and commuted to Logan on the weekends.

* * *

Doyle's Hardware was just two doors down from the bar—very convenient for our first place in Logan, though it was also very small. To get to the apartment, you climbed a long staircase that led to a doorway halfway down a hallway between the second story of the hardware store and the Farm Bureau Building. That door opened to a hallway that took you to a door into the apartment. We had a bed in the hallway, which is where Deke slept. Mom slept on the sofa, and Brian and I shared a bed in the back of the apartment. The kitchen was tiny, just a few cabinets, a sink, a small stove, and a refrigerator. It didn't matter, though, since we ate most of our meals in the bar.

Two windows faced Main Street overlooking Highway 30, which ran through town. It was good for hours of gawking at people on the street.

We hung out of the windows. In the fall, we even rolled our jack-o-lanterns down the back steps to watch them explode as they tumbled toward the alley. In the winter, we would go out the back to the landing, scoop up all of the snow there, and toss snowballs at people on the sidewalk. We also built a snowman on the backstairs landing, too, and pushed that down the steps.

I didn't want to move to Logan. I had friends at Florence Elementary School, and I had been elected president of the Sixth Grade Red Cross for all of Omaha. I had to give up my post—though, to this day, I don't know what my responsibilities were going to be. Shirley told me to get over it with a little bit of her homespun wisdom, "Nobody likes a change but wet babies."

The first day in Logan was scary. I didn't know anyone except my cousins who had moved to Logan in 1964. At first, they rented the upstairs apartment in a big rambling house that was once used as a maternity ward. Sometimes after school, we would gather at their house and watch *Dark Shadows*, which was a popular afternoon soap of sorts about a vampire. Sometimes, I went out to explore.

I walked the half block from Shirley's bar to the city park. The west end of the park had a big stucco band shell dedicated to the soldiers in Logan who fought in World War II. And in the middle of the park, which all the sidewalks led to, was a water fountain. I always stopped to get a drink before I was off to do more exploring.

My first friend in Logan was Penny Christo. When I met her on my first excursion into town, she was wearing a white brocade dress with a light blue geometric design—very short, they were all short in those days—and she had big, bright blue eyes and her light brown hair was cut into a short bob. She walked up to me and asked my name, which I told her. She said, "You're cute." She pinched my cheek and walked off. My first experience in town was positive, but they weren't all that way.

When Brian and I ended up at the schoolhouse playground, we were confronted by a couple of kids who said point-blank, "Our parents told us we can't play with you because your mom owns a bar."

Small towns have a definite caste system—led by the old rich families with long histories wrapped around the town, then came the professionals, the school teachers, the ministers, the farmers, and at the lower end, folks who worked in factories or ran taverns. Even though Shirley's family had been in Harrison County since the first year of its settlement, one of the first three or four families to settle, and Wilbur's family came twenty years later, we were new to Logan and still considered outsiders. It was something you could feel.

Shirley had worked in taverns for years and knew her way around a sloe gin fizz. She was pretty sure that she could make a go of one of her own. Wilbur was probably more excited about owning a bar than Shirley—but he had never worked in one, though he had plenty of experience on the customer side of the business.

Shirley purchased the Farmer's Northside Tavern from Dave and Helen Smith. Helen was more or less the front of the house for the bar.

She was a little ol' lady who had her hair teased and lacquered with hair spray, which formed into a sort of helmet. She called everyone "honey" or "sugar" or "darling." I am not sure she knew anyone's names. It was phony, but because she used it so much and to everybody, it just seemed natural. Shirley wasn't swayed by it though. Her take was a little different, "Helen is so sweet shit wouldn't melt in her mouth." Shirley didn't really do *sweet*.

After Shirley bought the tavern, she promptly renamed it Shirley's Northside Tavern. The building that housed the bar was divided, with two separate histories. The east part housed a series of restaurants. The west part of the building operated as a bakery for a long time. In the 1930s, the building evolved into a tavern in the east part, billiards in the west. In October of 1965, both sides were taken over by Dave and Helen Smith and converted into the Farmer's Northside Tavern. The Smiths broke two door openings from one building to the other. The east part of the building had the front bar and the back bar, where the drinks were mixed and the beer was poured. It also had a lunch counter. Shirley opened the bar at 5:00 a.m. to serve coffee and breakfast. The lunch counter had an industrial stove with a griddle and four gas burners. It seated ten.

Hanging above the middle of the bar was an ancient electric relic—rumored to be the first electric fan installed in Harrison County. The great fan once had four wooden paddles, but now two remained, making it look more like the propeller from the *Spirit of St. Louis* than a fan. The fan had two speeds—whirlwind and tornado. With the fan on either speed, no ashes were left in the ashtrays. On hot days when it was quite necessary to turn the fan on, customers often had a layer of ash in their eyebrows and hair and even on their faces when it caught on sweat. People were literally ashen when they left the bar.

The west part of the building had some orange booths, big round tables, a pool table, and the men's bathroom. Both sides were fairly narrow and long. The back room was where a group of old men usually came in to drink coffee and play cards. After they cleared out, I would go back there with Brian to clear the cups and bring them to the sink for washing. One afternoon, I went back to clear the cups long after the card players had left and saw a man on top of a woman in one of the booths. I could hear the woman making a low moaning sound. The man was making the same sort of moaning sound, too. It looked like a slow-motion scuffle. I was sure she was being hurt. I ran into the front room to tell Shirley.

"Mom, there are two people wrestling in a booth in the back room." Shirley tore into the back room to break up what she initially thought was a fight—I followed closely behind to see if I could help. When we got there, Shirley said to me, "Git back in the front room; they aren't wrestling!"

By the time Shirley purchased the business and the building in 1968, the building was in pretty bad shape. Shortly after she bought the building, she and Wilbur opened up the two rooms by removing all but the bearing wall in the center, which had a door opening in it.

They then installed a drop ceiling to hide the peeling ceilings, wires, and years of neglect. The first drop ceiling had names of local companies stenciled on each panel; for a nominal fee—$5 a panel—they had a little ad space. Wilbur, a master mason, plastered the walls inside and remodeled the exterior by covering the front of the building with white stucco. Two planters of blue stucco punctuated with pink quartz flanked either side of the front door to the east side of the building. The second doorway in the front on the west side was closed altogether.

One of the first things to go in the tavern were the spittoons. Shirley made up her mind she would not be cleaning those disgusting and feted sluice pots. Nor would she tolerate the geriatric group of card players in the back room spitting on the floor, especially a floor that she sanded and gym coated.

There was a little stage in the back room, so Shirley started hiring bands to come in on weekends. Farmers and their wives from all over the county came in to dance. She hired bands with names like the Country Gentlemen, the Country Playboys, Sloe Motion, the Peck Brothers, Okie Finokie, the Barn Doors, the Johnny Sunshine Band, the Road Rangers, the Ramblers, and the Country Revolution. Most of the bands were rinky-tink bands that carried a tune and a beat adequately enough to which farmers and the locals could dance. Some bands, however, were quite good and drew very large crowds.

There were times when the bar was so crowded that people sat on beer crates, elbow to elbow, in the blue haze atmosphere of the busiest bar in Logan. The back room, formerly a bakery, was now crowded with dancers pumping their arms up and down to the beat of the music, often clad in buckle-down overshoes and jeans, straight from the field, laughing and drinking into the small hours of the morning. At 1:30 a.m., Shirley would yell, "Last call for alcohol!" That was to let everyone know that they only had time for one more drink before she closed for the night. For some people, the party was just getting going and they didn't want the fun to end. When 2:00 a.m. came, it was difficult to bring the evening to a close. Customers clung to it as if they were afraid they could never recreate the magic and fun of the night they had just experienced.

One of the regulars was a tiny high-spirited woman in her early sixties, Teddy Sears. Teddy was a nickname for Tressa. As Wilbur would say, "SHE WAS NO BIGGER THAN A FART IN A WHIRLWIND." She was a twin—Essa and Tressa. Teddy had graying strawberry-blonde hair. She wore bright red lipstick, which was nearly as heavily spread on her teeth as on her lips. Sometimes there was even a dab on an earlobe. Teddy was married to an old farmer named Herman. The two had dated when they were in their late teens, and Teddy expected Herman to ask for her hand in marriage. After eight or nine years of waiting, she gave up and married a guy named Slim. When Slim died decades later, Herman mustered the courage to finally ask Teddy to marry him.

Teddy took a liking to me. She didn't have any children and liked to spend time with me. That first Christmas we were in Logan, she bought me the game Operation for Christmas. On Saturday afternoons, Teddy would put a couple of quarters in the jukebox and teach me the basics to the two-step to the beat of the "Jingle Bell Rock" by Bobby Helms. I would practice all week, and then on the following weekend, when Shirley had the bands come in, I would dance to live music, practicing what I had learned the week before. Teddy was a lively dancer who kept the beat by making a clinking sound while she danced. I was not sure if she did it for my benefit or if she did it every time she danced. Herman wasn't really a good dancer. When he did, he looked like a wind-up doll—he was stiff-legged and moved robotically across the floor.

Shirley said I could dance on the weekends with customers as long as I didn't turn anyone down—the good dancers and the bad—I had to dance with them all. It turned out to be a boon for my dance lessons because many of the women taught me different steps. Teddy was the first but not the last customer to give me dance lessons. Bev, whose husband was in one of the bands, taught me how to polka and to waltz. She was two axe handles wide but so light on her feet you'd never know that she was heavyset. Helen taught me how to Charleston and a few more steps to the waltz. Helen's daughter, Janice, who worked as a waitress in the bar, taught me how to jitterbug. At thirteen, I could keep up with almost any woman who came in to dance and lead them just like a grown man. As I got better, more and more of the women customers wanted to dance with me. It was a mixed blessing—it increased my ability to lead, but it also meant I had to dance with a lot of bowlegged farm wives still in their buckle-down boots. But Shirley kept to her guns—all customers got to dance with me, no matter if they were good dancers or bad.

On any given weekend night, Shirley's place really looked like the bar scene out of *Star Wars*. We had so many characters who came in. The Bices were a couple from Magnolia. He was a gravedigger and looked the part—one eyeball facing east and the other facing west. He was a gentle soul who would compliment those he was fond of by saying, "It would be an honor to dig your grave." Even though it sounded a bit ghoulish, he meant it in the kindest way. His wife was a large-breasted woman who wore costume jewelry broaches on the front of her dress—not one or two but many at a time. When the sunlight hit the front of her dress, it lit up like a disco ball. She walked with two red canes and listed from side to side as she walked.

Gabby worked in the rock quarry. He had a light dusting of limestone over him at all times. If you slapped his back, a cloud of dust would float from his clothing. He was loud and argumentative, and most everyone liked to tease him because he always took the bait. He often fell asleep after he'd drunk too much. One night, one of the customers lifted his cap off while he snoozed and drew an eagle on the top of his bald head with a marker.

Then there was Newt, reportedly one of the best carpenters in the county. Everyone knew, though, you couldn't pay him until the whole job was completed because he would take the money and go on a bender and you might not see him for weeks, leaving the job waiting, unfinished until he sobered up. He would lean back on his barstool and shake his chest and bellow, "HOOOOOOO!" Once when a customer commented on my curly hair, Newt said, "I'll show you curly hair." He started to unbuckle his pants when Shirley smacked the back of his head and yelled at him, "Newt, knock that shit off." He laughed and buckled up.

Penny, my friend, came in with her parents, too. Her father, Don, was a kind man who worked at a manufacturing company in Omaha. Her mother, Fern, was a sweetheart. Shirley worked all the time, so Fern would bake cookies for me to take to the Boy Scout bake sale so I would have something to contribute. Sometimes some of their kids would be in tow—Boone, Penny, and Betsy. Their oldest three, Donna, Tom, and Jerry, were already out of the house.

Our neighbor June was a regular on Wednesday nights. He would drop his daughter Jane off to catechism and have a couple of drinks in the bar while he waited for her. She would walk down from St. Ann's afterward, and we shot pool until June was ready to go home. June and his wife, Barb, often came on Saturday nights, too.

Every weekend, Wilbur made the forty-minute drive from Omaha to Logan to spend the weekend in with us. He drank in the bar on Friday nights, then would open the bar on Saturday mornings. It gave Shirley a small break. She slept in but also took care of various errands she couldn't do during the week.

At the end of a Saturday night, Brian and I would clear tables, wipe them down, and stack the tables and chairs so it was easier to clean the next morning. It was also a way to get the partiers to understand it was last call and time to go home. By 3:00 a.m., we would be ready to head out. Often, we headed nine miles to Missouri Valley, the next town south on Highway 30, to have breakfast at Sunnyside, a twenty-four-hour truck stop at the edge of town. The place would be packed after the bars closed—we would see many of our customers sitting there, too.

Wilbur never cared how much you ordered for breakfast. But he did care about how much you ate. "YOU ORDER IT AND GODDAMN IT YOU HAD BETTER EAT IT!" he would bark as a preemptive strike with Norma, the waitress, standing there taking our order. I liked lots of different flavors, so I usually ordered a salad with Italian dressing, French fries, a side of bacon, French toast, and a hot chocolate—sometimes I would add one egg over easy if I was particularly hungry. Wilbur would sit and eat—very fast—and get refills on his coffee while he waited for everyone else at our table to finish. To get Norma's attention, he would raise his coffee cup straight up in the air and wait until she noticed and came over with the pot.

* * *

The bar for us was the hub of the family activity. We sat in the back booth during weeknights when it wasn't as crowded and ate dinner, did our homework, and sometimes even fell asleep in the booth waiting for Shirley to close for the night. Then we would walk up to the apartment together and call it a night.

The other bars had regulars that started coming into Shirley's bar. Her place had a newness about it with bands, fish fries, and the crowds. Her competition across the street was the most vocal, often conjuring up nasty-sounding names for the bar. A couple of the names that went around town were Squirrelly Shirley's and Shirley's Slippery Tit—the latter epithet reemerged several times while Shirley owned the bar.

Around when I was twelve or thirteen, I was looking to collect something. Brian had a collection of 45s and of glass cats and kittens. But I never seemed to have any money for anything but matchbox cars, which cost fifty-five cents, and Eskimo Pies, which were a dime. If I found and turned in enough bottles, I could keep myself in both! I bought so many Eskimo Pies at the Candy Kitchen that the owner told me she thought I was going to turn into one.

Soon, the bar napkins in Shirley's bar caught my eye. There was a wide range of them to collect. Some had beer names on them—Hamm's, Miller, Falstaff, Olympia, Blatz. Others had funny cartoons, funny sayings, and some had trivia. I started my collection in earnest, and my biggest contributor was Wilbur. He brought me napkins from all sorts of places: Crackers, Spankey's, Twig's, Granada Royale Hometels, King Crab Lounge, Rusty Scupper, Partner's Lounge, Mr. Whipple's, Nashville Club (which was actually in Council Bluffs), The Tic Toc Club, Ak-Sar-Ben—the race track in Omaha, The Pink Pussycat, the Mermaid

Supper Club, Mirrors Image Lounge, The Warehouse, Peony Park, the Minne Lusa Tavern, the Trail Dust Steak House, and the Cheshire Inn and Lodge. He made lots of stops. I would see him at the end of a night, and he would reach into his shirt pocket and pull out a bar napkin and hand it to me.

"DO YOU HAVE THAT ONE?"

"Nope," I would say, neatly adding it to my ever-growing collection.

The bar napkins could be categorized into major themes—such as sports with titles printed on the napkins like, "SOME FINE TIPS ON HOW TO IMPROVE YOUR BOWLING," "BOATING TIPS," "OH SAY CAN YOU SKI," "SPORTS NUTS," "SPORTS TRIVIA," "NEBRASKA—FOOTBALL CAPITAL OF THE U.S.A." (with the football season schedule), "SPORT RECORDS," "SPORTING YACTIVITY!" (the cartoon on the front of which pictured a small boy who had caught a shapely mermaid and as two grown men looked on at the catch with envy, the boy said, "I GOT IT WITH A BENT PIN AND A WORM!"), "THE RULE BOOK SAYS," "AT THE TRACK," and "FOOTBALL CLASSICS."

Fitting to any tavern were the bar napkins that really focused on the topic at hand—drinking! The titles were not subtle, either. "HOW TO DRINK," "HAVE ANOTHER," "HOW TO BE A BARTENDER," "BOOZE IS THE ONLY THING," "SIP! SIP! SIP!" "A LITTLE HUMOR WHILE YOU DRINK," "HANDY LIST OF REASONS FOR DRINKING," "THE COCKTAIL CROWD," "THIRSTY MOMENTS," "BAR TYPES," "PARTY MANNERS," "EXCUSES ALMOST EVERYBODY HAS FOR BEING LATE!" My personal favorite was, "DON'T JUST SIT THERE . . . DRINK!" The napkin had a cartoon of a bartender showing the customer a picture of his family with a cash register with cobwebs in the background. The message, of course, was that if you don't order a drink, my wife and my little urchins are going to go hungry!

My collection of napkins had really taken off, and Wilbur made sure it grew steadily. Again and again, he would bound in after a night of drinking and inevitably ask, "DO YOU HAVE THAT ONE?" Even though I had multiples of some napkins, as many as five in some cases, my answer was always the same: "Nope. Thanks, Dad." And then my latest acquisition to the collection would go neatly on top of the stack.

My favorites included a series called "DID YOU KNOW?" I was stunned to read about the fastest loser, Paul Kimpleman, who lost 357 pounds in eight months. Or the heaviest baby boy born to a family in Turkey who weighed over twenty-four pounds and two ounces. Ouch. Or that Cheryl Tiegs was the highest paid model—paid $1.5 million dollars for five years!

Two of my very favorites, though, were "DAFFYNITIONS" and "HAPPY DAYS." I thought they were clever. I tried to memorize them so I could have something funny to say in my mom's bar. The "DAFFYNITIONS" bar napkins had some of the following definitions:

"HAWAII: WHERE MEN MAKE PASSES AT GIRLS WHO WEAR GRASSES"
"STAGNATION: COUNTRY WITHOUT WOMEN"
"WILL: A DEAD GIVEAWAY"
"YALE: A SWEDISH PRISON"
"BIGAMIST: AN ITALIAN FOG"

The "HAPPY DAYS" napkins had funny quips and truisms:

"NOTHING IS OPENED MORE BY MISTAKE THAN THE MOUTH."
"KNEES ARE A LUXURY. IF YOU DON'T THINK SO, JUST TRY TO GET HOLD OF ONE."
"WHEN MODERN GIRLS WEAR SWEATERS, MOTHERS BEGIN TO SWEAT."
"CHOOSE NEITHER A WOMAN NOR LINEN BY CANDLELIGHT."
"NO MAN EVER CONVINCED HIS WIFE THAT A PRETTY STENOGRAPHER WAS MORE EFFICIENT THAN A HOMELY ONE."

* * *

Deke wasn't at all happy with being in Logan, and he mostly took it out on me. Even though our parents weren't having the same kind of bacchanalian brawls they'd had in Omaha, Deke's festering anger was still being directed to me. It was as if he was caged and didn't know what to do about it. So, he struck out at me—literally.

One afternoon as he was coming after me, I picked up a butcher knife and Brian came to my aid with a broom, which he shoved up under Deke's neck. We backed Deke into a corner.

"Don't hit him," Brian said.

"Shut the fuck up."

"I mean it," Brian persevered.

I had the knife in Deke's side. The bristles of the broom were poking Deke in the neck, and he was uncomfortable.

"Get back," Deke ordered.

We didn't let up.

"Listen, if you *ever* hit either one of us again, we are going to kill you in your sleep," Brian said.

"Okay?" I was looking for Deke to agree.

Deke grunted.

Brian brought down the broom, and I took away the knife. The showdown was over. And we never had a replay. We entered an uneasy armistice.

Teri and Douglas

15

"When they're nose to nose, his feet is in it, and when they're toes to toes, his nose is in it."

Barflies and Butterflies

I started seventh grade in Logan still living above Doyle's Hardware Shop. I was practicing my trombone to the amusement of hardware customers below, though they couldn't describe what they heard as music.

The space was cramped but workable. Our little dog, Fritzy, even liked it until the accident. We took Fritzy out to the sidewalk for his daily poos. Sometimes we leashed him, and sometimes we didn't. One day, Brian and I took him down the stairs to the sidewalk below, and he sprung out into the highway and a car tire brushed the side of his head—hard. At first, we thought he was dead, but he moved. Brian and I picked him up and carried his black and white limp body to the bar to ask our mom what to do. He was bleeding out of his mouth. It didn't look good.

"JESUS CHRIST, THAT LITTLE SON OF A BITCH HAS BITTEN NEARLY EVERYBODY IN THE WHOLE FAMILY. NOW WOULD BE A GOOD TIME TO PUT 'IM DOWN," Wilbur roared. His view of animals was utilitarian, not sentimental.

"I'm not going to have him put down, Wilbur," Shirley snapped back. She loved the little dog. They were often curled up on the sofa together sleeping. Only Fritzy could sleep through Shirley's snoring, which sounded like an intermittent buzz saw—occasionally jammed but would always start back up again.

A customer told Shirley that there was a good vet in Woodbine, and Wilbur took over tending the bar while we drove the nine miles north to Woodbine.

The vet delivered the bad news—Fritzy would most likely die because of the internal bleeding, and the best thing was to put him to sleep. Shirley wouldn't hear of it.

We drove the nine miles back to Logan and then another twenty-nine miles to Blair for a second opinion. This time, the vet was more optimistic. If we left him, they would watch him, give him medicine, and see what they could do. We ended up leaving him with the vet there. It was going to be an overnight stay, at least. They nursed him back to health. He drank and took the medicine but would not eat. The vet said some dogs were like that. We picked him up two days later and stopped at Burger King in Blair on the way back to Logan. He ate two hamburger patties in the car.

The incident with the car didn't make him any less feisty—he still went after my cousin Shelly every time she came to the apartment. For some reason, he never did like her and ran toward her with every intention of biting her. If we knew she was going to stop by, we would put him in the bathroom and shut the door.

While his spirit wasn't tamped down, he did become scared to go outside. He started going to the bathroom in the apartment, and we were forever cleaning up behind him. The trick was to spot it before you stepped in it. Early morning was the worst.

Shirley decided we needed to move to a house, so she rented what we called the "two-blue-door house" just over the viaduct and across from the limestone quarry east of town. We were so close to the rock quarry that when they dynamited, a fine layer of limestone dust would gently descend on our house like a light fog covering everything.

We now had a garage and much more room. So much room that Shirley bought a barrel racer named Shane. We kept him tied to a stake in the backyard. Shirley had had two horses as a girl—Eenie and Trudy—and liked to ride, and Wilbur trained horses and mules in Fort Robinson, so there was a lot of enthusiasm for having a horse but not much for taking care of him.

Fritzy was not amused by Shane and would bound off the porch of the house and run toward him, barking. Shane wasn't skittish but would move around, trying to avoid Fritzy. One afternoon, Shane's hoof came down on Fritzy's back leg. Fritzy let out a sharp yelp. It was back to the vet in Blair. After three days, we headed over to pick him up. The vet patched up Fritzy with a cast on his back leg. He told us that Fritzy would not eat, so we made our usual stop at Burger King.

I wasn't the only one preoccupied with a dog. My very first girlfriend, Teri, was begging for one. Her mother's concern was age old—where the dog was going to choose to poop, and if it was in the house, who was going to clean it up? Teri and I started dating early in the year. We had been elected officers of our seventh-grade class—I was president; Jean, one of her best friends, was vice president; and Teri was secretary. In fact, our picture made the *Logan Herald-Observer*, our local paper, which caught Wilbur's eye.

"SAY, SON, I SAW YOUR PICTURE IN THE LOGAN BLAB. SO YOU'RE CLASS PRESIDENT?" Wilbur asked. "I GUESS YOU'RE FAMOUS," he said with a chuckle.

"Yep."

"ISN'T THAT NINA'S DAUGHTER IN THE PICTURE WITH YOU?"

Nina owned the tavern in Magnolia. Teri was a bar owner's kid just like me. We were both barflies. Since Magnolia was six miles from Logan, most of our "dating" was me walking Teri between classes and an exchange of letters. Most of the letters recounted favorite episodes of *Gilligan's Island* or Teri telling me she wanted a puppy but her mother was not going to let her have one.

Magnolia was a town of about two hundred people six miles northwest of Logan on Highway 127. Our two towns consolidated schools in the early '60s to form the Logan-Magnolia Community Junior Senior High School—Lo-Ma was shorthand.

"Yes, Dad," I answered, "and, she is my girlfriend." We were going steady—I had given her a ring that I bought in Darner's Hardware Store that turned her finger green! It was official, I had left my mark.

Teri, hands down, was the cutest girl in seventh grade. She had blue eyes and blonde hair that curled into a little bob. I was shy, and so was she. Almost as a cliché, I was elected president of the seventh-grade class and she was elected secretary.

The Homecoming Dance was *the* school dance of the year. Since I couldn't drive, her mom had to bring Teri over to Logan. About a half a block away from the Lemuel R. Bolter American Legion Hall, where the dance took place, was Jeannie Foutch's house. Jeannie was a friend of Teri's. Teri, Jean, and Jeannie all agreed to meet there before the dance to get ready. The boys could come pick up their dates at Jeannie's. I walked the block and a half to Jeannie's to gather Teri, and together we walked back to Shirley's bar so Shirley and Nina could see both of us all dressed up for the dance. Teri was wearing a dark blue turtleneck and a matching plaid vest and skirt. She looked beautiful, and I was totally smitten. I was wearing a brand-new camel-colored double-breasted suit coat with big brass buttons. After I pinned her homecoming mum on, Shirley snapped a couple of pictures with our brand-new Polaroid camera. I was about an inch, maybe two, shorter than Teri. So, I stood up on my tiptoes just before she started snapping pictures.

Wilbur caught me. I saw him wink at me, but I knew what he was thinking. He always thought it was funny when he saw a man with a woman who was taller than he was. He had a picture from World War II at an USO of Fred dancing with a woman who was nearly a head taller. All you could see was the back of Fred's head in the picture, but Wilbur always said, "YOU KNEW FREDDIE WAS SMILIN' CUZ HE WAS

AT EYE LEVEL WITH HER TITTIES." If the difference in height was greater, he'd say, "WHEN THEY'RE NOSE TO NOSE, HIS FEET IS IN IT, AND WHEN THEY'RE TOES TO TOES, HIS NOSE IS IN IT!" Then he'd laugh.

After the picture taking was over, we walked across the street to the dance. Junior high kids had to leave the dance at 11:00. So, Teri and I, and Jean and her date, Mike, walked back to Jeannie's. Her front porch was screened in. You walked through a screen door and then about twelve feet to the front door. I walked Teri to the front door. Mike and Jean lingered at the screen door and started kissing goodnight. It looked like it wasn't their first time kissing. I looked at Teri, and she looked at me. We both looked at Jean and Mike and back at each other. It was now or never, I thought. I was scared. Gulp. I leaned up and forward, closed my eyes, and we kissed. It was over in a flash.

I skipped all the way back to the bar.

Fred Rife, Wilbur Rife, and Ronnie Gillette

16

"If they didn't have a pussy, I wouldn't even talk to them."

Uncle Ron Returns

My mind wasn't really on the road or the frozen scenery of the rolling Iowa landscape. My thoughts kept drifting away. I was thinking of the people who'd be coming to the funeral as we drove down the highway.

* * *

My dad's younger brother, Ron, came in and out of our lives—often on his way to somewhere else—usually with the law in hot pursuit. When I was a kid, that made him seem like Jesse James to me.

Ron had a rap sheet a mile long. He was arrested in Dallas, Texas, for larceny and delinquency in 1943, when he was only twelve or thirteen years old. But, his first "job" took place in March of '44 in Stillwater, Oklahoma. He and his friend, Jackie Owens, decided that they were going to burglarize a house. Unfortunately for them, they picked the wrong house. They got in and out of the house without notice all right, and on the way out of the house, Ron grabbed a large black cowboy hat and put it on as a memento. A short time later, the wife reported that the house had been broken into, and the sheriff took it personally—because it was *his* house. Not only that, when the two boys were caught, Ron was still wearing the sheriff's hat. The two were sentenced to eight years in the Boys Training School in Paul's Valley, Oklahoma, but not before they were both severely beaten by the sheriff.

Ron and Jackie served only a year.

After Ron was let out, he went back to live in Dallas, Texas, where Ada was living at the time. He was on probation and was to be on good behavior, but he started skipping school. He was arrested again for burglary and truancy and sent to Gatesville Prison for nine months.

By this time, Wilbur thought the best place for Ron to get three square meals and some discipline was the army. Ron reluctantly joined and went to Ft. Louis in Washington for basic training. He was transferred to Ft. Warren, Wyoming, later that year. He went AWOL and was sentenced in 1947 to serve his sentence in Gatesville Prison in Gatesville, Texas. He served eight months and one day.

In early October 1950, Ron and his friend Henric Marincic, nicknamed "The Professor," robbed the Town Theater in Omaha of $271—they were both nineteen years old at the time. Ron and The Professor named a third man, Matthew Greer (who had worked at the theater as an usher and custodian), as the "finger and getaway man." The Professor testified that Greer purchased the guns and also the getaway car used in the robbery, but the jury did not believe him. The judge sentenced Ron and Henric to five years in the Federal Reformatory at Lincoln, Nebraska. In

1951, Ron was transferred to the Nebraska State Penitentiary, where he served out the rest of his term—he was paroled and served three years of the five-year term.

While out on parole, in late December 1953, Ron was arrested in Los Angeles. He had a .22 caliber pistol on him at the time of his arrest. A gun of the same type had been used in the Thanksgiving eve murder of Colorado Highway Patrolman Richard Burchfield of Colorado Springs. Ron and his friend Tommy Warlington were both picked up and held under suspicion of the crime but later released. The Monday, December 21, 1953, edition of the *Omaha World-Herald*, page seven headline reported the story of their release: "Lincolnites Freed of Killing Charge." The Colorado Springs Police Chief, I. B. "Dad" Bruce believed the crime was committed by a "local punk," not out-of-towners. Not all of the police involved in the case were as sure as "Dad" Bruce. Some believed that there was a strong possibility that Ron shot and killed the police officer in Colorado Springs. Even though there were no witnesses to the murder, a claim was made that while sitting in jail, Ron told Ada, who had come to see him, that he killed the officer—shooting him nine times. No evidence connected Ron to the shooting. The crime remains unsolved.

What was clear was that Ron had been arrested in Oklahoma, Texas, Nebraska, and California. He had been under investigation for burglary, robbery, assault, and had been an army deserter and a fugitive. The Omaha Police Department considered him a hoodlum and believed that he was a member of various gangs and had committed crimes for which they had no evidence to convict him. If robbery was his art, then this was the most prolific time of his career. He was crisscrossing the country involved in all sorts of nefarious acts, with all sorts of nefarious criminals. And often, after a big robbery, he would take off for Las Vegas, Havana, or Tijuana to spend the money lavishly on alcohol, women, and gambling.

On January 7, 1954, two Los Angeles police officers approached him. Ron was armed and pulled his gun. He disarmed one of the officers, but the other officer moved quickly to take the gun away from Ron. In the scuffle, Ron was shot in the shoulder and apprehended. He was returned to the Nebraska State Penitentiary.

Less than a year later, the December 16, 1954, edition of the *Omaha World-Herald* ran with the headline "Omaha Car Thief Given 18 Months," with a dateline of Sioux City, Iowa. Ron had been robbing liquor stores in Elk Point, South Dakota, with Burton Kinney. Law enforcement authorities noted that Ron was "a member of the Burt Kinney group involved in a 1953 liquor store holdup in North Sioux City, South Dakota."

Burton Kinney had been an honor student and president of his high school class in Sioux City. Kinney had been a promising boxer, first as an amateur, then as a professional, fighting in seventeen professional bouts. But something went wrong. Kinney had been arrested after he was caught breaking into businesses in Sioux City. He was convicted and served two years in the maximum security federal penitentiary in Terre Haute, Indiana. After his release, he and Ron stole a car and drove it across the state line into Nebraska.

Ron was sentenced to eighteen months in a federal prison for a charge of interstate car theft. He was already serving time in the Nebraska State Penitentiary at Lincoln. He was to start the federal sentence on expiration of the Nebraska term in 1956.

* * *

When I was a small boy, the police surrounded our house with their guns drawn. They believed that Ron was inside, and they had come to arrest him.

Wilbur walked out in front of the house.

"Are you Wilbur Rife?" one officer shouted.

"YEAH."

"You got a brother named Ron Gillett?"

"YEAH."

"Do you know where he's at?"

"THE WHOLE WORLD'S HUNTIN' FOR HIM AND CAN'T FIND HIM AND YOU EXPECT ME TO KNOW?"

"We think he may be hiding here at your place."

"PUT THE GUNS DOWN—YOU CAN SEARCH WHATEVER YOU WANT, JUST PUT THE GUNS DOWN. I'VE GOT FOUR LITTLE BOYS, AND I DON'T WANT NOBODY GETTIN' HURT."

The police told Wilbur that they thought Ron had stashed the money in our house or yard and they were going to have to dig up the yard to find it.

"WELL, GET OUT THERE AND START DIGGIN'. IF YOU FIND ANYTHING, I'LL SPLIT IT WITH YA."

He leaned toward Shirley and whispered in his way, "MAYBE THEY'LL DIG UP THE WHOLE PLACE, AND WE CAN SEED AND GET SOME GRASS TO GROW IN THIS GODDAMN YARD!"

The police searched the house and worked their way over the yard and found nothing.

Ron was also arrested that year for assaulting Charlie Hicks. Charlie was Lucy's husband. Ron never cared for him. He had gone over to Lucy's house because he had gotten word that Ada was going to be coming to town from California for a visit, and she wanted Ron to let Lucy know. Ron got over to their house and everyone was eating supper at the time. So, Ron reached over and grabbed himself a little piece of fish.

All of a sudden, Charlie jumped up and said, "I don't want you comin' in my house again."

Ron turned around to say something back to him, and Charlie had a gun pointed at him.

Ron looked Charlie square in the eye and said, "You ain't got nerve enough to shoot me."

That's when Charlie whacked Ron across the head with the gun. The two of them got into a kerfuffle. Ron wrestled Charlie to the ground while Jewell was hollerin', "Don't hurt my daddy!"

Ron took the gun away.

"What the hell?" he said. He took off and later was arrested.

When they went to court, Charlie took the stand and began telling one lie after another, completely mischaracterizing the events of the evening.

The judge asked Charlie, "Well, if Mr. Gillett did everything you claim, how did you finally get him out of your house?"

Charlie testified, "It was just brute strength!"

The case was thrown out of court.

* * *

On August 30, 1957, at 8:55 p.m., Ron and George Bevins robbed the Safeway Store in Long Beach, California. They drove a blue Plymouth coupe. The store manager, Thomas Wood, testified that the two gunmen who robbed his store got away with $4,418 in cash and checks. Wood testified that Bevins and Ron "entered the store as he was in the process of putting the money from the check stands into the safe, preparing to close the store at nine." As he closed the safe and turned toward the check stands, a man approached him and put a gun in his side and told him to open the safe. Wood observed that the gun was a chrome-plated revolver. Upon Wood's opening the safe, Bevins held out a bag and told him to put the money into it. Wood began to pull out the drawer that he had just placed in the safe, whereupon Bevins said, "No, not that, I want the big money." Wood then started to put the drawer back, but Bevins told him that he would take that also. Wood took the drawer out again, removed the currency, and put it into the bag. Wood then opened the combination side of the safe, where there was a box about six by eight inches containing currency in $100 bundles. Bevins told Wood that was what he wanted. Wood started to take the money out of the box, but Bevins had him put the box and its contents into the sack.

Bevins also told Wood he would take all of the rolls of money, including half dollars, quarters, dimes, nickels, and pennies. Wood started to pick them up one at a time, but Bevins told him to hurry; finally, Bevins stepped in and took the rolls of money and put them into the bag himself, while Wood stood back. While this was going on, Bevins was inquiring of Wood the time the police checked the market. Wood informed Bevins that he did not know. Bevins stated to Wood, "My buddy is standing behind you. Don't try anything funny." At this point Bevins left the store. Wood observed that Bevins was wearing a hat but had no mask. Wood gave a description of Bevins to the police when they arrived.

Around this same time, Ron was also working with Paul Small. Small was described as a slight, red-haired, freckle-faced man. He was best known for his 1955 burglary of the Margaret Kellogg home. Mrs. Kellogg and two of her friends, who were in the house at the time, knew that the robbers meant business. When Mrs. Kellogg asked that they show mercy for her Chihuahua, Monca-Pu, Small and his cohort ripped the diamond-studded and bejeweled collar from around its neck. That heist was valued at between $125,000 and $175,000.

On September 4, 1957, at 7:45 p.m., Ron and Small robbed the Safeway Store in Long Beach. The store manager, Henry Barber, testified that $5,500 in cash was stolen along with four hundred American Express money orders totaling $40,000. On September 20, at 7:26 p.m., the Greater #11 American Market was held up in Corona Del Mar. Almost $6,000 in cash was stolen.

The September 26, 1957, edition of the *Omaha World-Herald* ran the following headline: "4 Omahans held on Coast; 2 Charged in Holdups; Small Also Accused."

Ron was found guilty and sentenced to seventeen years in Folsom Prison. During that time, he was transferred to various prisons in the California system—San Quentin, California Men's Colony East San Luis Obispo, Susanville, Southern Camp Center, Chino, and even the Soledad Baking School. The prisoners were often expected to fight fires, clean up after oil spills, and shovel snow. The Santa Barbara Oil Slick in the early sixties got him out and onto the beach to help clean up. It was dirty, messy work, but he appreciated that it was outside. He was also shipped up to Lake Tahoe to move snow after a blizzard—and he fought numerous California forest fires. The best part of that was how well they fed the forest firefighters—steak!

Ron was transferred to Chino in '71. In February of that year, he saw a chance to escape. He rode out in the back of a furniture truck. He worked his network to end up driving a semi-truck and made his way to our house outside of Logan.

We were sitting one morning drinking coffee when the phone rang. It was the Harrison County sheriff's wife, Mary. It was a small town, and we all knew each other—at least seemingly so. I picked up the phone and said, "Good morning."

"Who is this? This is Mary Allstot."

"Mary, this is Douglas. What can I do for you?"

"Dougie, I know you won't lie to me, so when I ask you a question, you'll tell me the truth."

"If I can, I will."

"Well, there is an APB out for your uncle Ron. He has escaped from prison out there in California. Have you seen him?"

"No, Mary, but if I do, I will call you and let you know." I hung up the phone and turned to Ron. "You'd better head out; they know you are here."

He headed out of town that morning.

* * *

In some ways, he was glamorized for his free-spirited ways. It seemed pretty exciting to us. But not to Wilbur. Wilbur didn't understand why Ron wouldn't go to work with him. Wilbur told him many times, "HEY, LOOK, ART, I CAN GET YOU STEADY WORK ANYTIME YOU WANT TO WORK." It was clear that wasn't the life that Ron wanted. He wanted easy money, though that came with quite a few occupational hazards, not the least of which was being shot at by the police or jailed. And jailed he was, with many stays in the "gray bar hotel." Wilbur more or less gave up when he told Ron, "YOU KNOW YOU WERE BORN ABOUT A HUNDRED YEARS TOO LATE. YOU WOULD HAVE BEEN BETTER OFF IN THE OLD WEST DAYS."

Nineteen seventy-one was a big year for our family. Ron showed up with his go-go dancer girlfriend, Judy. He was married four times during his life, but Judy was not one of his wives. He didn't really think much of women—oh, he treated them okay when he was with them, but he said, "If they didn't have a pussy, I wouldn't even talk to them." Not exactly an enlightened way of thinking about the opposite sex.

Ron was slender with enough charm to get out of nearly any situation. Judy was five-foot-nothing and, as they say in these parts of Iowa, built like a brick shit house. Though that doesn't sound like much of a compliment, it was. She was curvaceous—the kind of body you would expect to see on a go-go dancer.

On his way to our house that year, Ron had staged a car accident up by Carroll, Iowa. The day after the accident, Shirley, Brian, and I drove up to Carroll to search a road ditch near the accident for guns that Ron had thrown out of the car before the police showed up.

Judy had broken her back as a young girl, and Ron and Judy knew that the x-rays would show the breaks. They were going to say Judy had broken her back in the car accident and claim the insurance—which they were hoping would be $25,000 or more for pain and suffering. I wasn't sure of all of the moving parts of the scam. In fact, I thought it was real—at least for a while.

Judy and Ron moved into the downstairs bedroom in our house. They rigged up a pulley system above the bed. She wore a neck brace that was connected to the pulley system to put her in traction. She may have had some whiplash, but judging by the muffled sounds of glee that came from the room when Ron was there, Judy definitely had not broken her back.

Judy would call out for things. "Could someone bring me a glass of water?" When I took the water in to her, she was hooked up to the pulley, lying there splayed, wearing a matching tiger print bra and panty set. I scanned her scantily clad, overstuffed body as I handed her the water—I could hear Wilbur's description, "SHE'S BUILT LIKE A BRICK SHIT HOUSE!"

She was unabashed about it, too. She never even attempted to cover up. She didn't put on any more clothing when Shirley was in there teaching her how to crochet afghans. They worked on a black afghan with bright red roses for several weeks. The only change in appearance was the matching underwear sets.

* * *

Nineteen seventy-one was also the year that Fred and Amy got a divorce. Another messy divorce in the family.

The end result was that we got two more houseguests—our first cousins, Shelly and Reynie, came to live with us. Shelly and Reynie were Fred and Amy's two youngest children.

Shelly was tall with long, dark brown hair, alabaster skin, and bright blue eyes. Shelly's features were a perfect blend of Fred and Amy. In many ways, she brought some stability to the house by adding a touch of mothering. For one thing, she cooked on a regular basis. Beef chunks and macaroni and tomatoes was a standard evening meal. Shelly was also a great baker—she made fantastic gooey chocolate chip cookies that were unbelievable right out of the oven. She made her granny's German chocolate cake on a few occasions, and it was first-rate even though not many of us were coconut fans; somehow it worked for all of us. Shelly was also a leavening force in the house. She was the oldest of the kids still living in Shirley's house and had a judicious way about her, mediating disagreements in a disarming way.

Reynie Shawn, the youngest of our cousins, was not as tall as Shelly. Reynie had light brown hair that was straight and long, as was the fashion. She had a little bit more color in her skin—she could carry a tan better. She also had bright blue eyes, one of the characteristics all the girls in Fred's family shared. Reynie was a giving and loving girl. She would scrape and save, and with whatever little money she had, she would buy little bits and baubles for everyone else. She had a fiery and volatile temper, and she and I, while very close, could fight like cats and dogs. Those arguments seemed to start out with a smart remark—we always tried to best each other.

"If your brains were made of cotton, there wouldn't be enough to weave a Kotex for a pissant," Reynie screamed at me.

My comeback was quick, "If your brains were made out of gas, there wouldn't be enough to power a pissant's motorcycle around a Cheerio." Pissants seemed to play a central role in our point-counterpoint arguments. Often those arguments escalated to shouting matches and finished with slammed doors as we retreated to our own spaces to stew and sulk. Reynie Shawn and I both had short fuses, blew lots of smoke, and then cleared up quickly. Shelly, though, could hold a grudge—you didn't want to mess with her.

So, when Ron showed up with his girlfriend, Judy, we had a full house. And the whole time they lived with us, Ron and his girlfriend didn't lift a finger to help around the house—they were consumers but not contributors. That was getting under Wilbur's skin.

One Saturday, when Wilbur had come up from Omaha for the weekend, he had no place to sleep. He was pissed. Practically in the middle of the night, he roused Ron out of bed.

"LOOK, ART, I GOT NO PLACE TO SLEEP HERE. YOU ARE GOING TO HAVE TO PACK UP AND GET THE HELL OUT. WE DON'T HAVE ENOUGH ROOM."

"Okay, Walt."

"I WANT YOU OUTTA HERE FIRST THING IN THE MORNING. I GODDAMN OUGHTA HAVE A PLACE TO SLEEP IN MY OWN HOUSE."

The next morning, at daybreak, Ron and his girlfriend took off. Judy took our best towels on her way out—and the black afghan with the red roses.

Brian, Shirley, and Douglas Rife

17

"She got the gold, and I got the shaft."

THE DIVORCE

"How is Mom doing?" I asked Brian.
"She's okay, though, I think she feels guilty."
"Guilty? I don't get it."
"She mumbled something that if she'd known Dad was going to die so soon, she'd not gone through with the divorce," Brian added.

* * *

I was sitting in my room one Sunday morning looking out of the window as I worked on some homework for the next day at school. I was a junior in high school at the time. I thought it was pretty odd to see

Shirley circling the house. It seemed as if she had gone around the house four or five times when I finally raised up the window.

"Are you okay?" I asked her.

"You'd better come down here," she said.

"All right, I'll be right down." I knew something was wrong, but I had no idea what she was stewing about.

"I've told the other kids, so I better tell you," she said. "I know how close you are to your father."

For a moment, I thought she knew something about Wilbur's health that she was keeping from me. Thoughts flooded into my head—was he sick? Did he have the Big C? People didn't even want to say the word *cancer*, so they said the Big C instead, like that made it better or less terminal or less foreboding.

Then she said, "I have been thinking about divorcing your father for a long time, and now I am going to do it."

As strange as it sounds, that was a relief. I was aware of their discontent. They had financial and fidelity issues that were not helped by tumblers of alcohol. Their relationship was bad, and it was getting worse, if that was possible. They seemed like two people who had a vague knowledge of the other but by now were completely disconnected, only held together by worn bonds of family obligation and habit more than anything else.

By this time, Shirley's dislike for Wilbur was active. It wasn't like two people who had drifted apart. These people had been paddling in opposite directions as quickly as they could for years. Wilbur spent most of his week in Omaha and only came up on the weekends. When Shirley would hear his pickup truck tires hit the gravel as they turned into the driveway, her whole demeanor would change. She physically changed. You could see her body tense up. Her mood certainly went south. So, it was no wonder that she had decided to get a divorce.

"Why are you going to get a divorce?" I asked, even though I had lived through the first seventeen years of my life experiencing their marriage firsthand.

"Your father and I don't love each other anymore. We argue and fight, and I can't stand the drinking, the cheating, and the gambling. I've had it."

I wasn't blind. None of us were. It wasn't like they hid it either. They snapped and sassed each other and hardly exchanged a civil word. They swore and cussed. None of us could stand to be around either of them when they started to argue.

By the time Shirley was telling me this, I knew what Wilbur was doing. For one thing, I had seen the gambling and its effects over the years and had become repulsed by it. I couldn't stand to see hard-earned money lost because of a card game or a football score. There was so much wasted on gambling that often there wasn't much left for other things.

And Wilbur's addiction to gambling seemed to have no bounds.

I grew up in bars, dodging drunks, and watching what went on in the back room, where men gathered 'round tables to play cards. The card room was long and narrow, about fifteen feet in length, with big round tables in it. Over each table, a long cord hung from the ceiling with a bare light bulb on the end. The tables, littered with beer bottles and whiskey glasses, were surrounded by old men, chewing tobacco and spitting out big brown globs that went ker-plunk as they landed in the spittoons scattered around the room. The poker players huddled around the table, each armed with cards in hand, waiting for that great hand, confidence building as their whiskey glasses emptied. Each drink made them bolder as they bet. I couldn't begin to count the times Wilbur was right in the middle of it all. He would sit at one of the tables, his eyes intensely gazing on the five cards tightly clasped in his calloused and bulky fingers. I heard my dad bellow, in a familiar gruff voice, his bid, "I'LL RAISE YA A HUNDRED!"

By the end of the night, what started out as a friendly game of poker had turned into a fiercely competitive game of five-card draw by men who couldn't afford to lose. It seemed like the more my dad lost, the louder he became, and the wilder he got with his bets.

Friendships strained, and losers, pledging that they'd get even at the next game, sullenly shuffled away from the tables.

Staking your fortune on the turn of a card is not the only way to gamble money away. There are horses and dogs at the racetracks, and a whole gamut of sports—basketball, football, hockey, and baseball—to bet on. One of the most widely watched and gambled on sport was the

World Series. Men swarmed to the tavern to give their undivided attention to quenching their thirst and watching the World Series as they sat securely on bar stools, elbows resting lightly against the bar, their eyes glued intensely on the television set. In this kind of setting, it never took long for my father to sift out the betting men; then the whole ritual started over again.

Early that spring, Wilbur got in a crap game. His penchant for rolling dice, hoping for lucky seven, cost him $3,600.

When conventional betting wasn't enough, Wilbur would get creative. He would pick a family on Family Feud and lay $5 at the beginning of the show! Once he bet a local farmer $400 that our guys would land on the moon. The farmer didn't believe they'd make it. When they showed the moon landing on television and we heard those famous words by Neil Armstrong, "One small step for man, one giant leap for mankind," Wilbur was licking his chops at getting his money. He told me he didn't care if it was filmed in White Sands, New Mexico, he had $400 coming!

Shirley had had enough, and she wanted to explain it to me.

Even at seventeen, you want your parents to be married and live happily ever after. I knew that was my fantasy and not hers. She was done and had been for a long time.

Now she just had to tell my dad and file the paperwork. Shirley took a needed and cautious approach—because she wasn't sure how Wilbur would react. Or more likely, she did know how he would react. She drove to Council Bluffs, checked into a motel, and then called him. She had told us that she would be gone for two weeks until he settled down. She gave us money to cover whatever we might need—groceries and whatnot—then took off.

Wilbur wanted to know where Shirley had gone. "GODDAMMIT, TELL ME WHERE YOUR MOTHER WENT."

"We don't know," I said, Brian nodding his head in agreement. And that was the truth. Shirley knew not to tell us in case Wilbur got it out of us. If we didn't know, we couldn't spill the beans.

In his frustration, Wilbur said, "WOMEN, YOU CAN'T LIVE WITH 'EM, YOU CAN'T SHOOT 'EM!"

***

That Friday night, Tana, a school girl friend, pulled a wagon with food in it out to our house to make sure I had something to eat. Sometimes when you are in darkness, you don't recognize light. The next few months or so were going to be rough for Shirley and Wilbur and Brian and me.

Wilbur wasn't taking it too well and would show up at the house or Shirley's tavern drunk and wanting to argue. If his normal voice was loud, it literally boomed when he was angry. Everybody could hear it. It was disruptive in the bar. Customers couldn't help but hear it, and Shirley was fed up. So, she filed for a restraining order.

The restraining order was followed by a letter from Wilbur's attorney, whose verbal and written warnings to Wilbur to behave were falling like snowflakes:

> *November 12, 1974*
> *Re: Rife v. Rife*
>
> *Dear Wilbur:*
>
> *Having received a letter from Shirley's lawyer I have to assume that perhaps you were a little loaded Saturday night or Sunday morning as she claims you were in the bar harassing her and the help and also were out at the house.*
>
> *This is directly in violation of the agreement we made last week and the Court, having entered an order on it, would not hesitate to find you in contempt of court and "jug" you for being in contempt.*
>
> *Don't do it anymore as I think, up until now, we are in a pretty good position with the Court to get an equitable result. Don't blow it.*
>
> *Yours truly,*
> *Bill*

That Christmas was a bleak affair for Wilbur. He couldn't come to the house as usual. Shirley, however, felt pretty good knowing she was going to have this holiday without him. She went ahead like she did every Christmas. She rolled out homemade noodles and made mashed potatoes and yams with marshmallows on top. She fried two or three chickens and baked a ham. She cooked corn and beans. She baked apple pies, pumpkin pies, and mincemeat pies. And, she mixed up a batch of eggnog with a heavy dose of rum and sprinkled some nutmeg on top. Beautifully wrapped packages with bows, bells, and baubles were under a Christmas tree lit and laden with all of our family's ornaments to make our holiday festivities complete.

Due to the restraining order Wilbur was sharing a small apartment with Fred on the weekends. It was above a house about a block north of the city park. It didn't feel like Christmas to me without Wilbur, so I went up to see him. When I walked up the stairs, I didn't think he was there at first because there were no lights on and the room was dark. When I got to the top of the stairs, though, I saw Wilbur sitting at the table eating by himself. He turned and looked at me and said, "MERRY FUCKING CHRISTMAS."

It was a sobering moment when I saw him, someone who had never been vulnerable, sitting there with a tear streaking down his unshaven cheek. He continued to eat. "WHAT ARE YOU DOING HERE, SON?"

I told him I just wanted to check to see how he was doing and to wish him a merry Christmas. He told me that Fred was off somewhere and he had whipped up a little something to eat. He asked me how I was, and we talked for about a half an hour before I decided to head back home.

As I started to leave, Wilbur pointed to a stack of bar napkins on a side table. During the holidays, the bar napkins took a festive turn. One Christmas napkin had four reindeer on it that said, "MEET SANTA'S RAIN BEERS! HIGH-BALL—LOOPED—TIPSY—SPIRIT." Another was printed, "'TWAS THE NIGHT BEFORE CHRISTMAS" with a little mouse sleeping in a glass. The stir stick was a candy cane. Or "HOLIDAY CHEERS" with a Christmas ball hanging off a martini glass.

"DO YOU HAVE ANY OF THOSE?" Wilbur asked as I leafed through them.

"Nope." The napkins turned out to be a bright spot in an otherwise dismal holiday.

I gave him a hug. On my way toward the stairs, I looked over and said, "I love you, Dad." He looked at me and said, "I LOVE YOU, TOO, SON." His voice was a few decibels lower than usual.

* * *

In January, they each got a notice to pay a fee so the divorce papers could be filed.

Paying his half of the filing fee pissed Wilbur off. "SHE WANTS THE GODDAMN DIVORCE AND I HAVE TO PAY ATTORNEY FEES AND HALF THE COURT COSTS. LIKE I ALWAYS SAID, SHE GETS THE GOLD, AND I GET THE SHAFT."

And then finally it was over—at least the paperwork.

When it came to settling finances, the judge might have well saved his breath and the paper the judgment was written on. Shirley never paid Wilbur any alimony. Wilbur never paid any child support. The property was divided as the judge ordered, but that was it. The ongoing fight continued, but the marriage was over.

In fact, Shirley and Wilbur threw a party together that following spring at Shirley's house to celebrate the divorce. They roasted a hog, had kegs of beer tapped, and the drunken bacchanalia was on.

I left the house for the day and drove to a spot on Willow Creek between Logan and Magnolia that I liked. When I returned late in the afternoon, the yard was littered with beer cans and soda bottles—and even a girl asleep and draped across our front step. I stepped over her and walked up to my room. I heard later that they had four picnic tables lined up for people to sit around, Wilbur at one end and Shirley at the other. Even that distance couldn't stop them from getting into a screaming match. I was glad to have missed it.

Illustration by Votto Boock, sent to Mom from him

18

"She had more meat showing than a butcher's window."

CITY HALL

Shirley's bar had been a very lively place and a good business. But it died down a bit and folks were looking for something new. Like most things, after a while the novelty wore off. The bands Shirley brought in on Friday and Saturday nights weren't drawing the crowds they used to. So, she was looking for something new to rev up the business when she struck on the idea of having topless dancers.

She didn't come to the decision lightly, but the bill collectors were at the door—or more precisely on the phone. It got to where Shirley wouldn't answer the phone because she didn't want to talk to the bill collectors. She would scream at us to pick it up. When we asked what we were to tell the person at the other end, she would yell, "Tell 'em I went to shit and the hogs ate me." If she did happen to be on the phone and needed a cigarette, she would hold two fingers in a *v* shape and mouth, *You little house ape, get me a cigarette or I'll kill you.* Always with a grin, but the financial strain was getting to her.

Shirley and Brian went to a beverage convention in Des Moines to check out new things going on in the bar business. They tried new drinks and ate ham and cheese sandwiches that could be cooked in minutes in a little oven and served piping hot in inflated plastic bags. Absolute cooking wizardry.

She toyed with many ideas.

I had some suggestions, too. "Why don't you get a projector and rent films and show the films in the bar? I've been to the Shakey's Pizza in Des Moines on Hickman Road, and they had Laurel and Hardy movies playing."

"Jesus Christ, Douglas, are you kidding? No one wants to sit in a bar and watch old movies. Besides that, people can't hear themselves talk over the movies. They want to drink and talk, not stare at old black-and-white films."

Shirley wasn't having it.

"No, what we really need is something that will really stir things up. Something this town hasn't seen before."

"People really come in for your fish fries," I offered again. "When the farmers castrate and you cook the mountain oysters, they like that."

"I hate cleaning those goddamn turkey fries and pig nuts. Slimy shit anyway," she retorted.

"Or maybe you could put in a pizza maker." It seemed like all of my ideas were centered on food and were a complete failure.

None of the other ideas we talked about seemed like they would really draw a big crowd—shake things up. When Shirley first started having the bands, the crowds were huge. But people were looking for something different from country and western bands or fish fries.

"Nope, the same old stuff won't do. We are going to have to do something that gets the town talking and brings in the drinkers."

Topless dancers were her answer.

In the first week of April 1975, she employed her first dancers and all hell broke loose in our little town of Logan. I was a senior in high school. No one talked about anything else. It is hard to imagine that unleashing two C-cups would also unleash a torrent of criticism and anger. But it did, and it did quickly.

Even the bar napkins in Shirley's bar took a turn—girls, girls, girls. The napkins were illustrated with cartoons of women with exaggerated proportions in tiny bikinis. The cartoon women had micro bikinis in hot pink ink. Or one titled "BIKINI TALK"—same theme, same kinds of cartoons. Along with the "GIRL WATCHER'S GUIDE" and "GO-GO GIRLS!" which were both confections of top-heavy and curvy line drawings of bathing beauties, and tag lines something like: "SHE HAS THE KIND OF HOUR GLASS FIGURE THAT MAKES YOU WANT TO PLAY IN THE SAND" or "SHE'S GOT THE KIND OF FIGURE THAT YOU LIKE TO BARE IN MIND!"

"DO YOU HAVE THAT ONE?" Wilbur asked me as he gave me a napkin that said, "GIRLS WITH CURVES ARE USUALLY SURROUNDED BY MEN WITH ANGELS." He always winked at me when he handed me these.

"Nope," I said, as I stuck it in my shirt pocket to add to my collection later.

Shirley had a number of dancers. The best was a young woman from one of the little towns just north of Logan on the Lincoln Highway. She was tall and lanky, with auburn hair, alabaster skin, and the freckles that usually come with milky white skin. She had a beautiful body. She was the most requested and sought after of the dancers, by far.

It was hard to see her sitting with her deaf, blind son and imagine that she was the same woman strutting energetically around on stage. But with her son on her lap, she was calm and serene. She constantly massaged his joints, moving his legs up and down. She sat facing the sun, so his little body could feel the warmth of it on his face. She was the dancer that people, men, mostly remember when they think back on the flash of time when Shirley had dancers.

When I think back on my memory tapes, some of them are scratchy, but there are those moments in your life when the tape, played back years later, stays crystal clear.

One such moment was a Saturday afternoon. I was standing in the kitchen.

Shirley and I had had had an argument that morning. One of the topless dancers who had been staying at the Logan Motel had evidently had sex in the motel while she was on her period. Blood was all over the sheets. Harriet Dunlap, my high school English teacher's older sister, ran the motel. Harriet was old school. She wasn't happy having the "pillow cases" as she called them, stay in her motel. She ran a respectable establishment, and it was going to stay that way. I suspect she didn't want to clean up after them either. With the local motel closed to them, the only place in town for them to stay was at our house.

"Why do they have to stay here?" I asked.

"Because Mrs. Dunlap isn't going to let them stay in the motel anymore."

"Well, who is going to wash the bathtub after they get out of it? We don't even know these women you are bringing into our house."

"Jesus Christ, Douglas, get over yourself. What is wrong with you anyway? These girls aren't going to bother you."

"Mom, don't you care about what it means to have them in our house?" I asked her point-blank.

"I don't give a shit about what people in this one-horse town think of me. I have to make a living. Do you think any of those assholes making a stink about these dancers are going to pay our mortgage payment if I go out of business? You know goddamn good and well that most of the men lining up against it in Logan drive down to Omaha and Council Bluffs to see dancers down there. They just don't want anyone to see them go in. All of these bastards are hypocrites."

That evening, the dancers started staying at our house. We had a very small bedroom just off the kitchen and the bathroom. It had mainly been used as a sort of junk room, but we put a bed in there and straightened it up, so it was suitable—certainly not luxurious. The dancers were, for the most part, young and very attractive. They were also fairly unabashed. One night as I did the dishes, one of the dancers came out of the bathroom only wearing powder-blue panties and a towel wrapped around her head like a turban. She looked at me and smiled and turned into the spare room to get ready to go up to Shirley's to dance. She had more meat showing than a butcher's window, I thought, as I remembered the line from an episode of Andy Griffith. I kept doing dishes but the image stayed with me.

Then the city got involved.

From practically first wind of the dancers in Logan, people started talking about it. Immediately letters were mailed to the paper.

April 2, 1975, *Logan Herald Observer*

Dear Mr. Bloom,

We have always been proud of our town and community. We think it is the very best place to raise our children. We've been for everything that would improve it.

Is this type of entertainment in town this week what we want for our young children?

Is this a good follow-up for Holy Week?

Mr. and Mrs. Charles Kersten

April 10, 1975, *Logan Herald Observer*

Dear Editor:

I was brought up to believe this is a free country, freedom of speech, freedom of choice.

If the people's choice is to spend their hard-earned money to see topless dancers then this should be their choice.

No one should be able to keep them from their choice.

If you don't want to see topless dancers, stay home. If you do, then go while we still have our free country, what there is left of it.

Mrs. N. Kidd.

To the Editor:

I feel that all the hassle about Logan having topless dancers is a bit ridiculous. No one is forced to go watch them, so if some of the townspeople don't want to see it, don't go.

No minors are allowed in to watch them, so there should be no trouble about children growing up in such surroundings. Also, anyone 18 years of age is old enough to make their own decisions, and there is nothing their parents or friends can say to sway their decisions.

Every person that owns a business has some way to draw people to make some money. This just happens to be one way of doing it. I think it won't hurt Logan.

Penny Christo.

We also received a letter. It was from an artist in Omaha who included two pencil sketches—one of a woman with pasties and one profile of a nude woman:

April 14, 1975

Dear Mrs. Rife,

I heard and read about your situation over there in Logan, well let me tell you something, I am for you all the way and 100 percent, so keep up the good work.

We have a radio station here in Omaha, a talk station. This one man on the show was sure rubbing your policy the wrong way, well he is one of these fellows that also likes to see Omaha be a cow town. One of these petty kind that is forty years behind. Keep up your good thinking and stay in there and fight. You can take it from me, I consider Omaha a one-horse town that is overstuffed with prudes!

Now I shall say a few words about myself. Painting and art work (but it is mostly painting) is a hobby of mine. I paint mostly nudes, and I think the female is beautiful, I adore the female body. Prudes can think what they like, I think it is beautiful.

This man criticizes everything of that nature, he was looking for people that agreed with him on the talk show. That is his thinking on gambling, prostitution, topless girls, and so on. I don't know the age of the girls but it must be legal. If they are interested in some fairly good money to make on the side, I am very interested. Omaha is not too far away and it is good for 75 to 100 dollars, could use a model too. I am sincere, reliable, and not some kind of jerk.

Paintings of a dancer has always been one of my main interests, veils, plumes, furs, and the go-go type of stance. I will say that some of my work is out of this world, use pastel colors and that makes them very life-like and alive.

So stay right in there and keep fighting as I adore the female body like many others. God Bless You.

I am Very Sincerely,

V.H. Boock

The Logan city councilmen almost immediately began considering a proposed ordinance to ban nudity at places that sold alcohol in an effort to stop the topless dancers Shirley had hired.

If that passed, it would be over.

The president of the Federated Women's Club in Logan and the wife of my high school band director had circulated petitions throughout the town to gain support for a ban on the topless dancers. Approximately ninety people signed the petitions that were presented to the Logan Town Council at their regularly scheduled meeting the second Monday of April.

The reverend of the Methodist Church began his own campaign against the topless dancers, saying that he considered it a form of sexploitation. The reverend was talking the issue up in the pulpit and with the other clergy in Logan. He had a two-point charge—the Logan Methodist Church and the Magnolia Methodist Church. He would preach first in Magnolia and then drive the six miles to preach the same sermon to the Logan congregation. He was given to a bit of theatrics and often cried during his sermons—always in the exact same spots in his sermons in both churches. I had a firsthand seat listening to him rail against the topless dancers in Logan; I was a member of the Magnolia Methodist Church congregation. Some of those Sunday mornings were fairly uncomfortable.

A special session of the Logan City Council was called for Monday, April 14, at 7:00 by Mayor Olson. That was the night I went to give a speech in defense of Shirley's right to have the topless dancers. Even though I disagreed with her at home about the dancers, I decided to support her publicly—blood being thicker than water and all that.

The council room was quite small and crowded, even though it only had the mayor and the council members in the gallery. A row of folding chairs at the end of the council table, where participants in the meeting and the lookers-on sat, was full. Shirley, Kay Freymiller, Carole Schaeffer, Mrs. John Benedickt, Penny Christo, Brian, and I sat waiting for our turn to speak out in favor of the topless dancers.

The first order of business was a discussion about two building permit applications. After much discussion, a motion was put on the table and voted on—one was denied the building permit, and one was granted. I was squirming in my seat in anticipation of my turn.

Finally, it came. This was my speaking debut. This was my entrée into local politics. I was just eighteen years old. And I was nervous. On top of that, I was about to employ a high-risk strategy for dramatic effect during my speech, and I didn't know how it was going to go. My hands were sweaty. I could practically feel my heart pounding out of my chest. As I stood up to give my speech, everyone turned to look at me. I could feel my face and ears turn red hot as the blood rushed into them.

I cleared my throat and began, "Anyone in business knows that a business depends on the promotion of new customers and the continuance of old ones for their livelihood. This and only this will sustain a business, and that's why my mother had topless dancers. Merely as a business promotion, and it worked. It stimulated her business and brought more money into Logan. There was nothing shady or underhanded about it. There were no minors allowed, and no Iowa state laws were broken.

"Some people in Logan and organizations in this community think that the presence of these dancers was immoral and obscene. Well, obscenity is only relative to how you are raised anyway. This is a new and permissive society, and times are changing. Is our town going to give businesses air to breathe, or are they going to smother them with the Victorian morals and ideals of the 1890s? I agree that there should be a decision made whether or not people should see topless dancers. But this decision shouldn't be made by the town council; it should be made by the people. If they want to go in, they should be able to, and if they don't want to, they don't have to.

"If the town council says no to topless dancers, they will be depriving the people of making the decision for themselves. The town council will deprive the Logan people of one more freedom and cheat them the right of choice.

"Everyone who goes in to see this entertainment is eighteen years old and considered an adult by law. These people are old enough to vote, drink, and fight in wars. They are old enough to choose what they want to do and certainly old enough to choose what they want to see.

"Anyone who has ever paged through some of the magazines that are sold locally knows that worse than bare-breasted girls can be seen in the centerfold of *Playboy* magazine, which is sold coast to coast as well as in our town. If the topless dancers are stopped, it would only be justice to ban the sale of magazines that expose bare breasts and bottoms. Treat all as equals under the law."

At this point, I reached into a paper bag that I had, which contained the April issue of *Penthouse* and the April issue of *Playboy*, which I had purchased earlier that day at Eby's drugstore.

I had never bought a magazine like that before, and I was actually flushed when I went up to the counter to pay for it. I knew everyone in town, and they knew me. So, I had purposefully waited until there wasn't anyone in the store before I went up to the counter to pay for the magazines. Mrs. Mertz worked at Eby's, and up until that point, I think she had a fairly good opinion of me. When I put the money out to pay, she said, "I didn't know you were the kind to read this sort of thing." I mumbled something about a civics project and quickly stuck the magazines in the brown paper bag and got out of there. Her husband, Don, who was a councilman at the time, would find out firsthand what I meant by that.

I had done my homework earlier in the day and rifled through the magazines very *slowly* and *thoughtfully* to find the most explicit photos and marked them with little slips of torn paper.

I opened the *Penthouse* to one of the marked pages, and several of the slips of paper fell out like snowflakes to the floor. I opened to the centerfold. Judy Clayton was featured that month. Except for a small white "wife beater tee" that she had pulled up over her breasts, she was completely naked. She was pictured leaning back and sitting on the edge of a chair with her legs spread slightly, exposing a triangle of dirty blonde pubic hair. Her tan lines made her look even more naked because they spotlighted what the bikini had kept covered—the sun had been nature's highlighter so to speak. There were a couple of audible gasps in the room!

Mayor Olson gaveled the room back to order and ordered the city clerk to take the magazine away. I wasn't given a chance to pull out the April *Playboy*—but the first magazine had its desired effect of shock. After the hullabaloo died down, I continued.

"The mass of the people who signed the petition that the SOS Club put out have never been in my mother's tavern, and more than likely, they never will be. They wish to stop these dancers, but not one of them has offered to put food on my table, pay my mother's bills, or offered to send her two sons through college. It may be a noble thing to stop these girls from dancing, but is it so noble when you might cause a business to lose a large amount of its income? My mother is just trying to make an honest living—can anyone blame her for that? All she is trying to do is bring more money to her business, and at the same time, it would be wise to remember that she is also bringing money into Logan. Granted, there might be other ways money could be brought in, but none of them have been pursued.

"All who entered Shirley's tavern came in on their own accord. No one was forced and it was all voluntary. Men and women alike came, and none of them could see anything wrong with these dancers, and some of them made the comment that the girls were such good dancers that they didn't notice when they took their tops off! One of the local townswomen made the remark to me that 'Nothing is as beautiful as the human body.'

"The SOS Club petition advocated that nudity not be seen where liquor is served. How would the absence of liquor change what is being viewed? These petitions were put in various businesses around this town. The Chamber of Commerce should have realized that that was a violation against good business policies, and it should have never been allowed. It was like business against business and was out and out wrong.

"All my mother is asking is that Logan 'one hundred years old and geared to grow' does grow. Grow with the changing times. That Logan allows this type of entertainment. Other Iowa towns have approved it and brought more money into their communities. Why should Logan people who want to see this form of entertainment have to drive to other towns and spend their money elsewhere? Why don't we try to keep our people in our town and bring others to it, too? My mother isn't asking that everyone come in but only those who want to. She knows that everyone doesn't approve, but she does ask for the right that her ideals are allowed to coexist with everyone else's and that people in town make the decision for themselves.

"Last, I would like to ask if any of the council members were in to see the dancers. If you didn't see them and make a ruling against them, it would be like saying someone is guilty without hearing the evidence."

I was relieved to get it over with. I sat down and didn't hear much else of what was said for the rest of the meeting. Another meeting was scheduled for the following Monday, April 21.

* * *

The letters kept coming in, with such gems as "The basis for morality is found in God's word, and He does not change. Only people do. You are now a slave of sin or Satan, and scripture says that he is your master. But you can be free because Jesus Christ has paid the penalty for your sins." Of course, that writer included a pamphlet called the "Meaning of Life." Shirley read that letter and rolled her eyes. "Now the Christians and the Jesus freaks are coming after me."

The *Logan Herald Observer* also covered the meeting, as did the *Omaha World-Herald*. Jeff Withrow, *World-Herald* reporter, started his article with the provocative first line, "Topless entertainment has bounced into this western Iowa community, and according to one bar owner, has caused some cleavage among the residents." The dancers were the talk of the entire town and the school. One of the council members was a school bus driver during the day. He noted that he shouldn't have to drive a bus and hear school children talking about topless dancers on their way to school.

I was dating at the time, and my girlfriend's parents were none too happy that their daughter was dating the son of the bar owner who was employing topless dancers, not to mention letting the dancers stay at our house. It was all too unseemly for a modest farm couple.

My minister was also not satisfied with just delivering sermons from the pulpit—he got active in the resistance. The Des Moines *Register* quoted the reverend, "Anytime sexuality is exploited for financial gain, the whole basic sexual nature we are born with is cheapened." He began calling on the other ministers in Logan to talk to Shirley and plead with her sense of morality and good citizenship to stop the topless dancers on her own.

The first pastor to show up at our house was the Lutheran minister. The night he came to talk to Shirley, it was dark and stormy—the sky seemed to open up and let it rip. Torrents of rain fell. We heard a knock on the door, and there he stood, wet and dripping on the rug as he stepped into the alcove.

"Shirley, I was hoping I could have a word with you regarding the entertainment at your tavern."

Shirley was polite but visibly irritated. She was gracious enough—even offered him coffee, which he waved away. They talked for a few minutes, and it was clear that the pastor wasn't making any headway. His parting shot was more or less a plea for her to reconsider. Then he walked to his car. We had a gravel driveway with a gravel turnaround, but when he backed up his car, he missed the turnaround and sunk into the mud. We could hear his car as the wheels spun fruitlessly. We went to the door to see if he was going to make it out, and it was clear he was in pretty deep. Shirley told Brian and me, "You boys better go out there and give him a push, or he's going to be out there all night."

We ran out to help. With a couple of pushes timed with him giving the car some gas, the car lifted out of the mud and up onto the gravel where he got some traction. He rolled down the window. "Thank you two for the help," he said.

Brian couldn't hold back and quipped, "We were glad to help, pastor." Then added, "The Lord does work in strange and mysterious ways, doesn't He?"

He drove away, and we hurried back into the house laughing.

The next confrontation came from the reverend when he told Shirley he was going to bring in a group of the local clergy to sit in the front row while the dancers were dancing, supposedly to embarrass the patrons into not watching. Shirley generously offered to waive the cover charge and said she would supply the group coffee. The ministerial conclave and sit-in never materialized.

When questioned by reporters, Shirley made it clear it was strictly a business decision, not a statement on public morality. She also made it clear she had gone to great lengths to cover the windows with paper and post a person at both doors to keep anyone underage from seeing anything untoward. "I'd never seen topless dancers myself before. These girls are not vulgar or suggestive." Her main point being that no one was forcing anyone into the bar; it was clearly a matter of one's individual choice whether or not they came in to see the dancers since it was obviously they would not see anything accidentally. Shirley fought back by delivering a petition of her own in support of the dancers with a total of 207 signatures. She also made it clear that she would fight the ban, in court, should the ordinance pass.

***

The April 21 meeting of the city council was crucial. They were going to take the deciding vote on the topless ban—officially embodied in Ordinance #203.

Many weighty issues were before the council that night—there was a request to widen a drainage ditch, a man was there to report that his survey stake had been pulled up by his neighbor who had planted the area with beans again, one woman requested permission to make her trailer permanent by removing the hitch and wheels, and the Methodist minister requested that the alley between the church and the lumberyard be closed for a summer recreation project. It seemed like it was taking forever to get to the main event.

Finally, the vote. Councilman Watts moved to bring forward his motion to adopt City Ordinance #203. Clevenger seconded the motion. There was a motion to dispense with the reading of the Ordinance by Councilman Murray and seconded by Councilman Adams. Mayor Olson called for the vote—Watts, aye; Mertz, aye; Murray, aye; Clevenger, aye; Adams, aye. With the vote five in favor to zero opposed, the ordinance passed.

Shirley lived up to her threat and employed attorneys who successfully argued for an injunction to be put in place. She hated to be told what to do and was not going to be bullied by the city council. Contradictions abounded—Shirley was an otherwise shy woman yet ran the tavern. She also hated to argue but relished the fight with the city. For her, it was David and Goliath. Her against the man, her against the system. How dare they tell her what to do?

District Court Judge E. F. Hanson signed a temporary injunction, halting enforcement of the anti-nudity ban while Shirley's claims could be considered. She had won the first battle.

The judge considered the ruling and later reversed the court decision, reinstating the ban on nudity saying, "The court does not have the power to question the wisdom of the city council in its exercise of its legislative prerogative."

Logan Herald-Observer printed the headline that summed up the finale, "Judge halts topless dance ban in Logan." The paper ran a few of the details:

> *The council members last week had voted 5–0 in favor of the ordinance, which was a completely new liquor control ordinance for the city of Logan and which has a section, 19(8) which bans nudity in any business establishment licensed to serve liquor or beer.*
>
> *In his decision, Judge Hanson said, "The Plaintiff's attack on the propriety of the ordinance focused entirely on the proscription against the exposure of the human female breast including the nipple or any portion below the nipple with less than a full opaque covering."*
>
> *The decision reads in part: The court finds that the ordinance does not violate any constitutional rights of the plaintiff.*

The battle was over.

* * *

Funny, though, how the fact that Shirley owned a bar practically assigned a reputation to her—as if because you owned a tavern you were automatically a tramp. I was in driver's ed when I first came face to face with it. I was driving down Main Street in Logan when the driver's ed teacher said, as we drove by my mother's bar, "Hey, I hear the night bartender puts out."

I was pissed. I pulled the car into the nearest parking spot. My teacher looked at me as I put the car in park.

"What are you doing?"

"I want you to apologize for what you said about the night bartender."

"What do you mean? I didn't mean anything by it."

"You know my mother is the night bartender, so apologize." I sat there humiliated. I couldn't let him get away with it. "You can either apologize here or in front of the school board. Your choice."

"I certainly didn't mean anything by it, and if it sounded like I was talking about your mother, then I am sorry," he said sheepishly. I pulled back into traffic—still fuming.

* * *

Lessons from Shirley's foray into having topless dancers abounded. We all got constant advice about marriage and sex from both Shirley and Wilbur.

Shirley's idea of marriage was not to do it—avoid it. Over the years, she had really soured on the idea of getting married at all. In fact, she would often say things like, "If I had to do it all over again, I would just shack up with your father long enough to have you boys, then I would kick his ass to the curb." A real Hallmark moment.

It was not really the romantic ideal that so many young people hear from their parents. After all, even if the parents' marriage isn't great, the parents hope for a better marriage for their children than they had. Shirley hoped for no marriage at all, just the byproduct of children—she did want grandchildren, plenty of grandchildren.

She also gave plenty of advice along the way.

"If you can't stand to look at them every morning across the breakfast table, don't sleep with them." That little gem was meant to discourage us from sleeping around. Be committed or don't have sex. Be selective. You never know if an accident is going to happen and you have to do the right thing—marry the girl and raise the baby. God forbid you are fooling around with someone you wouldn't want on your arm and she got in a family way. What then?

"Marry in haste, repent in leisure," she would say, with an all-knowing look on her face, an expression born out of her own experience.

"Flies spread disease" she would bark, "so, keep yours zipped up." That bromide was to teach us that promiscuity could lead to all sorts of trouble, not the least of which was gonorrhea or syphilis. The ultimate was a baby.

One of the salty lessons Brian and I got from Shirley came when it was rumored that one of the girls in the sophomore class of our school was pregnant. The story that one of the teachers had impregnated the girl made its way all over town. Supposedly, according to the lurid details making the rounds, the teacher and the sophomore had done it in his classroom at school. To this day, I'm not sure if that part of the story was true or not, or if it was part of the embellishment that happened as the story was passed on from one person to another around town. Those stories got better each time they were told and retold.

As time went on, more and more details trickled out. The girl wasn't from a family that had much money, so she went up to the social services office to apply for aid to dependent children (ADC). Small towns were notorious for being class conscious. If you were on ADC, that meant you were on the bottom rung. Folks in small towns thought everyone ought to be able to get a job and pay their own way.

Once she got to the aid office, one of the ladies behind the counter there told the girl, "You have to identify the boy who is the father."

The girl pleaded that she didn't want to do that.

"But you have to."

"Why?"

The lady behind the counter explained that the aid office would sue the father for child support.

The young girl paused for a long time in silence. Then she sobbed.

"I know this is difficult for you, but you really do have to tell us."

"I can't, I just can't!"

"You don't want to get the boy into trouble, I can understand that, but he must take care of his responsibility."

"No, it's not that."

"Is it because the boy is married?" the lady behind the counter asked. By this time, everyone in the office was listening to this highly emotional and highly charged conversation.

"No, it isn't that, either."

"Well, you just have to give us his name, or I am afraid we are not going to be able to help you."

She gulped, a long pause, and said, "It is just that I had sex with about eight guys during those two weeks I got pregnant, and I don't know who the father is."

When Shirley heard this last bit of the story, she said, "Well, Jesus H. Christ! If a buzz saw hit you in the ass, how would you know which blade cut the deepest? There is no way to know who the father is. Keep away from girls who carry on like that, or you are going to end up raising someone else's kid."

Wilbur's approach was completely different than Shirley's, though the advice was about the same—"DON'T GET MARRIED ANY SOONER THAN YOU HAVE TO." Wilbur believed that the main objective was just to have as much sex with as many women as you could possibly have. He wasn't all that discriminating about it either. When he spotted a pair of legs he liked, he said it very directly—"SHE'S GOT LEGS JUST LIKE I LIKE 'EM, FEET ON ONE END AND PUSSY ON THE OTHER." It would seem any legs would do as long as they ended up where he was going. Objectification—pure and simple.

"I WAS DRIVING TO WORK, AND I SAW A WOMAN HITCH-HIKING ON HER WAY TO OMAHA. I PICKED HER UP AND ASKED HER WHERE SHE WAS GOING." Wilbur said that he had asked her how she got around from place to place without a car. "SHE RAISED UP HER BLOUSE AND SHOWED ME HER TITTIES AND SAID, 'THESE GITS ME EVERYWHERE I WANTS TO GO!'" Wilbur was disappointed that he didn't have time to have sex with her because he was on the way to work, but he dropped her off and gave her $20 to help her out. "OPPORTUNITY KNOCKS, AND YOU HAVE GOT TO TAKE ADVANTAGE OF IT WHEN YOU CAN."

Wilbur was the fat guy at the Chinese buffet. You don't go to the buffet looking for gourmet food; you go in because you want food by volume. Wilbur was the volume guy. He would say, "I'VE NEVER HAD BAD SEX. I'VE HAD SEX THAT WAS BETTER THAN OTHER SEX BUT NEVER BAD SEX."

That explained his approach to asking women if they were interested. He was direct. For him, it was a numbers game. If you posed the question

"DO YOU WANNA FUCK?" to enough women, there would be a high enough percentage of women who would say yes that it was worth the rejection of the ones who turned you down. And he rarely missed a chance to ask the question.

Sometimes Wilbur would make an attempt at flirting—his version of it anyway. By the time he was middle aged, he had quite a large paunch, which looked like a large helium balloon inflated to the limit about ready to explode. He would pat his stomach, lean forward, and say with a smile, "I'M GOING TO HAVE A BABY ELEPHANT. DO YOU WANT TO SEE HIS TRUNK?"

One night after the bar closed, he and I drove down to Missouri Valley to have breakfast at the Sunnyside Café. On the way to a booth, Wilbur grabbed an *Omaha World-Herald* to look through while we ordered and waited for our food. He had breakfast, and I had my usual—a salad with Italian dressing, french toast, french fries, and hot chocolate.

As I was eating my starter—the salad—Wilbur found an article in the paper that took his interest. Splashed on the front page was an article about a Lutheran minister and his son from Decorah, Iowa, I think, who had been arrested in Omaha for soliciting an undercover prostitute. The storyline captivated him: father and son arrested trying to hire a prostitute. We talked about the story, and he laughed as we ate through our early morning breakfast feast. At the end of the meal, Wilbur turned to me and said, "SON, LET'S GO GET ARRESTED!"

"What are you talking about?"

"LET'S GO DOWN TO OMAHA AND GET WITH SOME GIRLS. I KNOW SOME WORKING GIRLS WHO WILL MAKE YOU FEEL GOOD. IT'LL BE GOOD FOR YOU."

"I don't really want to go."

"NO WORRIES, I'LL PAY. YOU'LL LIKE THESE WORKING GIRLS, TOO. THEY WILL MAKE YOU FEEL GREAT."

Wilbur tossed me the keys to his car.

"YOU DRIVE."

I got behind the wheel of his Pontiac Lemans and pointed the car in the direction of Omaha, traveling down I-29. It was only about twenty-five or thirty minutes to get into the city. St. Mary's Street was where the action was at that time.

As we drove toward Omaha, I broke into a sweat. I did not want to go.

Wilbur could see that I was nervous. "WHAT'S WRONG, SON?"

"I don't really want to go down there and sleep with some woman I don't even know."

"WE AIN'T GOING TO DO NO SLEEPIN'!" Then he laughed.

"You know what I mean, Dad."

"IS YOUR LITTLE GIRLFRIEND UP THERE IN MAGNOLIA PUTTIN' OUT?"

"I don't really want to talk about that."

"LET ME TELL YOU, SON, YOU DON'T WANT TO BE WASTIN' YOUR TIME ON A WET FISH. THERE ARE PLENTY OF GIRLS OUT THERE WHO WANT TO DIDDLE."

"Dad, this isn't really something I want to go do."

"DON'T WASTE YOUR TIME NOT GETTIN' SOME PUSSY. WHEN YOU GET MY AGE, YOU AIN'T GOING TO REMEMBER THE TIMES YOU WAITED OR PUT IT OFF; YOU ARE GOIN' TO THINK ABOUT THE TIME YOU WASTED NOT GETTING EVERY BIT YOU COULD."

"I don't really want to go."

"WELL, SON OF A BITCH! THEN TURN THIS FUCKING CAR AROUND!" Wilbur was fuming.

I got into the left lane, slowed down, and turned across the grassy median separating the ribbons of highway and up onto the other side heading back toward Logan before he changed his mind.

"YOU THINK THEY ARE SPECIAL, BUT LET ME TELL YOU SOMETHIN'. YOU TURN 'EM UPSIDE DOWN, THEY ALL LOOK LIKE SISTERS."

Douglas Rife, senior class picture, 1975

19

"When it rains I think of you, drip, drip, drip."

Yesterday's Dream

It was a tough year. With everything going on with the city council and the talk at school, my high school girlfriend's parents had completely soured on the two of us dating. They saw me as a barfly and really wanted us to break up. They made it clear to both of us when I would show up for a date. Her mother would say to me nearly as soon as I walked in through the doorway, "Have you left yet?" Not exactly inviting.

In spite of some of my personal setbacks, there were a few moments that made me stand a little taller. For instance, in preparation for graduation, our class held a meeting to pick our class colors, our class motto, speakers, and so on. One of my classmates stood up and nominated me to give a commencement address. It came out of the blue. Our valedictorian and our senior class president were slotted to speak. But I was just sitting there minding my own business. Our principal asked me to leave while the class took a vote on my nomination to speak. When I returned, he said I was on the slate to speak. Our motto had three parts to it; my speech was to address "yesterday's dream."

On Wednesday May 21, 1975, in the Magnolia School Auditorium, where we held our graduation ceremonies, I walked up to the podium. I was petrified as I looked out at the faculty, the families, friends, and classmates and delivered my second public speech of the year—but this one was of a very different nature.

"Our dream began as we hesitantly started off to school on those very first days, reaching out beyond the narrow security of a mother and a father. For the first time we were going out among people alone. For the first time we had begun to expand our horizons. We encountered a world of varied faces, of different places, and of new challenges. We had severed the home ties.

"Elementary school wasn't all skipping rope, climbing the jungle gym, and playing ball. This was a time when we started to develop. Our elementary years were formative, not only educationally but socially. We made friends and, needless to say, enemies, too.

"About the beginning of our junior high years, somewhere during the rustling of papers and the slamming of lockers and the scurrying to class, the boys discovered something new—girls. It was the dawning of the girl-boy relationship. We had, so to speak, opened Pandora's Box and didn't quite know what to do with what we found.

"At this time, I would like to share a little memorabilia with you. Something poetic but far from the original. Something we boys were reciting to our newfound dreamboats. It typifies the emotion of a seventh or eighth grader:

> Roses are red
> And grow in the region
> If I had a face like yours
> I'd join the foreign legion.

"Or maybe a little quip like this:

> When it rains
> I think of you
> Drip, drip, drip.

"But that didn't compliment the girls too much, and when we realized that wasn't the way to romance a girl, we wrote something like this:

> I clutched a daisy in my hand
> When I was two or three.
> And lisped 'she loves me—loves me not'
> As I tore the petals free.
> With more concern through teenage days
> I sought a petaled head.
> But when I found my true love
> I counted I confess
> Before I plucked the petals
> To make sure they would say yes.

"Of course, junior high and high school weren't all romancing. It was a time when we were striving toward one ultimate goal. Now we can look back and reflect and see that many of our dreams haven't yet come true, all of the fruits of our labors won't quite be known yet. All of our rewards aren't material, many of them are intangible, some of them may be unreachable, and our biggest dream is yet to come—our future.

"We have worked to make today, graduation day, a reality. Our dream has brought us to where we are now. We have laughed and cried, labored and learned, excelled and failed, and now our high school years have ended. But it is only a beginning. A new plateau, a milestone. In these thirteen years of growing and maturing as young adults, we have developed distinct personalities and characteristics that make us unique.

"With our personalities and talents, we will recall our youthful dreams and look forward to the future with optimistic aspirations."

> Memories, still moist in my mind,
> Of the days of yesteryears.
> Fragments of what we left behind
> Release a flood tears.

With the exception of the last four lines, which came from a poem I read in the *Omaha World-Herald* by Marilyn Van Fleet, I scratched out my speech and gave it with all of the heart I had. I scanned the audience and spotted Shirley but couldn't see Wilbur anywhere. Where was he? Why wasn't he at the graduation ceremony?

I saw him in the bar a few days after graduation.

"Hey, Dad, I looked for you at graduation, but I didn't see you."

Wilbur looked up and said, "HEY, SON, I HEARD YOU DID A GREAT JOB GIVING THE SPEECH AT GRADUATION."

"Thanks, but where were you that you couldn't make it?"

"YOU KNOW ME, I DON'T LIKE THOSE KINDS OF THINGS."

"Yeah, I know, but I was graduating and giving a commencement address. It was kind of a big deal to me." I looked back at him and said, "Yeah, it turned out pretty good. You should have been there."

The worst part was that he wasn't doing anything that night. He just sat in the bar and drank.

* * *

I worked in the local publishing company warehouse in Logan, picking orders and stocking shelves after school. I worked all summer to save money. Our school counselor had suggested that I might want to go to a vocational art school, since I had taken four years of art in high school and my work was exhibited in school art shows. It was natural for him to suggest it. He even sent away for a brochure for an art school so I could become a graphic artist.

The Omaha Art School (OAS) was located in the old Woodmen of the World Building on 14th and Farnam Streets in Omaha. It was a magnificent Italian Renaissance-style building built in 1912 with the exterior adorned with a pink granite and terra-cotta base of three stories and ornamental brick on the rest of the building. At the time it was built, it was not only the tallest building in Omaha but also the tallest between Chicago and the West Coast with eighteen floors originally, and a nineteenth added later. The brass mailbox in the lobby weighed three thousand pounds and gleamed of an earlier time. The building had a two-story entrance that was thirty feet high, with an arched marble mezzanine and marble staircases on each side of the lobby leading up to the mezzanine level. The art school was located in the mezzanine on the left side of the lobby.

There were two banks of three elevators facing each other in the lobby. By the time I started going to school, two of the elevators on the left side of the lobby were still manned with operators, one of the last buildings in the city not to change over. The sweet little ladies running the elevators could stop exactly on the floor—it was their art. They were also happy to let me tour the abandoned penthouse apartment on the nineteenth floor.

I started art school that September and still worked a night shift picking orders in the warehouse in Logan, sometimes running and collating orders in the computer room. But in November, the night shift was shut down, and I lost my night job. After a quick search in the want ads, I had an interview at the *Omaha World-Herald* to work in the print shop mixing inks and doing odd jobs but didn't get the job. I interviewed at the Frito-Lay Company to work on the line, but I didn't get the job. I hated not getting that job because I love Ruffles potato chips—my weakness, my kryptonite. I interviewed at Blue Star, a frozen foods company in Council Bluffs, but I didn't get that job either.

A few weeks later, I was hired at a plant that made frozen TV dinners and pot pies and had an experimental soup line. I was placed at many different stations, depending on where I was needed. One night it might be on the line dumping Salisbury steak patties out of 220-pound boxes for the line workers to put into the tins for frozen dinners; the line ran at 120 dinners per minute. Or maybe I worked on the pot pie line pouring the chicken, turkey, or beef onto the assembly line. Sometimes I worked in the quick freezer chipping the dinners off the floor that fell off the cooling racks or in the butter room mixing water, butter, and garlic concentrate for the spaghetti dinners—the garlic butter mix was splashed on the slice of bread in the dinners. I also got tagged as nimble enough to be a lump buster. I would have to reach my arms into a large vat to find the macaroni lumps that were big enough to clog the machine squirting out the concoction into the tins while dodging the hydraulic paddles that mixed and stirred the seven hundred gallons of macaroni and cheese. If your fingers got between the paddles and the edge of the vat, the paddles would clip off your fingers. I worked with a guy whose right hand was missing three fingers. He only had his thumb and his little finger—it looked more like a claw than a hand.

I went to school from 8:00 in the morning to 2:30 in the afternoon, slept in my car for a quick fifteen minutes, and then clocked in for my night shift from 3:00 to 11:00. Then I would make the half-hour drive from Omaha to Logan and catch as much sleep as I could before it started all over again.

My program at school was twenty-two months. I was to learn how to paint and draw with commercial art mediums such as gouache, watercolor, colored ink, and pen and ink. My first teacher was a small grayhaired woman named Lois. She was gentle and encouraging but tough. She set high expectations for the quality of the art and also the speed at which it was done. She stressed one could not be successful at a job without the ability to conceptualize a piece quickly and then have the ability to execute it flawlessly. Lois led us in our life drawing classes—we were expected to know musculature and the skeleton so that we would be able to draw the human body accurately.

I only made it eleven months. With school during the day and work most of the night, I was exhausted and contracted mono. The doctor told me I could either go to school or work but I couldn't do both without continued problems with my health.

I hated working at the food factory, but the people I worked with were incredible. And their spirit was amazing. I worked with a woman named Alberta who had been there for over thirty years. She said she went to work there one summer to buy a new refrigerator. Then as she paid for that, school was close to starting, so she stayed to buy her six kids new school clothes. She discovered there was always one more thing to stay for to buy for her family and the dual income with her husband became a necessity. I asked her how she had managed to be there for so long. She said, "This company and this job has been good to me, all six of my kids have gone to college." Alberta had a great sense of humor, too. Often when the line broke down and we stood around waiting for the mechanics to fix it, she would tell jokes.

"Douglas, I have a new one for you!" she said with a bit of a giggle. "This bashful boy took all of the courage he could muster to finally ask this beautiful girl out who he had had a crush on. She said yes. He decided he would make it the best date ever! He took her out for a nice dinner, a drive-in movie, and pizza afterward. They ate rich food and drank some beer. During the movie, he started to get a really bad case of gas but did not want to let it out in front of her, so he decided he would get her home, walk her to the door, give her a quick kiss, and get to the car as quickly as possible to get some relief. The gas pains were nearly unbearable. He drove her home and walked her up to the door and just as he was about to kiss her goodnight, the door opened and the father was standing there. 'So, you are the boy dating my daughter. Come in and let's get to know you.' The young man sat in a big winged-back chair when a very old and large basset hound came and sat directly on his feet. The kid couldn't stand it anymore. He raised up a little and let some of the gas out. The father raised up and looked at the dog and yelled, 'Duke!' The kid thought, he must think it is the dog. So he raised his butt cheek up again and let out a little bit more. Again, the father looked at the dog and yelled, 'Duke!' By this time, the kid was practically doubled over with gas pain and decided to let it out since it was clear the father thought the dog was gassy. He raised up and let it all out. After the prolonged blast, the father leaned forward, looked at the dog, and yelled,

'Duke, you'd better get out of there before he shits on you!'" Then her shoulders bobbed up and down as she laughed at her own joke.

The lead lady on the line was a sixty-five-year-old woman named Kathryn. She had a ready smile and calming disposition. She lived in Missouri Valley, which was nine miles south of Logan and on my way to work. We started commuting together. I would pick her up on my way to work. As it turned out, Kathryn and my hometown banker had dated when they were young. She said he was a natty dresser and drove a new car. I asked her why they stopped dating, and she said they broke up because he kissed like a wet fish.

On our way home, we often stopped at the bar right next to the factory. It was a tough bar, and we fit in. We would stop and have a couple of shots of whiskey to brace ourselves after our shift was over. The bar had poker games in the back room. Her son was involved in one of the games, and he caught one of the other players cheating and confronted him about it. The other player broke the top of his beer bottle and gouged her son's eye out, peeling off his eyelid in the process.

The factory was rough. I worked with a guy who got mad at me because when I was wheeling pallets of peas out onto the seventh floor to screen them, I inadvertently wheeled out the bottle of vodka he had hidden in the pallet. Now all of a sudden, he had to sneak the bottle out of the pallet and back into the freezer to another hiding place. He decided to take his revenge by throwing pan acid on my hands. I could feel the burn instantly. I dashed to the sink to wash the acid from my hands. Fortunately for me, a woman in the washroom saw the whole incident. She told me to wash my hands in the water fountain because the cold water deactivated the acid.

I decided I had to get out of the place. I started interviewing for jobs, and I applied at the Harrison County Courthouse in the assessor's office. I applied at Arthur Murray as a dance instructor. Then something unexpected happened. I got a call from Clinton Keay, who said that Perfection Form was looking for an art "type" and asked if I would consider the position, which would start in the Logan office and possibly move to the Des Moines office. Mr. Keay remembered my artwork from the high school art shows. All I had to do was interview with the art director, Denny Clark.

A couple of weeks later, I accepted the graphic art position. Around the same time, Shirley was having financial trouble with the bar—she couldn't seem to manage her expenses, so the parking lot, which she was buying, was under foreclosure. If someone else bought it, her customers might not have a convenient place to park, so I paid the notice but asked her to assign the deed to me, which she did. On one end of the parking lot was a small brick house that had been abandoned for years.

I imagined that I was going to restore the house to its former glory. I went up to the post office and asked what the address of the house was. The postmaster said, "Pick a number between one and ten."

I said eight.

"Okay, the address is 108 North 3rd Avenue."

The house was an Italianate design. All traces of the Victorian era embellishments were gone—the bric-a-brac front porch, the tracery in the gables, the shutters, and the white picket fence. The house had soft double brick walls—eighteen and a half inches thick. The interior was virtually gutted. I decided I would get a bank loan and fix it up and live in it.

Wilbur plastered the ceilings in the house. I had contractors wire it, plumb it, put a new floor in the front room, carpet it, drywall, and repair some of the windows, and finally put in kitchen cabinets.

When I got the offer to move to Des Moines and work in the creative offices there, I made the decision not to let the house determine my future. I rented the house out, and a brother and sister opened a unisex clothing store in the bottom floor. I became a landlord.

Wayne De Mouth

20

"Douglas, oh, Douglas, we got lumps."

The Unexpected Benefactor

Mr. De Mouth was a gruff man with a very large commanding presence. He was wide but not fat—stout, the body of a linebacker. He had a gentle manner but could be rigid and unyielding. No one doubted who was in charge when he was in a room, and he was addressed as Mr. De Mouth by all of the younger staff members.

The small publishing company office was besot with an unusual cast of characters. Gail, the secretary, was young with long, light brown hair. She was vivacious and pretty, and Mr. De Mouth was completely smitten with her. Ginger, a fiery redhead, was a keen developmental editor. Nervous, she chewed her fingernails until they bled. Peggy, the line editor, managed the editing for nearly every product and catalog we produced. She was the first militant feminist I had ever met. Sometimes she wore army boots to work. She also smoked at her desk. Bob was the creative force behind many of the company's award-winning filmstrips. Jean, his sidekick and co-creator, kept Bob on track—well, as much as that was possible. Denny, the former *Look* magazine artist, was the company's art director and my direct supervisor. Denny often worked at this desk with a toothpick in his mouth and was always quick with a joke—"Do you know the difference between a baby and a seagull? A seagull flits on the shore." Then Denny would get a big grin and chuckle breathlessly. Michelle, a sassy blonde bombshell, wore her jeans so tight if she put a dime in her back pocket you could tell which direction FDR was facing. She entered all of our manuscripts and copy into the Wang, our word processor. And then there was me, the graphic artist.

The summer staff swelled. Mr. De Mouth would hire teachers and college students to work on various products—Jerry, with a deep rich baritone voice that sounded like God, had the ability to work on any project handed to him. Jackie, a tall blonde statuesque woman regal in bearing and manner, created some of the company's most memorable and iconic products. Kathy, a college girl who often wore a skin-tight black zip-up cat suit, filed and took care of office odds and ends. Carol also worked on various products that required writing and editing, and she and I both starred in some of the filmstrips.

I didn't have a car or a phone and felt isolated most of the time. That summer, I read voraciously. Peggy volunteered books from her collection for me to read. She introduced me to Boccaccio, Colette, Isaak Dennison, Saki, Hemmingway, Fitzgerald, Faulkner, Chaucer, and a dozen others I had never read before. She insisted that I not waste my time reading trash fiction when there was so much good literature to be consumed.

Since my studio "garden apartment," a euphemism for basement apartment with a Murphy bed that never sat solidly on the floor, was at the bottom of a hill only about a half mile from the office, it was just a short walk to work. The only time it seemed arduous was during inclement weather—Iowa winters were especially tough. Otherwise, the walk was quite enjoyable.

I went to the dances on Wednesday nights at the Val Air Ballroom. On those nights, they had an "over twenty-eight dance night," signaling the type of music that was going to be played, not the minimum required age of those admitted. If you had the eight-dollar cover charge, you could get in.

About a year into my tenure in the Des Moines office, Mr. De Mouth called me into his office. He had heard I had written a couple of short stories, which I had shared with Peggy. He said he wanted to read them. I told him that they weren't very good, but he said, "Hey, I'm the old English teacher here, I'll decide if they are good or not. You just bring them in." I did. A few weeks later, Mr. De Mouth called me into his office to talk about one of the stories. I pulled up a chair to the side of his desk. He opened the folder with one of the stories—it was blood red with comments, editor's marks, and notations. I could feel my heart sink.

The story was a sketch of my grandma Ada. It dealt with her senility and my dad's frustration with it.

"This story is an outstanding character sketch with some very nice details. You are at your best when writing straightforwardly. As in the passage describing the photograph of your grandmother. Perhaps," he paused for a second, "the paragraph is overlong in terms of the rest of the story. Perhaps, it could have been two paragraphs, but this is good." I listened as he read my own story back to me.

"You have some stray sentences. You also have a problem with switches in tone. Sometimes it is too formal and feels out of step with the informal."

It seemed he went on for hours. I felt like the bone didn't have much chicken left on it when he got done picking it apart. But then he ended his critique by saying, "But, these are minor problems. The important thing is to show, not to tell, the reader. Good job."

I was heartened by his last few sentences. Then he said that he thought I had talent as a writer and that I could be an editor right here at the company. But, he could only hire me as an editor if I had a college education. "You won't have any credibility without a degree."

"Mr. De Mouth, there are two problems with what you are suggesting," I said to him.

"What are those?"

"First off, I have something money can't buy—poverty. I can't afford to go to college. Secondly, I am not sure if I am smart enough to make it through four years of college."

"Let me tell you something." Mr. De Mouth leaned forward and looked at me directly. "If you have to live in my basement, I will get you through college. I will make sure you have a job every summer and every break. Secondly, do you know how many dumb sons of bitches I know who have a college education? If they can get through college, you can."

"Okay, I'll look into it."

"See that you do. One last thing, I would keep this story and use it for an assignment in narrative writing in your freshman English course. It will score very well . . . especially if you boiled it down. Save this."

It had not really occurred to me that I was smart enough to get through college. I had been a National Honor Society student in high school, but no one in my family had encouraged me to go to college. And no one in my family had gone to college, save my brother Deke. At the time, he was enrolled in college and was doing really well and liked it. So it started to become a possibility to me.

Over the next year, I found out what the requirements were and how much it would cost, and I applied to Iowa State University in Ames. Surprisingly, I was accepted. I was to start in March of 1979. I was twenty-two years old and getting ready to start my first quarter as a college student.

* * *

Shortly before I quit working full time at the publishing company to pursue a degree in American history, Mr. De Mouth invited me to go to lunch with him. Then, when the day came, his boyhood friend Robert Hullihan showed up for lunch. I told Mr. De Mouth I would be happy to go some other time, and I didn't want to interrupt their get-together. Mr. De Mouth assured me that I could tag along, and off we went to Chi Chi's, which was just down the street from our offices.

When we got to lunch, Mr. Hullihan started asking me quite a few questions, and then he took out a notepad and started writing down the answers. I knew that he was a feature writer for the Des Moines *Register*, but I wasn't sure what was going on or how I could help. Finally, Mr. De Mouth said, "I asked Bob to lunch to meet you. Bob, if you can't find an article in this young man, it's time to quit."

I told him I was sure there wasn't anything about me worth the ink. Bob told me he would make that determination for himself. Mr. De Mouth stood up after he finished lunch and told me I could take the rest of the afternoon off, since Bob had some follow-up questions. We spent the next couple of hours talking about what seemed like nothing and everything.

The following week, Bob and his wife came to the Val Air Ballroom. He watched me dance during that evening and asked some of my dance partners questions. Then, in the middle of the night after the ninth dance, he and his wife were gone. Two weeks later, on February 4, 1979, in the Sunday edition of the Des Moines *Register*, the following article was published:

Douglas takes his partner on a dance back in time

On nights when Douglas Rife is Prince of the Val Air Ballroom here, it is difficult to see him as the youth who came running when the cry of "lumps!" arose along the processing line in a frozen foods plant in Omaha where he once worked.

Come on, Douglas, we got lumps!

Shirley's reaction was typical—she was low-key but positive and proud. Wilbur did something rare—he called me, which was expensive in those days. He treated long-distance phone calls as a luxury only to be used in rare cases and sparingly. "HEY, SON, SEE YOU BACK IN THE PAPER. THIS TIME IN A REAL PAPER. GUESS YOU ARE FAMOUS NOW!"

* * *

That March, I began studies at ISU in Ames. While at Iowa State, I continued to work at the publishing company during summers and spring holiday breaks. I worked in the Logan office but still as a production artist, pasting up workbooks, designing book covers, and study guides. I also worked for the food service department of the Iowa State Memorial Union, serving food at catered events at the Iowa State Center. By the end of the summer, I was still short on tuition. I went to Wilbur to ask if he could help me out. I hated asking.

When I caught up with Wilbur, he was walking out of the back door to his car, which was parked behind Shirley's bar.

"Hey, Dad, can I ask you a quick question?" I could feel my heart start pounding as the words came out of my mouth. I felt trapped. What was I going to do? I needed the money and didn't have anywhere else to go.

"SURE, SON, WHAT IS IT?"

"Well, I have been working all summer." I paused for a second to gain my composure. "Even though I have saved everything I've made this summer, I am still eight hundred short for college tuition." Another long pause. "Uh, would it be possible for you to help me out?"

"JESUS, SON, THAT'S A LOT OF MONEY. I'D LIKE TO HELP YOU OUT, BUT I WAS IN A CRAPS GAME LAST NIGHT AND I LOST THIRTY-SIX HUNDRED BUCKS. I'M TAPPED OUT."

I hung my head and said, "Well, that's okay, I'll think of something else." The truth was I wasn't sure what I was going to do. I felt desperate. I didn't want to quit art school and now college. I didn't want to be a two-time loser.

In the end, a student loan paid my fall tuition.

* * *

After the fall quarter, my landlord told me I had to move out of her house. She said I was missing out on the campus experience by not living with students. I first moved into temporary housing in the basement of Friley Hall, a sprawling labyrinth of rooms under one of the largest dormitory buildings in the United States. We were packed in. The place was wild, too. The freshmen would drape sheets around the bottom bunks and bring their girlfriends for a romp. Some of the guys would sit nearby and cheer the happy couple on while they listened to the lovers grunt and groan from inside their tented bliss. A hundred and thirty freshman boys were waiting for room assignments for the first few weeks of the quarter. It was misery. Finally, I was assigned to Merrill Hall—the last man in a three-man room.

It wasn't too many weeks before the Christmas break. I was happy to be headed home. By this time, Shirley and Wilbur had cooled off from the divorce. Wilbur was dating a woman, Lorena Keele, whom he had known and had a crush on as a kid, and Shirley liked Lorena. In fact, by this time, Shirley and Wilbur were actually doing things for each other. Shirley mended clothes for him. And he, who always had a big garden, would bring her fresh vegetables—kohlrabi, tomatoes, cucumbers, radishes, sweet corn. And now Wilbur came to Shirley's house at Christmas to spend the day with the whole family.

Wilbur bounded in around noon. He threw cards for each one of us on the tree and got ready to eat Shirley's cooking. He didn't bring Ada—it was too confusing for her and too much of a bother for him. He fixed her breakfast before he left the house. Mike, his wife, Carol, and their son, Tim, were there. Brian and I were both there, and so was Deke, his wife, Delila, and their baby girl, Laura. Laura was scared to death of Wilbur and his booming voice. "COME TO PAPA!" he would bark in his most soothing voice. Even still, nearly every time he talked, she would cloud up like she was getting ready to cry. But Wilbur kept trying to get her to come to him. He reached out his arms, and that Christmas morning, she reached her little arms out toward him. In a flash, Wilbur scooped Laura up. He took her over to a bookcase in Shirley's front room that had whatnots on the top of it. He pointed to each one of them and explained what each and every one was. He took her to other parts of the house, telling her what this and that was—he didn't want to set her down. He was beaming. He cuddled Laura and carried her until it was finally time to eat.

Before Wilbur left for the day, he loaded up a plate for Ada—some mashed potatoes, noodles, fried chicken, and a piece of apple pie.

In less than a month, he would be dead.

Wilbur Rife's grave

21

"For all I care, you can run my body up a flagpole after I die."

Buying a Plot, Picking the Casket

From Ames to Carroll, the ground is fairly flat, but the closer to western Iowa you get, the hillier it gets. Harrison County is home to the Loess Hills. The hills were made millions of years ago when the receding glacial winds deposited fine silt known as Loess. The wind dropped the silt forming a line of hills like a spine that begins in Pottawattamie County through Harrison County and goes up to

Monona and Woodbury Counties. Because of that geological phenomenon, as you get closer to Logan, the expansive prairie gives way to the Loess Hills.

I would get more anxious the closer to home I would get. As I'd drive over the viaduct going over the railroad tracks and the Boyer River, I would look to the north to see Wilbur's trailer. I would always look that way when I came home for a break from college to spot his car. If he was home, I usually went down for a visit with him. If his car wasn't there, more often than not, he would be uptown in one of the bars having a drink. He liked to drink, but he also went to the bars to see his friends and to get away from Ada.

After Ada had her stroke, Ron sold her trailer in California and made off with the money, but not before he deposited Ada on Wilbur's doorstep with only her clothes and an old beige suitcase full of photographs she had carted around with her for her entire life.

She was crazy—though, I think the clinical term is *senile*. However, her body was in great shape. She could out-walk most twenty-year-old women. She talked incessantly about things that didn't matter or make sense and that no one cared about. And she had that irritating habit that senile people have of repeating themselves over and over to the point that you couldn't stand it anymore. Wilbur had to get away, or he would have killed her. The bars were a place to go. He knew everyone there, and he liked to drink, even though he wasn't supposed to. Even after he found out about having diabetes, which in part was why he had recently been in the hospital, he didn't quit drinking. At first, he tried, but it was hard for him not to have a drink when he was in the bar with his friends. He would buy them a drink, and they would send him one back. He finally gave up on moderating his drinking or eating habits.

He would say, "WELL, IF YOU GOT TO QUIT LIVING TO KEEP FROM DYING, YOU MIGHT AS WELL BE DEAD." That was the philosophy he had always lived by and consequently the one he died by. His philosophy was "bite down hard." That marked the end of him trying to watch his diet. Moderation wasn't one of the hallmarks of his character. He had "bout hundred and ten years on a fifty-six-year-old body," as Jack Hampton would later say at his funeral.

He hadn't begun to save money for his retirement. I suppose he figured that Social Security would have to do. Just weeks before he died, he was in a big crap game where he lost $7,200. He was a firm believer in those who were alive being allowed to live. "I AIN'T NEVER SEEN A HEARSE FOLLOWED BY AN ARMORED CAR!" He would sip another drink. "COFFINS DON'T HAVE POCKETS, YA KNOW!" Then he would let that sink in a moment and then say, "YOU CAN'T TAKE IT WITH YA!"

The bus stop ticket office in Logan was in Doyle's Hardware store on Main Street, but the bus always turned the corner onto 3rd Avenue to let people off. Shirley's house was the first house on 3rd, right across the alley from Doyle's. Mrs. Doyle came out when it was slow and pulled weeds by the fence. Sometimes she and Shirley would strike up a conversation about the flowers or the yard or just things going on in town—though there usually wasn't much of the latter.

* * *

"We are finally home. I didn't think we were ever going to get here," I said as we crossed the viaduct into Logan. Passing over the bridge, I looked north at Wilbur's trailer as it came into view. I knew he wasn't going to be there, of course, but I looked out of habit. My heart sank. Emptiness.

We drove the last two blocks of the trip and turned the corner onto 3rd Avenue. I couldn't wait to get to the house.

Deke's car was already there—Deke, Delila, and Laura had come down from Lake City, a small neighborhood in Storm Lake, Iowa, where Deke and his family were living at the time.

We pulled up to the curb. Kitty said she had some stuff to do at work and would see me later. I grabbed my bag, and Brian and I hopped out of the car.

I told Kitty I would catch up with her a little later. Then Brian and I walked into Shirley's house.

Mike, Deke, and Delila, along with their baby girl, Laura, were already in the house.

I think we were all in shock.

"Do you boys want coffee?" Shirley asked.

"What happened? I can't believe Dad's dead. Brian and I were just at the hospital two days ago. He was supposed to get out today."

Brian added, "I guess he did get out."

It all seemed impossible. Like this couldn't really be happening.

After an hour or so of turning things around in our minds and talking, we knew we had to start making some decisions.

Mike, Deke, Brian, and I headed out to the graveyard. For most of us, the last property you buy in your life is your cemetery plot. You don't get much land in the transaction, but you get the land forever, so it makes up for the size. Wilbur, however, had not prepared much for dying. He had no plot and hadn't said much about it. In fact, most everyone thought that Wilbur would be buried in the Little Sioux Cemetery. It wasn't really very far from where he was born on Gus Pearson's farm along the foothills, and most of his family were buried there. His great-grandfather Levi Smith and great-grandmother Anna Fowler, parents of his father's mother, were buried there. His paternal grandparents, George and Annie Smith Rife, and his maternal grandparents, Amos Harrison and Sarah Caroline Harrow Anderson, were buried there. His father, Clyde Rife, was buried there with a plot empty next to him for his mother. And there were cousins, aunts, uncles, and friends there, too. I remember so well going to that cemetery with my dad on Memorial Day. He would spot a grave of a friend or a relative and then tell me a story.

"SEE THAT GRAVE OVER THERE?"

"Yeah," my response was less of a response than it was a signal that I wanted to hear the story he was going to tell me.

"HE WAS MY COUSIN. HE ALWAYS PISSED THE BED. WHEN WE WAS KIDS, FREDDIE AND ME HAD TO STAY AT THEIR PLACE, AND ALL THE KIDS SLEPT IN ONE BED. WE WOULD SLEEP CROSSWAYS IN BED. WE WAS STACKED UP LIKE CORD WOOD." Wilbur motioned with his hands, showing the direction of the bed from the headboard to the foot, and then he motioned the other way to show how all of the kids in the bed were laid out. "MORE OF US WOULD FIT THAT WAY. ANYWAY, YOU NEVER WANTED TO SLEEP NEXT TO HIM 'CAUSE HE ALWAYS PISSED THE BED AND YOU'D WAKE UP SOAKED. GAWD, YOU HATED TO WAKE UP COLD AND WET."

"SEE THAT GRAVE OVER THERE? HE WAS MY COUSIN. HE WAS KILLED WHEN HE WAS A LITTLE KID. HIS MAMA WAS BOILING WATER TO WASH CLOTHES." He shook his head and grimaced. "WHAT AN AWFUL WAY TO DIE. HE WAS ONE OF UNCLE DAVE'S KIDS."

"COME ON DOWN HERE. MY DAD IS BURIED DOWN HERE."

We walked down the slope of the hill to where his father, Clyde Rife, was buried. There was a simple stone with just his name, dates of birth and death, and one other word—*Dad*—chiseled into the gray granite gravestone. We stood there for a few minutes. I could tell that Wilbur was standing there thinking about his own father and how much he had meant to him. Clyde had not been the greatest father in the world by a long shot, but he was still one of the most supportive and loving people who had been in Wilbur's life. He had been a hero in my dad's eyes, probably because Wilbur's memory was sufficiently lax enough for him to remember his own father better than the reality had been. People tend to wear better after death than during their lifetime, and Clyde had undergone the same sort of revisionism after he died. He hadn't been sainted *yet*, but he was certainly in the process of being canonized.

"NOW HE WAS QUITE A GUY," Wilbur said almost wistfully. He wished at that moment, I thought, that I could meet his father, that we could have known each other. And in a way, we were meeting. Not face to face but through him. I could feel the flow of generations past. This was my introduction to another generation of Rifes. This was my first meeting of Clyde Rife.

Then Wilbur repeated a story I had heard told and retold.

"I REMEMBER WHEN DIPHTHERIA WAS RAGING. WHEN I WAS A KID, IT WAS A BIG KILLER. NOBODY DIES OF THAT ANYMORE, BUT FOLKS WAS SCARED OF IT WHEN I WAS GROWING UP. MY DAD HAD HEARD ABOUT A VACCINE WHEN HE WAS WORKING ON THE RAILROAD UP NORTH. HE DROVE ALL NIGHT LONG AND WOKE UP OL' DOC CUTLER AND MADE HIM GET UP AND GIVE ME AND FREDDIE THAT VACCINE THAT NIGHT."

That deed of a normal parent had been turned into a heroic moment for my father. It wasn't a great act of strength. It didn't represent great courage. There weren't any big struggles that Clyde made. He hadn't fended off bandits who were threatening the family or their property. He hadn't saved anyone from drowning. Clyde merely showed those little boys that he loved them, and it was emblazoned forever on Wilbur's memory.

"Is this empty spot here next to Grandpa Rife for Grandma Ada?" I asked.

"YES, BUT I THINK DAD WOULD JUMP RIGHT OUTTA THERE IF WE PLANTED ADA NEXT TO HIM."

Then Wilbur thought a few minutes and said, "ACTUALLY, I THINK DAD WOULD KINDA LIKE IT IF MOM WAS THERE. I'M NOT SURE IF HE EVER QUIT LOVIN' HER."

Probably the natural response of any kid with divorced parents. You always have a heartfelt desire to see them together, if not in this life, maybe in the next one. And if you are visiting graves, on a practical level it makes it easier to have them be together. Not far from Clyde's grave were his parents' graves—George and Annie Rife. Wilbur remembered them pretty well. He had known each of them, since he had lived with Annie after his parents were divorced.

"GRANDMA WAS A LITTLE BITTY THING, NO BIGGER THAN A PINT OF SOAP AFTER TWO WEEKS OF WASHIN'. SHE HAD A LITTLE PINCHED FACE AND WAS CLEAN AS A PIN. SHE TOOK IN BOARDERS AFTER GRANDPA RIFE DIED. HE DIDN'T HAVE MUCH TO DO WITH US," Wilbur said. "I SUPPOSE HE WAS TIRED OF KIDS SINCE HE HAD SEVENTEEN OF HIS."

"Do you remember much about him?" I asked.

"HE WHITTLED PEACH PITS INTO LITTLE BASKETS AND STUFF LIKE THAT," he said. "OF COURSE, LIKE MOST OF US, HE LIKED TO HAVE A DRINK. NEARLY ALL OF THE RIFES LIKE TO DRINK. HIS PROBLEM WAS THAT HE WOULD ONLY QUIT ONCE THE BARREL HE WAS DRINKING COMPLETELY TAPPED OUT."

"Did Annie Rife drink?"

"OH, NO, NO, NO. ANNIE DIDN'T LIKE DRINKING, AND SHE WOULD LOCK THE DOOR WHEN HE GOT LIQUORED UP. HE'D FALL ASLEEP SOMETIMES IN THE FRONT YARD. US COUSINS WOULD SIT AROUND AND COUNT THE FLIES GOIN' IN AND OUT OF HIS MOUTH." Wilbur chuckled. "HE'D GET LIKE THAT ONLY ONCE OR TWICED A YEAR, BUT WHEN HE DID, HE REALLY TIED IT ON."

We always visited Ada's parents' graves on Memorial Day, even though Wilbur didn't remember his grandma Anderson and didn't like his grandpa Anderson. I'm not sure if he did it because it was tradition, or if he thought it was the right thing to do, or if he knew it would prompt a memory.

"THAT OLD HARRY ANDERSON WAS A SON OF A BITCH," Wilbur told me. "WHEN HE DIED, HIS KIDS WERE TOGETHER AND WERE TRYING TO FIGURE OUT WHAT TO DO WITH THE FUNERAL ARRANGEMENTS AND ONE OF 'EM SAID, TED, I THINK IT WAS TED, SAID, 'I DON'T CARE WHAT YOU DO WITH HIM, YOU CAN FLOAT THAT OLD SON OF A BITCH DOWN THE MISSOURI RIVER FOR ALL I CARE.'"

With all that history, it was pretty easy to assume that Wilbur would be buried in the Little Sioux Cemetery with the rest of his family in Harrison County. But a few weeks before Wilbur died, he told Fred that he wanted to be buried at Frazier Cemetery. Frazier Cemetery is next to the Logan-Missouri Valley Golf Course, the country club that Fred and he belonged to and golfed at. They had had plenty of fun there, and he said to Fred about half-jokingly, "HEY, BURY ME AT FRAZIER, THAT WAY IF A STRAY BALL COMES UP BY ME, I'LL JUST GET UP AND PLAY A ROUND!"

So, we contacted the gravedigger and caretaker at Frazier. We met him at the graveyard so we could pick a plot for Wilbur. I rode out with Deke. Mike and Brian rode with Fred. Fred said that he and Annie, his second wife, wanted to be buried at Frazier, too, and while he was at it, he would buy a plot for Ada.

Frazier was a nice little country cemetery on a hill, as all country cemeteries were, with a handful of evergreen trees, symbols of what else but everlasting life. We walked around the cemetery while we waited for the gravedigger to show up. We looked at some of the gravestones in the cemetery. Henry Reel, the founder of Logan, was buried there next to his wife, Catherine. Logan had been named Boyer Falls, but Reel changed the name to Logan in honor of the people's general of the Civil War, John Alexander Logan. It was a relief to look at the stones and have my mind on something else besides Wilbur being dead.

The road that went up to the cemetery was surrounded by woods on three sides and a cornfield on the other. The road wrapped around in a rounded square, encircling most of the stones. We picked out a space for Wilbur to the right of the gravel road.

As we stood there, we tried to figure out if we should buy Shirley a plot next to Wilbur. There were actually plenty of pros and cons to it. After they divorced, Shirley made it clear she had no interest in being buried in Harrison County or next to Wilbur Rife. As she said, "If you were married to Wilbur Rife for twenty-six years, you wouldn't want another man!" That sentiment followed to the grave.

So, there we were debating whether or not we should buy Shirley a rectangle of earth for her next to Wilbur. The very natural inclination of children is to have their parents together. Since we couldn't seem to get them back together in life, at least we would be able to get them together in eternity. We decided to go ahead with the decision and pay the thirty-five dollars.

As we were choosing the place, Fred said, "This one is nice. This little tree is going to get big, and it will give Wib plenty of shade." Obviously, the coffin lid closing would provide all the shade that Wilbur would need, but it was a warm and wonderful thought.

"Be sure to take shoes up to the undertaker. Your dad's feet was always cold." Then Fred teared up and said, "Why did I have to take your dad's marbles and hide them in the attic? You could get ten of those little marbles for a penny. They cost nothin', but it was all he had—them marbles. It was all that little kid had to his name, and I took his marbles. I would just grab them all up and say 'grabbies' and take them all. Now why would I do that?"

"Uncle Fred, I don't think there was anybody he thought more of than you," I said, trying to comfort him.

"Oh, gawd, no, I'd get 'em all, we get all in that big circle, ya know, and I'd see him put 'em out there, and I'd just grab 'em. And away I'd go. He used to just cuss me. Ya know, he was something else. He wanted me to let him ride my bicycle, and I wish I'd just let him, but I didn't. I'd lock it up, just like a kid would. And he'd just take it anyway and put his foot though there and coast it and he'd be gone."

With tears in his eyes, Fred said he wanted to pay for Wilbur's plot. He said it would be the last thing he would ever be able to do for his brother Wib. Then he began to cry.

It deeply affected me. I think we were all choked up because it was so unexpected. Fred was stoic. Men from his generation did not exhibit emotion, much less cry. And yet there he was in an unguarded and honest moment, completely exposed.

I was connected to him by shared grief—his brother, my father. We were both going to miss the robust and full personality of Wilbur Rife. The loss of my father left a hole in my life. My father lived large in his own way. He loved living; he loved life.

On the way back to Shirley's house, I rode with Deke. Mike and Brian rode back with Fred. I really lost control and may have cried harder than I ever have. Deke looked at me in despair and didn't know what to do. He asked, "Should I pull over?" Neither of us knew what good that would do, so he kept driving the four or five miles back to Logan.

Once we got to Shirley's house, I walked in the door and screamed, "We got you a plot next to Dad, and goddamn it, I don't want to hear you bitch about it either. You are going to be buried next to him, and that is all there is to it!" I was not going to hear any pushback about it. We had made a decision, and she was going to have to listen to it.

Shirley looked at me like I was out of my mind. And maybe I was a little bit. She said, "That's okay, honey, I'm fine with it."

And then I said, "And besides, the plots were really cheap, too." We burst out laughing. We all needed the laugh, and it sort of broke through the overwhelming grief. It was a relief.

* * *

That day continued to be grim. Next, we had to go pick out the casket. Oh, god.

When rich people die, fortunes are at stake. Families quibble and spit at each other for money, land, and heirlooms. Lawsuits and lawyers cheat money from brothers and sisters fighting over the details of the will, forever left bitter. But in poor families, it's different. We worry about how we are going to pay for the funeral. You don't want your loved one repossessed if you miss payments to the funeral director. We wanted to provide a decent burial, but we couldn't go whole hog. It cost too much. When poor people die, there is sadness and a fear that you won't be able to do right when burying your loved one. Our family was no different. Every cost, every consideration had a price tag that we might not be able to afford. We still had to go on living, and living right now seemed harder than dying.

We went to the local undertaker's office to pick out the casket. Mike, Deke, Brian, and I went to look at the different options we had. Shirley deferred to us to make all of these decisions. She was in a strange position; the father of her four sons had died, but she wouldn't be considered a widow. She and Wilbur had divorced five years before he died, after twenty-six years of a tumultuous marriage.

We all knew the undertaker. And he knew Wilbur, too. He and Wilbur golfed together once in a while. "I knew Wilbur was in the hospital, and I woulda gone to visit him, but I didn't want people to think I was down there trying to drum up business." Then he laughed.

So, there we were at the coffin showroom, looking at models of caskets like you would at cars. Sleek, stainless steel, highly polished metallic boxes to carry you into the next life. I think at the beginning we were all dumbstruck. We were looking for our father's final resting place. A place that was supposed to offer comfort, but to whom? He was dead. Comfort, I suppose, to us, that in the end it was the last thing that we could offer him, the last thing that we could do for him.

"What color of suit is Wilbur going to be buried in?" the undertaker asked us. Wilbur didn't like wearing suits; he was hardly ever seen in anything but the work clothes he wore for everything he did. It was almost as if he was always ready to work, always ready at a moment's notice to jump up and earn some money. But in reality, he didn't much care about his appearance. He was short on fashion, long on the practical. If it was usable, it was good enough for him. He had been a survivor of the

Depression. The kind of survivor who was haunted by the hunger and the abject poverty he had known. He had survived, but he had not conquered the fear that it could come back, that he could be hungry, cold, and homeless. He could never quite bring himself to throw anything out if there was any possible use left. He never felt like he was more than a paycheck or two away from where he started as a kid.

When he died, he probably had ten or fifteen tires with hardly any tread on them. Perhaps someone would need threadbare tires. He bought much of what he owned at the Goodwill because he could get a shirt for a dime and a pair of shoes for a quarter. He was proud of these buys, too. He would walk right up to you and say, "SEE MY NEW SHOES, A QUARTER." More often than not, the shoes looked worn, they needed to be shined, were badly scuffed, and had already conformed to someone else's foot. Even the heel had worn a certain way because of the previous owner's gait. But the virtue was in how inexpensive they were, how usable they still were, and how good a shopper he had been. Wilbur didn't say, "THESE ARE GREAT-LOOKING SHOES I GOT!" He said, "A QUARTER." By god, those big retail stores like K-Mart weren't making money off him.

"Well, what color is his suit?"

The selection of possible clothes to bury Wilbur in was pretty limited. He had a black Botany 500 suit that he wore at my brother Michael's wedding in 1969, but the truth was it was probably not going to fit and was in bad shape from being at the bottom of his closet. But he did own a relatively new blue double-knit leisure suit. Thank god it didn't have white edging. But it was fashionable, still disco-era stylish, and we wouldn't have to put him in a tie.

"Blue," Deke said.

"Well, I've got this nice midnight blue metallic casket over here that will match Wilbur's suit and his tie."

Wilbur was going into the next life color-coordinated, something he hadn't much given thought to while he was alive. All of that fashion and for only $1,998, including the funeral service, of course. There weren't any Goodwill bargains to be found in dying.

"Dad wouldn't want to wear a tie, I mean he didn't much like ties, so we'd rather not bury him in a tie."

"You'd better bring a tie—sometimes those pathologists cut pretty far up on the body when they do an autopsy," the undertaker told us, completely devoid of compassion.

We hadn't thought about the pathologists until that moment. We hadn't thought of Wilbur being cut up.

"Are you going to buy a vault?"

"Is there anything such as an inexpensive funeral?" I asked. The cost of the funeral was starting to scare us. I was a broke college student, and my brothers weren't loaded either. Mike was living in Omaha with a wife and son, making ends meet on a roofer's salary. Deke had a wife and a young daughter, and Brian was working in a packing house.

None of us were flush with extra money.

"Yeah, you can wrap your dad in a white sheet and put a pin through it if you want to," the undertaker snapped back at me.

"That's not what I meant. It's just that we don't know how we are going to pay for this."

"You'll get $255 from Social Security as a death benefit. Let's see, there will be money from the Veterans Administration. Your dad was a vet and died in a vets' hospital. You'll get $150 because we had to transport him from the hospital to here. There'll be other money; you'll be fine." The undertaker had already figured where his money was coming from. This was his business, but it was new to us. At this time, we didn't know if Wilbur had life insurance, union benefits, or anything put away, though we doubted the latter.

"Why do we need a vault?" Mike asked.

"The vault protects the coffin."

"Do we really need a vault? Will they make us have a vault?" Mike asked.

"Legally you don't need a vault in Iowa unless you die of some sort of contagion like typhoid fever or malaria. Some cemeteries have rules about it because after a number of years the coffin collapses and it leaves a depression in the graveyard, but Frazier doesn't require it. But let me tell you a story." He lowered his voice a bit and leaned in to us as he started the story, "A few years ago, we had to exhume a body." The emphasis in that sentence was on *exhume*. He kept the sales pitch going. "They didn't have a vault, and when we got down there where the body was supposed to be, all there was down there was salamanders."

I think we probably all knew that was a story told to sell vaults. But at the same time, you couldn't help but picture all of those salamanders gnawing on Wilbur. The thought of it was too horrifying, and after all, this was the last thing we could do for him. At least we could protect him from salamanders. This fuss for a man who said, "WHEN I DIE, YOU CAN RUN MY BODY UP A FLAGPOLE FOR ALL I CARE, I'LL BE DEAD. AND WHEN YOU'RE DEAD, YOU'RE DEAD FOR A LONG TIME."

I had talked Wilbur out of donating his body to science. He had been dating a nurse, Lorena Keele, when he told me about this idea. It was a noble thing to do. He said that if someone could learn something from his dead body, that was great. He didn't need a funeral, he said.

I told him about the story Lorena had told me. I don't know if it was apocryphal or not. There was a medical student who had cut the penis off a well-endowed cadaver. As a prank, the college kid slipped it into his pants and took it to the bathroom with him at a hotel, somewhere there was a lot of traffic. He stood at the urinal acting as if there was something wrong, making enough fuss to draw some attention and the whole time tugging at his penis, squirming. The unwritten rule in a man's bathroom is that you never look to the right or to the left at a urinal, just straight ahead. Firstly, you wouldn't want anyone to think you were trying to peak at their thing, and secondly, you wouldn't really want to see anyone's thing either. But the medical student was making too much commotion to go unnoticed. Men were breaking the unwritten rule, albeit nervously and reluctantly.

When enough people were looking at him, he yanked at the penis, groaned, and threw it into the bottom of the urinal. "Damn thing never worked anyway," the college kid yelled. He turned, zipped his pants, and walked away from the urinal, looking at the expressions of the men's faces as he exited from the bathroom. He howled later as he told his friends about the horrified looks and gasps of disbelief as the men in the bathroom looked into the bottom of the urinal and saw the gray, limp, useless severed penis. I told Wilbur I didn't want that to happen to him.

"WHAT DO I CARE IF SOME SON OF A BITCH COLLEGE KID HAS A LAST LAUGH WITH MY DEAD BODY?"

"I care," I told him. "The funeral isn't for you, and you'll be dead. It is for us, the living. And by God, I don't want you to donate your body and cheat me out of mourning for you and being at your funeral."

I knew I would need it to accept that he was dead. I would need to see him one more time. I would have to see him dead to make it real and believable, or it would be hard for me to accept it. The funeral would be a time for us to gather as a family with friends to think about him and to remember him and to celebrate his life and what he had meant to us.

He said, "WELL, SON, IF YOU FEEL THAT WAY, I WON'T DO IT." I think deep down he was happy someone loved him enough to care whether his body would have a place safe from college pranks and, for only $250, safe from salamanders, too.

Ben Cooper and Ada Anderson

22

"Boys will be boys, if girls will let 'em."

Cleaning the Trailer

The screen door opened and before me stood a spry eighty-year-old woman. Her yellowish-white hair was pulled back into a ponytail and tucked up under a tightly knit red stocking cap that held the locks from hanging in her face. Ada was totally indifferent to her condition. Since her stroke, her penchant for being neat, orderly, and clean was completely gone. She had been a good housekeeper but not now. She had been a stylish dresser but not now. The stroke, while not changing her feisty, aggressive, and belligerent personality, had rendered her totally unable to care for her own cleanliness. Age had been unkind to her.

Her old face was carved with lines, and her skin had grown to look like worn leather. The freckles of her youth had given way to liver spots that dotted her hands, forearms, and face. Her once beautiful smile was replaced with a toothless grin. She didn't have a tooth left in her head and hadn't now for so long that her toughened gums could chew meat like her jaws were sporting molars. The charms of her youth—radiant skin and auburn hair—were gone, replaced by the ravages of gravity, dry skin that had been exposed to too much sun, and brittle white hair. The only glimmer of beauty that was left were her sparkling blue eyes. The eyes still had life in them, but they lacked understanding. She had a vacant look.

She stood there clad in two pairs of polyester pants—one coffee colored, peeking out from underneath a dirty red pair—neither of them fitting the once well-proportioned body. She wore a brown and white striped pullover sweater that was covered with clinging fuzz balls. Her eyes met mine and the corners of her bluish-red lips turned up into a smile. Ada was glad to see me.

As soon as I came into the trailer, she scampered back to her chair. She sat back into the padded rocker directly in front of the television, which was on and loud. As soon as she sat back into the rocker, she began to rock nervously.

Even at this age, Ada's restlessness was apparent. She couldn't relax, she couldn't sit still. She was on the move. The relentless need for her to be in motion was propelling the rocking chair in a frenetic back-and-forth movement. She was holding the arms of the chair as if she might be jettisoned at any second out of the rocker. Here was a woman who had been ready to go at a moment's notice all of her life. First as a sharecropper's daughter, later as the vagabond spirit she had inherited took hold of her.

When she was young, she would walk to the highway and hitchhike a ride with a car going in either direction. It didn't matter where they were going or who they were, so long as they were going. It was as if she was constantly running away, but from what? She was just seventeen when she married Clyde Rife, probably to leave home. Then she left Clyde to run to another man, who became her second husband, then to a third, then to a fourth . . . she was still running. Whatever she had been in search of, whatever she had hoped to find, had eluded her, but the need to move was still with her. It was as much a part of her as her father's need to go from one beet field to another, to live in one town after another. It was like the genetic code that is passed from one generation of dog to the next that makes it circle in the tall grass to pat it down to make a bed. Dogs that have been bred to live indoors their whole lives still do it. They circle on a rug before they lie down. They don't know why they circle on the rug, there is no grass, yet they instinctively do it. She didn't know why she felt a compelling need to keep moving, she just knew it and did it because she felt it. Ada felt it as much as she felt the wind. It was as sure as the wind, always with you, sometimes blowing harder one day than the next, but it could stir up at any moment.

Ada raised her blotched hand and pushed back a stray strand of hair and asked, "How is Sioux City?"

"Fine," I answered, in awe at the persistence of the question. She had asked the same question of me hundreds of times before, and I had quietly explained to her that I lived in Ames, not Sioux City. But this time I had resigned myself that her mind had made me a resident of Sioux City, Iowa, for no apparent reason, or at least not one clear to me.

One summer when Wilbur was going to an army reunion in Fort Robinson, Nebraska, he asked me to watch Ada. I was working in Logan for the summer and would be there the week he was to be gone. It didn't require much of me, other than making sure she had dinner every night and giving her walking-around-town money, which Wilbur supplied.

"NOT ALL AT ONCE," he said with a cautionary tone, "I DON'T KNOW WHAT THE HELL SHE DOES WITH IT, BUT IT CAN GO PRETTY FAST."

Fred had given Ada a red leather coin purse to keep her money in, but she preferred to keep it in a yellow and white margarine dish in her pocket. That was what I was supposed to keep supplied with a daily allowance, the margarine dish. When I asked her why she kept her money there, she said, "Who would ever think to look in here for money?"

She would take that margarine dish into the stores in Logan and buy this little doodad or whatnot. Sometimes she would try to pay twice. The great thing about a small town like Logan was that even though Ada was a pain in the butt to deal with, everybody knew who she was. If she tried to pay for something more than once, the storekeepers would only take her money once. And if she forgot to pay at all, they didn't turn her in for shoplifting—they would tell Wilbur, and he would pay the bill.

That week in August when Wilbur was at the reunion, I had a high school friend who had worked with older patients come in and give Ada a bath and cut her hair. Wilbur said he couldn't bathe his mother. "NO WAY I AM BATHIN' HER, SHE'S MY MOTHER FOR CHRISSAKE!" he said. "IF SHE WANTS TO GET CLEAN, SHE CAN DO IT HERSELF. I AIN'T BATHIN' MY MOTHER!"

When Barb got there, I asked Ada if she wanted to take a bath. "No, I just took one," she said. After several conversations about her bath, Barb convinced her that a good long hot bath would feel good. Barb assured her that she would be there to help her in and out of the tub and that she would not slip and fall.

Barb also talked her into a haircut. Ada's hair was long and needed to be cut. She had forgotten that she agreed to the haircut and by the next day was accusing Wilbur of slipping into her room in the middle of the night and cutting her hair while she was sleeping. He looked at her like she was nuts. "YOU THINK I AM CUTTING YOUR HAIR IN THE MIDDLE OF THE NIGHT? YOU HAVE LOST YOUR FUCKING MIND."

That summer was hot, so the short hair was better for her. The trailer in that heat was like an oven. Wilbur kept the trailer closed up and the central air-conditioning on to help. I would come and fix Ada's dinner at night. One afternoon when I got there, the doors to the trailer were open and so were a couple of the windows. On that August day, the temperature had climbed to about a hundred degrees in the shade. As I looked about the floor of the trailer, it had become apparent that all of the air-conditioning vents had been covered by numerous piles of newspaper.

I asked Ada, "What are you doing?" I knew Wilbur would want to kill her if he had found the trailer this way, doors wide open and the air-conditioning straining to cool the place.

She smartly replied, "The damnedest breeze comes up through those little holes in the floor."

About the same time that Wilbur had gone to the reunion, Ada had gone uptown and told everyone around town that Wilbur had thrown her and all of her clothes out onto the front yard. No one believed it, of course, except the goofy Methodist minister, the reverend, who was charged with ministering to the Logan and Magnolia Methodist congregations. He was also the same minister who had led the charge against Shirley and the topless dancers. Like a bad penny, he was back, sticking his rather large nose in our business.

That is where the problem started—when the church decided to get involved with my dad.

In the Methodist Church, the local ministers serve at the request of the bishop of the conference. Iowa has its own bishop. This minister wasn't from around Harrison County, so he didn't know Ada or Wilbur. His mistake wasn't necessarily that he believed Ada. She could be convincing enough if she was having a lucid moment. But if you pressed her for any length of time, it became clear that her body had outlived her mind. And if the gangly, busybody minister had asked around town even just a little bit, he would have found that out and left the whole mess alone.

But, compassion and caring for the sick and senile being his business, the reverend made it his mission to get Ada taken care of, to get her removed from the trouble just as soon as possible. He went to the Human Services Department at the courthouse, and they sent someone to Wilbur's trailer and removed Ada to a nursing home in Woodbine. Ada got scared up there, but the Human Services people, being good bureaucrats in the business of wrapping every situation up with red tape, asked her if they could pick up a few of her personal things from the trailer. When they showed up, Wilbur was there. They explained everything to him and told him that Ada wanted her medicine, a comb and a brush, and some of her clothes.

Wilbur called me.

"DOUGLAS, THIS IS DAD." Like I didn't know who was on the other end of the phone. "SOME GOOFY WOMAN WAS JUST HERE FROM SOCIAL SERVICES ASKING TO GET THINGS MOM

WANTED. SHE'S BEEN MOVED TO A PLACE IN WOODBINE. THEY HAD A LIST OF THINGS SHE WANTED. GUESS WHAT WASN'T ON THE LIST?"

"I have no idea."

"HER BEIGE SUITCASE FULL OF HER PICTURES. NOW, I KNOW YOU HAVE WANTED THEM, SO GIT DOWN HERE AND TAKE WHATEVER YOU WANT OUT OF THAT SUITCASE."

"I'll be right down."

I couldn't wait to get there and pick through the suitcase. I had looked at those old pictures many times, and there were a lot of family treasures packed away in it. Ada had all sorts of pictures of her sisters dead in their caskets—Aunt Mae, Aunt Nonie. I hated those and could never understand why anyone would want pictures like that—as a last remembrance of someone they loved. Why not remember them alive? So, I hurried down to Wilbur's. He was waiting.

"TAKE WHATEVER GODDAMN PICTURES YOU WANT. I DON'T GIVE A SHIT IF SHE COMES BACK OR NOT, THEY ARE YOURS."

There were hundreds of photographs in the suitcase. I started to look through them and sort them into a chronological order, separating the oldest out. Most of the early ones were picture postcards.

* * *

"It's so good to see you, honey."

"Well, it's good to see you too, Grandma. How are you these days?"

"Well, we's just fine, me and Wilbur. Wilbur takes good care of me. Eat all I kin eat. I don't know why they plant corn so close nowadays. That's right, too close, the rows are too close. How is my papa goin' to git his team and wagon 'tween the corn rows? How's he goin' to pick corn?"

Nonstop, she regaled me with stories from years ago that haven't been told twice the same way. Each of them retold with renewed vigor and enthusiasm.

"Grandma, I have bad news. Dad died." It hurt me immeasurably to hear those words, let alone say them. It was now real. I had spoken them. It must be true. Wilbur was dead.

"What? Who?" she asked me, as she lurched forward in the rocker.

"Dad, Wilbur died."

"Wilbur?"

"Yes, Wilbur Rife. Your son, Wilbur Rife, died." I felt like I would die myself if I had to say it again.

"No, that ain't so. He went to another one of them reunions at Nebraska." She never slowed the pace of the rocking, she just looked at me like I was wrong.

"Grandma, Wilbur died at the vets' hospital on Tuesday morning."

"It ain't so, and you stop sayin' it." Ada was defiant.

"Say, do you want to see something funny?" she asked.

"Sure." I wasn't making any headway explaining that Wilbur had died anyway.

Ada headed toward the bathroom. That was a scary proposition because she was likely to flash me, and that was the last thing I wanted to see. But I reluctantly followed her back there. We walked in. The tiny little trailer bathroom was a design nightmare from the seventies, the worse decade for art, music, architecture, and fashion. The simulated wood laminate on the cabinets was peeling. The bathroom had a matching tub and sink of avocado green enamel. The sink was immediately in front of you as you entered the bathroom, with a large mirror over the sink. To the right of that was the toilet, a mirrored medicine cabinet over that, and on the same wall was the bathtub, rarely used by Ada. The tub and the shower curtain had a white film of lime. The limestone rock quarries east of Logan settled a white dust on the town when the quarries were dynamiting, and the limestone deposits leached into the water table. The white film was not unique to this trailer.

Ada pointed to the mirror and whispered, "Do ya see that old woman over there?"

"Uh, yeah, I see her."

"Well," Ada said, still speaking in a hushed tone, "whenever I come in here, that old woman is always in here." Then she laughed nervously.

It was hard to know whether she actually didn't recognize her own image in the mirror or whether she refused to believe that she had grown so old and withered. She had been beautiful as a young woman, and now it was hard to see the remnants of her youth. I didn't know if this was her senility or if this was a lucid moment she was having. Who hasn't wanted to deny growing old? Who hasn't wanted to have their youth back? Maybe in her lucid moments she felt like a young woman who had been somehow trapped in a withered, dried-up old body.

I heard the front door open. It was my brother Brian. He had come to help me clean the trailer. He had also saved me from any more time in the bathroom with Ada.

"Where should we start?" Brian asked.

"I don't know, maybe Dad's bedroom. There isn't much in there to save." We were cleaning everything out so we could rent the trailer out. Shirley thought it might be a way to make a little bit of money to pay for Wilbur's funeral, though we wouldn't get much for a three-bedroom trailer in Logan down by the county yards. The front window, facing south, overlooked an oil barrel. It held the oil for the county trucks to spread over the dirt roads in the county to keep the dust down in the dry summer months of July and August. Just across the street to the east were some county sheds and the railroad tracks, and to the west was Bill Buffum's house. Just on the other side of that were the old Logan stockyards. The trailer and shed were on a small lot that was only accessible by a steep rutted driveway that had never so much as had a load of rock on it. After a hard rain, the driveway was like a mud slick. To get to the top, Wilbur would gun his car about a block away from the driveway. Sometimes he'd skid sideways all the way to the top of the driveway. That driveway was not a selling feature.

We also wouldn't get much in rent because the trailer wasn't in good shape. Wilbur could fix a lot of things, he was a master plasterer and was handy, but the old saying about the shoe cobbler's kids going barefoot was true. The last place he would work on was his own place. It needed fixing.

Wilbur and Ada had been hard on the trailer. The carpeting had never been shampooed since he'd moved in. And little things needed fixing. The dryer wasn't venting properly—we found out later it was because Ada had unhooked the vent hose and stuffed the opening with toilet paper and one- and five-dollar bills and no one knew why. And Ada never opened a door—front door, cupboard door, or refrigerator door—without slamming it shut. Trailers aren't built well enough to withstand that kind of abuse. And she abused it actively. Wilbur's abuse was neglect, Ada's was active.

She had to be aware of some of her abuse. She knew better than to swing cupboard doors shut or to let the screen door slam behind her, almost off their hinges. But sometimes the abuse was beyond her.

"I think Mike said something about wanting that long leather coat," Brian said. He had broken my train of thought. I came back to thinking about what to keep and what to throw out. We both knew there wouldn't be much to divide among the four sons that was worth keeping.

"Okay, we can put the coat aside."

Ada started babbling. "One time when I was a livin' in Californa, my papa came out to visit. He didn't have no razor with him, and we went to church. He had all that stubble and whatnot. Well, that afternoon those church folks brought him nineteen razors . . ."

We listened half-heartedly to her unending persiflage, to a story I had heard before in the car on my way to the Thurman Cemetery to find Ada's grandparents' graves. Great Aunt Myrtle was in the car that day, too. Only in that version of the story, it was a dozen razors. The whole time Ada told the story, Great Aunt Myrtle shook her head and mouthed the words, *No, it never happened.*

The toothless woman spilling out the endless narrative before us had little connection to her surroundings or reality. Even the truth was eluding her now. In her old age and senility, she had transformed her hideous father—a cheating husband, a child molester, and a sharecropper who never made enough to support his family—into something he had never been: kind, gentle, and someone who would inspire strangers to give him gifts.

Brian and I started to carry clothes out to the burn barrel. With each load, Ada would say, "You'd better stop that. Wilbur's going to be mad when he gets home." What was next to the burn barrel, Ada would try to carry back into the trailer. Brian intercepted a couple of loads of things, but his level of patience was wearing thin.

Wilbur had a bunch of magazines in his bedroom. Some of them were *Playboy* and *Penthouse*; others were more specific, like *Jugs*. He even had a soft cover book about the history of pornography in America. I put them by the door, and Brian was getting ready to carry them to the burn barrel when Grandma grabbed them up.

"Now them is mine. I'm goin' to read these here." She hadn't even looked at the magazines enough to know that there were naked women on the covers but had decided to take a stand against any more of the things in the trailer going to the fire. She clutched them tightly in her spindly arms, clutched them as if they truly meant something to her.

"Grandma," Brian said with authority but not with a raised voice, "you ain't goin' to read those, so give 'em here."

"Yes, I am; these is mine."

"No, you can't have 'em."

Brian wrangled them out of her arms and threw them into the fire. When he got back into the trailer, he said to me, "She's makin' this hard. She keeps carrying things back in here. We'll never get this done."

It was hard enough burning Wilbur's belongings without having to carry them out twice.

"Do you want to take her for a ride while I take things out to sort and to carry out to the trash?"

We both knew that even as confused and senile as she was, the lure of going somewhere in a car would outweigh any desire she had to protect her belongings or Wilbur's things that were in that trailer. She would be moving. She would be in motion. She would be in a car traveling somewhere. It could be in circles for all she cared but she would be going. You could put her in a wheelbarrow and she'd be happy as long as it was moving.

Neither job was going to be easy. Being in the car with Ada, though, was probably more irritating and more difficult than cleaning. But Brian agreed to do it. For the next three hours, Brian drove Ada around while she drove him crazy.

I sorted through Wilbur's stuff. I found things that surprised me about him. Not the dirty magazines. I knew he went to strip clubs, engaged the services of working girls, and liked girlie magazines and dirty jokes. But I found a Bible on his bedroom dresser. And hanging up on the wall above his dresser was a placard with the Ten Commandments printed on it. I also found a tiny little silver pin that had a cross with a sword at the end of it. He had said one time he was going to call in because he'd heard the TV preacher say the pins were free and he wanted to see if it was true. There it was on the corner of his dresser. Did he believe in God, or was it a social membership?

I found a card that my grandmother Rasmussen, my mom's mother, had mailed to him. Two pennies were taped inside it. He had it saved since before Michael was born. Wilbur wasn't the type of man you thought of as being sentimental but here this was. He had told me that the nicest woman he'd ever known was Grandma Rasmussen. The first birthday card he'd ever been given, he had received from her.

Brian showed up with Ada—he had had enough.

"She keeps asking me about Dad. She is driving me nuts."

"Hey, look, I found a Bible in Dad's bedroom, and the placard taped up above his dresser of the Ten Commandments. Do you think he believed in God?"

"I dunno." Brian started to say something else when Ada peered around the corner.

"Wilbur ain't going to like you messin' with his stuff."

"Grandma, Dad, is dead. I have told you, Dad is dead." Brian was getting pretty frustrated. "Douglas, let's take her up to see Dad in the coffin. Maybe it will finally soak in then."

"Okay, let's load her up."

"Hey, Grandma, let's go for a ride."

"Sure, honey, where's we going?"

"Grandma, we are going uptown," I said.

We got Ada in the car and drove the few blocks to the funeral home. No one was in the room where Wilbur's casket was. He was alone. We walked Ada over to the casket, and she looked in.

"Look, Grandma, that's Dad in the coffin." Here it was Thursday and we had been telling Ada since Tuesday, and she still didn't seem to comprehend it.

Her eyes started to tear up, and then she looked into the room opposite the room we were in and said, "Look over there, ain't nobody in that room." That was it; she was ready to go.

I decided to take Ada back to the trailer. I needed to look for my class ring anyway, since I'd accidentally left it by the sink while I was doing dishes earlier. I was anxious to get it—especially since Wilbur bought it for me. With him dead, everything he'd given me took on new and significant sentimental meaning. But when I got to the trailer, the ring was gone.

"Grandma, did you see a ring?" I asked.

"Was it a blue ring?"

"Yes, it was a gold ring with a blue setting."

"Oh, my, what a pretty ring!"

"So, you saw the ring. Where is it?"

"What ring?"

"The ring you said you saw."

"I never saw no ring."

"Grandma, you just said you saw a pretty ring."

"I never saw no ring." She leaned forward in the kitchen chair. "But," she said, "I'll tell you what, I'll help you look for it!"

"Okay." I could feel my blood pressure rising with each exchange.

I was looking around the kitchen. I opened the refrigerator door because Wilbur had told me that sometimes she would open it up and put things in there that didn't belong—like dirty dishes.

"Say, honey, what are you looking for?" she asked as she poked her head around the room.

"We are looking for my class ring that you said you saw—it was gold with a blue setting."

"I never saw no ring, but I tell you what I'll do, I'll help you look for it."

"Okay fine, it's gold with a blue setting, and it was sitting on the back of the kitchen sink." By this time, I was out of my mind with frustration. I was also feeling fairly hopeless about finding my ring.

Ada had moved her search into the trailer's living room. She was half-heartedly looking at the sofa with a blank look on her withered face. I was still concentrating on the kitchen when Ada asked the question, again.

"Say, honey, what are we looking for?"

I exploded at this point and hit my fist on the edge of the kitchen table and screamed in frustration, "Well, I'll be a son of a bitch!"

Ada looked at me stunned and surprised and said, "You sound just like your father."

It was at that moment that I knew exactly how frustrated Wilbur had been a thousand times a day.

I gave up explaining what I was looking for and decided to finish cleaning out the trailer, hoping I might stumble across it.

I rediscovered the beige suitcase that had Ada's photograph cache. Even though I had pilfered quite a stash of her pictures, I was anxious to see what else was in the treasure trove.

It was filled with old postcards and postcard pictures—literally hundreds of them. I started picking them up and reading them.

Postmark—Cedar Rapids, Iowa, May 28, 1911

Harry Anderson
Blencoe Ia
Hello I am in Cedar Rapids how did you get Home yours truly
Harry Long

The front of the postcard showed the Washington High School in Cedar Rapids, Iowa. This must be the oldest one in the suitcase, I thought.

I chuckled when I read the next one I picked up. The front of the postcard was a photograph of the main street in Blair, Nebraska. It was the forgotten instructions that I liked handwritten on the postcard.

Postmark—Blair, Nebraska, August 19, 1912

Mr. Buck Anderson
Blencoe, Ia.
Don't forget to feed and water the chickens I forgot to tell you before leaving. Earl

Many of the old picture postcards were of Ada and one of her many teenage boyfriends. One of her first boyfriends was Ben Cooper. On the back of the postcard, she wrote, "me & one of my First boy Friends Ben Cooper he has been dead a long time."

The postcard, one of the picture postcards that were so popular at the time, was of her and Ben. Ada was beautiful in this photograph. She was wearing an ankle-length, lightly colored dress with white pinstripes that gathered at the waist, and he was wearing a dark single-breasted, three-button pinstriped suit, with only the top button fastened. Ben and Ada were standing side by side, but they were not touching. Ben Cooper looked ill at ease. Ada was a beauty that was stunning but accessible—a little too accessible.

Another example—a postcard—no postmark—no date. Written on the back of the postcard in Ada's handwriting, "Red Thurman Ada Anderson." This postcard had a picture of a young Ada Anderson seated on a wicker settee. She was wearing a light-colored dress that was gathered at the waist. Her hair was kind of a mess. The front of her hair was combed straight back and held in place on top of her head with a barrette. She had bangs hanging back on both sides of her forehead. She had long hair in this picture. It was pulled back into a braid in the back. She was looking directly into Red's eyes. Red was wearing pants and a white unbuttoned shirt. He was holding the front of the bench with one hand and a cigarette in the other. The backdrop in this picture showed the walls and door of a log cabin.

This was a picture that elicited a story from Granny, Aunt Amy's mother, who knew Ada as a girl. She had told me this story years before, and I thought back on the story as I gazed at the picture.

"Ed Richards had these girls. He had Garnett and Pearl and Violet. Yeah and Garnett was sneaking out. I think it was with this Guy Brunstedt, meeting this guy on the railroad tracks. And they lived up north, you know, and a . . . north of town, I mean. And I don't know why Ed was a fighting that but she was a sneaking out a meeting him. She'd lost something along the tracks, a scarf I think. It was felt or something. Anyhow Garnett didn't want ol' Ed to find out it was her, to know that she had lost it up there 'cause he had forbid her from running with Guy so she give Ada a dollar to claim it."

Granny's soliloquy continued, "Oh, whoever had found it had hung it up down at Harry Hatheway's store, right up in the front window for the person who lost it to see it and come along and claim it. Of course, Garnett knew that ol' Ed would see that come to town the next morning, you know. So she got Ada, Ada Anderson, to claim it for her. She gave her a dollar if she'd claim it.

"Then Harry Hatheway used to tell that and laughed till he was full. Ada came in, she claimed that scarf, and after he handed it to her, she said, 'Well, this ain't mine,' but she said, 'Garnett Richards gave me a dollar for if I'd claim it, so I'm claimin' it.'

"Nobody really had the nerve to tell ol' Ed. Nobody 'cause it would make him so furious . . . no tellin' what he'd do.

"Oh, she was old enough to know better, 'cause she got a dollar for sayin' it. I think she must have been about fourteen.

"Yeah, but I'll tell ya, if you didn't want anything known, you never wanted to let Ada know it. You might as well put it in the *Little Sioux Hustler*."

Granny's thin blue lips turned up into a smile, and she chuckled.

Again, picture after picture of Ada with various boyfriends—all before she married Clyde when she was seventeen.

Brian came up next to me. "What are you doing with those postcards and pictures?" he asked me.

"I dunno. Trying to figure out something about Dad, I guess."

"That's Grandma's shit. All them pictures are of Grandma, Lucy, and her kids. There's hardly anything of us."

"I did find this V-Mail letter from World War II that Dad sent to Grandma. I'll read it to you," I said.

April 24, 1944
Mrs. Ada E. Proctor
3717 Commerce Street
Dallas, Texas U.S.A.

A Mother's Day Greeting

From our faraway place of service in China-Burma-India Theatre of operations our thoughts are centered at this season upon motherhood. Lives are strengthened, memories enriched, and purposes heightened by the sacrifices, Faith, patience, hopes, and prayers of mother. And now over the vast distance and intervening years, our thoughts, affections, and our prayers stream back in love, appreciation, and reverence, to mother.

"The happiest part of my life has been my mother, and with God's help she will be more to me than ever"—Phillips Brooks.
PFC. Wilbur M. Rife, 17011929
5321.O.M.DEP.DET.(Prov.)
A.P.O. 689. c/o Postmaster
New York, N.Y.
April 24, 1944
V–MAIL

"That sure don't sound like Dad."

"No, it sure don't. It's a preprinted letter that the GIs just signed and mailed. I don't think Dad much liked Grandma at the time. He might have been homesick or something. He was definitely pissed off at her when he got home. He said she spent every allotment check that he and Uncle Fred sent home."

"Are you going to keep all that stuff in that suitcase?"

"Not the pictures of Aunt Mae and Grandpa Hobart and Aunt Nonie in their caskets. Yeesh."

"Douglas, we got to get ready to go to the viewing at the funeral home. Let's go up to Mom's and get ready."

"Okay." I really just wanted to leaf through the photographs. "Except for the clothes, Grandma has her life all in this suitcase." Ada's life was reduced to a beige suitcase from the 1940s—her brothers and sisters, her teenage boyfriends, her four husbands, her kids and grandkids. That was it. And Wilbur's life was reduced to some work clothes, some rare coins, and a few odds and ends. I sat there wondering what, if anything, it all meant.

"Hey, Brian, look what else I found—this Thanksgiving program from Fort Robinson."

It was Wilbur's saved copy of the 1941 Thanksgiving program from Fort Robinson that listed a sumptuous holiday fare—oyster soup and crackers, roast turkey, sage dressing, baked ham, giblet gravy, snow flaked potatoes, cranberry sauce and whipped cream, candied yams, sweet pickles, stuffed olives, buttered peas, buttered asparagus, mince pie, brick ice cream, pumpkin pie, fruit cake, Parkerhouse rolls, white bread, fruit salad, assorted fruits, mixed candy, mixed nuts, butter, fresh milk, cream and coffee. After dinner, the soldiers were offered cigars and cigarettes.

That was exactly what Wilbur was looking for at Fort Robinson—three hots and a cot. This program was forty years old and still meant something to him.

I also found a small stack of bar napkins. I ruffled through them. The one on top had a drawing of a woman in a bikini sitting in a glass, her legs dangling over the rim. I read a couple of lines on the napkin, "AN ORDEAL IS WHAT AN IDEAL BECOMES AFTER YOU MARRY HIM." And "ALIMONY IS THE HIGH COST OF LEAVING." I thought to myself, I am sure I heard Dad say that during the divorce. Another was titled, "BE HAPPY . . . IT'S CONTAGIOUS." The line on the front of another napkin was, "NEVER ARGUE WITH YOUR DOCTOR—HE HAS INSIDE INFORMATION." It seemed appropriate. I put the stack of napkins in my shirt pocket. It was to be Wilbur's last contribution to the collection. I mumbled to myself, "Nope, I don't have those," as I walked out of the trailer.

Wilbur Rife

23

*"I ain't never seen a hearse followed by an armored car.
You can't take it with ya."*

The Last Chapter

By the morning of the funeral, we still had not heard from Ron. We didn't exactly know where he was or how to get hold of him. Deke had sent word through Jack Petersen to let Ron know Wilbur had died and when his funeral was being held. We wanted him to be there, but we couldn't hold off forever even if it was January in Iowa.

That morning, as I was drinking coffee with Shirley, I told her that I had a dream about Ron.

"You did? Did he show up for the funeral in your dream?"

"I dunno if he made it for the funeral or not, but I saw him walking up the sidewalk in a big cowboy hat with a young blonde who is not his wife."

"Yeah, that sounds like Ronnie all right." Shirley shrugged.

"I think he will be here."

Wilbur had died on Tuesday, and today was Friday. His funeral service was being held at a funeral home in Logan. It was a cold and bleak day. I was so very sad. I was just getting to know him, not as the towering figure we think of our parents but as a real person—foibles and all. I dreaded today because it made it all real and final.

Family started to come to the house. Deke, Brian, and Mike.

"You know," I said to Brian, "Dad asked me to paint a picture of a western scene for him. He wanted to show it to St. Onge, an old army buddy of his."

"When did he want it done?" Brian asked me.

"For the army reunion at Fort Robinson," I said.

"Yeah, but that wasn't going to be until this coming summer. You would have done it by then."

I questioned myself. I hadn't painted the picture yet. Surely, Wilbur knew that I was going to paint it for him. I was just busy with school and things and I would get to it. I was feeling guilty that I hadn't done it yet. Would I have gotten it done? Would I have finished it for him to take to the reunion? It was unfinished business.

* * *

We decided to head to the funeral home around 10:30 that morning so we could greet people who came to the funeral and so Wilbur wouldn't be left alone too long up there. The funeral was going to start at 11:00.

When we arrived, the funeral director was standing over the casket and picking lint off Wilbur's leisure suit. It made Wilbur look like some sort of mannequin. I hated it.

Through the double glass doors of the funeral parlor, we could see Ada lurking around in front of the home—pacing back and forth. She was wearing her long beige corduroy coat and red stocking hat. It was almost as if she could sense what was going on. Maybe something had stuck when we brought her up to see Wilbur in his coffin. Maybe it stuck.

Brian asked, "Should we bring Grandma in?"

"Hell, no," Shirley quickly said. "You know she has no idea about what is going on, and it would be a pain in the ass we don't need right now."

We were seated in the front row. As people filed by the casket, their paths brought them past us. People stopped and offered their condolences. The organ groaned, which was the cue for people to scamper to a seat. The organ selections were played by Donna Erickson, who was married to my high school physics teacher, the most boring teacher to ever stand up in front of a classroom. His classes were as colorless as his complexion. Once in class he was showing gory footage of car wrecks and Brian almost fainted. All went unnoticed by the teacher.

Donna finished the song on the organ, and those still up took seats so the service could start.

Reverend Robert Evans walked up to the lectern. Wilbur didn't much care for preachers, and this one would have been no exception. Rev. Evans was always so sure of himself and the rightness of what he said and did and believed that many of the people in town called him "Bob God," behind his back, of course.

He had come to our house to talk to us about the sermon he would deliver at the funeral and to ask us questions about Wilbur—where he was born and other basic facts about his life. While he was there, he ate two pieces of pie that Sheryl Lynn Schaefer brought to our house when she heard Wilbur had died. As I was listening to Bob God drone on, really trying to convert people in the seats to Jesus on our dime, I thought, This is not a two-pieces-of-pie sermon! He barely mentioned Wilbur, and when he did, it was not in a personal way. The sermon was canned and generic and could have been delivered for anybody in town. Just insert name here and drone on.

He could have talked about Wilbur's work ethic. How he never missed a day's work. How he always provided food and shelter for his family. How he was known throughout the county for his word. If Wilbur told you he was going to do something, it happened. You could bet on that. He was the strongest person I knew and wasn't scared of anything. I saw him stomp rats to death, I saw him grab snakes by the tail so hard their heads snapped off, I saw him walk out into the darkness to find the person who'd opened our front door and made my brother Brian scream bloody murder. He had no idea who he was facing—he was undaunted. He had no fear. A man who showed how much he cared not by words but by deeds.

Bob God never talked about his character much less anything more than when and where he was born and died—and I could read that in the funeral program. Bob God was just trolling for Jesus.

When it was all over, people began filing out of the funeral home. I walked up to the coffin and leaned in and kissed him on the forehead. He was ice cold. It felt like my lips had just touched wax. I shuddered.

We walked out into the driveway to wait for the casket to be loaded into the hearse. We could see into the funeral home and see the staff tucking in the cloth around Wilbur's body, then closing the lid. Wilbur was already starting to get some of that shade Fred had talked about at the cemetery.

Honorary pallbearers Carroll Waterman and Larry Petersen came out first. Wilbur and Carroll had a long-running feud about how much they hated each other. Carroll even cut out a valentine one year and gave it to Wilbur—it said, "I hate you."

Jack Hampton was Wilbur's best friend, Howard Johnson was who Wilbur worked for, Murel Schaefer was a friend and bowling buddy, John Turner worked with Wilbur at Howard Johnson's Plastering Company, Jim Guyette and Craig Strong were Logan guys Wilbur became good friends with—they all carried the casket to the hearse.

Wilbur was a member of the Fraternal Order of Eagles of Missouri Valley; the VFW Post 6256 of Logan, as a lifetime member; he was also a Master Mason in the Capitol Lodge 3 of Omaha; and a member of the American Legion Post 378 of Mondamin. Masonic services were by Chyrsolite Lodge No. 420, A.F. & A.M.

The Masonic service was all a mystery to me. One of the lodge members came out with an apron that they put on Wilbur. He held up a trowel and talked about it. Then they tucked in a sprig of evergreen symbolizing everlasting life. They had a full-blown service, but it was a blur.

The military service was conducted by Logan VFW Post No. 6256 at the graveside at the Frazier Cemetery. Bob God said a few words, then the color guard presented the colors. They played Taps and then shot a twenty-one-gun salute in honor of his service in World War II. The sound of the shots seemed to cut through my body. Each one made me wince.

Two soldiers folded the flag atop Wilbur's coffin in a white glove ceremony. They snapped the flag into a trifold and handed it to the commander. The commander walked up to Shirley and said, "On behalf of the President of the United States and a thankful nation for Wilbur Rife's service, we present this flag to you."

* * *

We gathered at the VFW after the funeral for a luncheon.

One of the first people I talked to was the woman Wilbur was dating at the time of his death, Lorena. They had been kids growing up around Sioux. She was a little older than him—maybe a year or two. Wilbur had had a crush on her, but he never felt like he could ask her out. After Shirley and Wilbur divorced, he ran into her somewhere. By this time, she was widowed, and they started dating.

"I am very sorry about your dad."

"Thank you, Lorena. You are going to miss him, too."

"You know, this last Christmas he brought a lot of color into my life."

"What do you mean?"

"Well, my husband and I always decorated our tree in all blue lights. Your dad was down to my place, and I was in the kitchen cooking dinner when he popped in the kitchen and told me he had a quick errand to run and that he would be right back."

"Where did he go?"

"Well, I am not sure where he went, but I heard him come back, and after a while, I walked into the living room to see what he was up to. He had taken all of the blue lights off my tree and changed them to red, yellow, green, and blue ones. He said, 'YOU NEED MORE COLOR IN YOUR LIFE!'" Lorena looked me in the eye and said, "He brought that color into my life on our Christmas tree and so many other ways. I'll never forget him for that."

I never thought of my dad as a romantic guy, but I guess it was there.

Mr. Buffum, who lived in the house right next to Wilbur's trailer, wandered over and told us a great story about Wilbur being out in his garden watering it last summer. Mr. Buffum halfway acted out the scene. He hunched over as he described how his son crept up on Wilbur with their garden hose to spray him. Just as his son was about to squirt him, Wilbur, who could see him out of the corner of his eye, waited just until the little boy got closer. Then Mr. Buffum whirled around like he was holding a hose and explained how Wilbur whipped around and soaked his son. Mr. Buffum's son didn't give up, though, and Wilbur was pretty wet before the water battle was over, too.

Then Jack Hampton came up to Deke and me. He shook his head slowly. He said in an almost hushed tone, "The only letter I got all the time I was in World War II when I was in France was a letter from Wilbur."

"Only one letter? Did you write him back?" Deke asked.

"Hell, it was the only letter I got from anybody," Jack said wistfully. "The captain told me one time, he says, 'Why aren't you writing your folks?' I said, 'I ain't got no folks.' He said, 'Well, I noticed you ain't been getting no mail.' But I did get one and that was from Wilbur and it took it about three months to get there. That letter come clear across the world."

Again, Deke asked, "Did you write him back?"

"Naw, he was in India. Oh, no, it was too late, then. Too late in the war, I wouldn't have known where to write him anyway."

"How did he know where to write you?" Deke persisted.

"Huh?" Jack stopped and looked at Deke. His mind was somewhere else—maybe it had drifted to the war, or his memories about Wilbur and Fort Robinson.

"How'd he know how to write you?"

"I don't know," Jack replied. "Oh, he probably knew better than I did."

"I guess he didn't get that wish of his," Deke added.

"What wish is that?" I asked.

"You know, he always said, 'I WANT TO DIE AT A HUNDRED AND ONE AND GET KILLED IN A WHOREHOUSE BRAWL!'

"Or his other one, 'I WANT TO BE A HUNDRED AND ONE AND GET SHOT BY A JEALOUS HUSBAND AS I AM CRAWLING OUT THE WINDOW!'"

Jack started laughing, "Yeah, Wilbur had a dream."

About that time, a tall man walked up to us and said, "You probably never heard of me, but I am Roger Vipond."

"Oh, yes, we have heard of you. Dad has talked about you many times," I said.

"Did your dad ever tell the story of how he shot me?" Clearly Roger wanted to tell the story, and even though Deke and I had heard the story, we wanted to hear it again and this time directly from Roger.

"Nope," Deke said, "I don't think Dad ever told us that one."

"Well, me and your dad grew up together in Sioux. And your dad had gotten a pump-action BB gun somewhere. We were out in the foothills climbing around, and I climbed up onto a big rock and was looking at your dad down below me. I yelled down at him, 'Hey, Wib, I'll bet you can't hit me!'

"'THE HELL I CAN'T,' your dad shouted back, and then he pumped that gun, took quick aim, and shot me and knocked me clean off that rock." Roger chuckled. "Your dad was something else!"

"That he was," Deke added.

Fred walked over and said hello to Roger and then addressed Deke and me.

"Where the hell is Ronnie?" Fred asked.

"I dunno," said Deke. "I got a hold of Jack Peterson, who called him somewhere and let him know 'bout Dad."

Then Fred went a different direction, "I think your dad knew more than he was tellin' anybody."

"I think so, too. I think he, I think he kinda knew he was going to die," I said.

"I do, too, in a way 'cause I told him, I talked to him Monday—the day before he died. I said, 'Wilbur, I'm comin' down to see ya. We'll be down.' And he said to me, 'Don't come down, Fred.' He said, 'I'm comin' home tomorrow.'"

Fred shook his head and then said wistfully, "I never . . . I never had anything hit me as bad as that did. Ever! I just . . ." His voice trailed off.

"Yeah, me neither."

"Wilbur and I used to argue and we'd fight."

"I know that, we all know that, but he loved you," Deke chimed in.

"Oh, gawd, I loved . . . I thought more of him."

"You know he did. You know he loved you, too. I got that five-dollar bill with you two on it. Ya know, from the country club?" I was changing the subject. I could see that Fred was getting emotional.

"Yeah," Fred quietly agreed.

"Gawd, Dad got a kick outta that. He got a kick out of, ya know, like when we used to have those picnics down there at the Milliman Park down from St. Anne's Church here in town. Oh, he loved getting together with you and tellin' stories. Jeez, he loved that. Remember that time we were there and Grandma was pacing around and gettin' impatient? She had kept hounding him, asking when they were going to leave. Finally, Dad yelled at her, 'WELL, GODDAMN IT, MOTHER, JUST GO SIT IN THE CAR AND WAIT THERE UNTIL I AM READY TO LEAVE.' Grandma went down to the car, and it was hotter than hell that day. She got in Dad's car and sat down on those leather seats and then raised up a bit and said, 'Oh, my, that is the hottest that's been in a long time!'"

Deke, Fred, and I all laughed which we needed at that point.

Then Fred added, "You guys was up to our place in Sioux, him and I used to go huntin' and we played golf and . . . we done everything together."

"And you remember being kids together, and you grew up with Dad, and you two were always close," Deke said.

"Well, it was just him and me. But, ya know, I've always cussed myself that I didn't tell him I loved him. People should be able to say it."

"Yeah, but it's, ya know, you get busy," I said, trying to give Fred some comfort.

"Just like . . . just like my mother now. I know she is wandering around town right now. And it's a bad thing to say, but I don't even think about her anymore, but I should, ya know?"

"Well, I went down to visit Aunt Lucy one time. Grandma and I went down," I added.

"I took her down one time, too," Fred added in.

"Well, that really bothered Dad when Lucy died. 'Cause he let us all know that he wanted all of us kids to be there."

"Well, you boys was all there."

"Ya know, Uncle Ron said this business about how they made a deal they wouldn't go to each other's funeral, but I don't believe it 'cause Dad wouldn't miss Uncle Ron's funeral if it were him in the casket. He would be there. And when Aunt Lucy died, he made it known to us kids he wanted us to be there. And when we went by and looked in her coffin, he said, 'IT DOESN'T EVEN LOOK LIKE PUSS.'"

Fred thought back to that day at Lucy's funeral. "I thought that was kinda a sad day. That's what made me think, ya know."

"Boy, that bothered Dad, too."

"Like that Charlie, they had him in the county hospital. What was her life like, actually? Just think of it. Lived there in River Sioux in that little brick house. All those years in that little brick house. She never had nothing, actually. She was ornery . . . but really that poor ol' gal never really did have nothing to be happy about. In a reform school all the time she was a little girl. Away from her family."

"That's pretty sad," I said, agreeing with Fred.

"Course, like I always said, after you get so old you should know enough to . . . to get over whatever happened to you and act like you know something. Take responsibility."

Fred changed the subject. "We leave outta here every morning. You know where that little road is around Euclid? A little bridge just this side of it. That's the closest I can ever get to my house, where we're at right now, 'cause I can see my house. And that's the closest I ever can get. And then we start right down below the county line there at Loveland. You know that big iron bridge down there."

"Yeah," Deke agreed faintly.

"Well, we're gonna put all the railroad ties in there. Three hundred ties we're gonna put in there."

"That'll take a lot of work and time, won't it?" I asked.

"Not that much, really."

"I've been there, too," Deke said, getting back into the conversation.

"Dad worked for the railroad for a little while, didn't he?" I asked.

"Yep. Northwestern."

"He didn't like it. They made him crawl in a tube to clean it out, and he said, 'I DON'T LIKE THAT SHIT. IT IS LIKE BEING BURIED ALIVE,'" I added.

"Your dad worked hard."

"He didn't want to be buried before his time. He didn't like crawling in that tube."

"Wilbur had clausta . . . whatdya call it, claustrophobia?"

Fred grinned. "If you think, it don't bother you. One time I was painting a bridge and these big I-beams they call 'em, 'bout this wide and 'bout that close together, but I wiggled up in there so I could clean it better and just lying there and it wasn't nothing, it was simple . . . but, ya know, I got to thinking and I almost went crazy gettin' out of that thing. Where if I'd just used my head, I would've knowed . . . you can do anything with your mind if you want to."

"Of course," Deke added, "if you got in, you can get out."

"Right, but I said, gettin' out is a damn sight harder than I got in there!" Then Fred laughed and said, "I got into some places where I couldn't get out!"

"Where you didn't want to get out?" I asked.

"I got in jail once and couldn't get out!" And we all laughed.

* * *

We talked to other people, and other stories were told and shared, but so much of it was an emotional blur. I was happy to hear people share their memories of Wilbur with us.

People eventually drifted away from the luncheon, and a few family members walked around the corner from the VFW to Shirley's house.

She put on a pot of coffee as we gathered around the kitchen table.

We were standing around the kitchen when I asked, "What are we going to do with Grandma?"

"Who cares?" Shirley replied.

"Well, Dad took care of Grandma. I guess he cared," I snapped back at her.

"He shouldn't have. That old blister never cared about anyone but herself," Shirley snapped back.

"I think someone in our family should take care of her. I think I should take care of her."

"You're in college," Shirley shot at me.

"Maybe I should stay home from college and take care of her."

"Bullshit. You are *not* going to quit college to take care of that old bitch."

"She is our flesh and blood. We have a responsibility to take care of her." I was really pushing Shirley.

"You don't have a responsibility to take care of her."

"What makes you say that?"

"You aren't her next of kin. She has two sons still living, and it is their responsibility, not yours, to take care of her. Let Freddie or Ronnie decide what to do with her. Let the county take her. I don't give a shit what happens to her. She never cared for anybody but herself, and you aren't quitting college."

She turned from me, angry, to look out the window.

"Well, Christ on a crutch!" she said.

"What, Mom?"

"Look out the window. It's your uncle Ronnie, just like you described in your dream."

I joined her at the window. "Cowboy hat and little blonde and all."

The door opened and in came Ron with a broad smile, wearing a brown cowboy hat and his latest and newest girlfriend on his arm. She certainly was new—maybe twenty-two or twenty-three at the very oldest.

"Where the hell you been, Ronnie? We didn't know how to get a hold of you," Shirley chastised.

"Yeah, Deke called Jack Peterson. He figured he would know how to find you," I added.

"I was down in Texas when Jack called me and told me the news—then I started making my way up here."

"You missed the funeral; it was this morning," I said.

"Well, me and Walt made a deal that we wouldn't go to each other's funerals." He said, and no one responded.

"Hey, Ronnie, do you want a beer?" Shirley asked, breaking the silence. "One of the bars in town sent over a case."

"Yeah, sure. Sounds good."

"What about you, hun?"

"Yes, thank you," the generic blonde answered meekly.

Shirley went to the refrigerator and pulled out two beers, popped the tabs, and set them on the kitchen table.

"Shit. I can't believe Walt is gone. I thought he was indestructible. What happened?" Ron said.

Shirley said, "He was having a hard time breathing, so he went down to the vets' hospital in Omaha. They took tests and what have you and decided to re-regulate his diabetes medicine. He was on pills, and they thought he needed to take shots. So, he went pert near a week without any diabetes medicine then they gave him a shot on Sunday. I think that is what did it. I don't think his heart could take it."

"Jack Hampton went up there to pick up Dad's things for us and to talk to some of them old boys in the ward with Dad," I added.

"Jack said that one of the vets in the ward said Wilbur was uncomfortable early the morning he died—say at five or so." Shirley said. "He got up and went to the nurses' station and told 'em, 'I AIN'T FEELIN' QUITE RIGHT, I'M HAVING A LITTLE BIT OF CHEST PAIN.' According to the old boy, them nurses told him to go ahead and lay back down, the doctor would be on duty at six and would take a look at him."

"Jesus Christ." Ron muttered.

"Well, by the time the doctor was on duty, Wilbur was dead."

"No foolin', I didn't think anything could kill Walt. Why I saw him one time in the bar you worked in, Shirl, on Nicholas."

"The Wander Inn."

"Yeah. This guy was mouthin' off to him. Walt told him, 'JUST SIT DOWN AND LEAVE ME ALONE. I'M JUST TRYIN' TO ENJOY MY BEER.' The guy had a hard on to fight Walt for some reason. He was itchin' to get him into a fight. Finally, Walt jumped up off his stool and squared off. 'Fore Walt knew what happened, this guy punched him in the side of the head so hard it woulda knocked a mule off its feet. But Walt was still standin'. Then Walt hit him so hard, it knocked the guy out. Goddamn, Walt had a hard head. He could take a punch like nobody. Then he turned around and got back up on that stool and finished his beer."

"I was working for Bus Triplette there—he owned the Wander Inn. Wib had a pretty hard head the night I tapped it with my high heel shoe." Shirley laughed.

"What's this, Shirley?"

"Wilbur pissed me off. I didn't want to go home, and he wanted to. So, I snuck up behind him, slipped off my high heel, and hit that son of a bitch three times on top of his head as hard as I could. He swung around and smacked me, then carried me out to our car and threw me in the back seat."

"Jesus Christ, Shirley, it is a wonder he didn't break your jaw. Boy, those days in Omaha were boozy. We all drank a lot. Hell, if there wasn't a fight by ten o'clock, somebody would start one. And ol' Walt might take some punches, but the next morning, we'd wake up bruised and Walt would say, 'WE HAD A GOOD TIME LAST NIGHT, DIDN'T WE?' Shit, I'd barely be able to move, and he was up at five getting ready to start the day."

"You got your share of licks in, too."

"Damn right I did," Ron answered Shirley with a big grin, the small gap between his teeth showing.

"I thought you were going to get my ass thrown in jail that time," Shirley said accusingly.

"When was that, hun?" Ron asked.

"That time you had me go to the airport and pick up your suitcase."

"Oh, yeah, when I had you go pick up my suitcase." He turned to me and his girlfriend to tell the story. "See, I got off the airplane and had a suitcase full of money and had some guns with me and I see a bunch of cops. I figure the whole police force must've been out at the airport. And I thought maybe they was after me, so I went and I put my money in the suitcase and checked the suitcase into one of them airport lockers."

"Then he shows up at our house," Shirley added.

"I checked out the deal, ya know, and caught me a cab and went out to Shirley's house . . . and I don't remember exactly, what'd I tell you?"

"You just asked me to drive out to the airport and get it."

"So, Shirley went out and got it. And I guess the police were after somebody else. I was a little paranoid about it. Hell, yes, I was."

"See, Ronnie had just robbed all them stores in California and got the money and the guns in the suitcase, but I didn't know that."

"Sixty-two thousand dollars. See, in them days, see, they didn't search you when ya got on an airplane. And you didn't have to go through metal detectors or nothing, so I just put the guns and everything right in the suitcase, and when I got off, there were police all over, apparently lookin' for somebody else. And then I told Shirley to go pick it up."

"Yeah, so he stayed with the kids, and I went over there like a dumb klutz and why, I could hardly lift that suitcase up. I came back to the house, and I said, 'Jesus Christ! What ya got in here? Lead pipes?'"

"Sixty-two thousand dollars and guns!"

"My god, my heart about stopped. They would have hauled me . . . they'd have put me away somewhere the snow flies, wouldn't they? And all I could think of was who is goin' to take care of my boys, because they would think I was some kind of accomplice."

"I'd have been there before you'd have went and told 'em." Ron laughed.

"They would have thought I was a gun moll or something because of all the money in the suitcase you had stashed in the locker."

"You woulda been fine since you didn't know you were helping me!"

"I don't remember, Ronnie, but was Paul Small involved in that?"

"Yeah." Then Ron hesitated for a minute. "You know Paul died a few years ago. He was all in the papers because he robbed Kellogg of all of those jewels—something like a hundred seventy-five thousand worth."

"Yeah, I saw it."

"They wrote an article about him sayin' he was tellin' his step kids to stay in school and do no wrong. Hell, I saw him not long before he died, and he said to me, 'Hey, Ronnie, let's go out in a blaze of glory with a great big shootout!'"

"He wanted to go on a robbing and shooting spree?" I asked.

"Ya damn right he did. I told him, 'Hell, Paul, you're the one dying, I ain't!'"

* * *

People buzzed in and out of the house, drank a beer or two, told stories, and then went on. I couldn't get enough—I wanted to talk about my dad all night, but, as they say, the jackal barks and the caravan moves on.

Cousins and friends needed to get back to their lives, and ours had to start again—differently, without the overwhelming presence of Wilbur. It was a blur, like most big events that go by too quickly. It was over in a flash.

"Well, Shirley, we're going to take off. I'll stop by in the morning," Ron said as he got up and headed to the door with his girlfriend.

The door shut. That was it—the day was over. The funeral was over. Wilbur was dead. Dead. Dead and buried. Dead forever.

My relationship with my dad and all of the things I knew and remembered about him could now never change. I just had my memories.

Epilogue

"The gun was in the waste of his pants."

Grandma Ada

After Wilbur's funeral, it was decided that Ron would take care of Ada. He moved her up to Onawa with him, his girlfriend, and her three little children. Since Ada received a Social Security check and a pension check from the State of California, that windfall now became Ron's.

Ada was immediately confused. She had been taken out of her home—Wilbur's trailer was familiar to her. As with many people suffering from dementia, when she was taken out of a place she had become used to, she no longer knew where she was. There was constant questioning of Ron's girlfriend when he was off doing whatever it was he was doing during the daylight hours.

"Where is Wilbur? When is Wilbur coming to pick me up? Where are we?" Ada would ask over and over.

Ron's girlfriend would answer the questions as patiently as she could until one day Ada became dissatisfied with the answers and decided she was going to do what she had done so many times before—head for the highway and hitchhike to where she wanted to go.

Unfortunately, Ron's girlfriend got in the way. She blocked the door and told Ada she could not leave and that Ron would explain everything when he got back. Ada pushed her to one side of the door and started out. When Ron's girlfriend resisted, Ada grappled her to the floor, slapped her a couple of times, and bolted. This happened several times before Ron's tiny little blonde girlfriend finally gave him an ultimatum—choose me or her.

Hmmm. The choice was between his eighty-one-year-old mother or a sex party with his twenty-something girlfriend. The thought process did not take long. Ron admitted Ada into the state nursing home in Cherokee, Iowa. It wasn't much better for Ada in Cherokee either. She was just as confused there as she had been at Ron's. She escaped a couple of times and was found on the highway heading out of town—wearing a hospital gown and exposing some pretty loose skin to unsuspecting drivers along the highway. By the time Fred was notified, her condition had deteriorated pretty rapidly.

A year later, Ada died. My college roommate at the time—Uncle Bob was his nickname—left a note for me that said succinctly, "Grandma Ada died. Call home."

Ada Elizabeth Anderson Rife Gillett Proctor Williams died March 27, 1981, in Cherokee, Iowa, at the state hospital.

The story that Ron told went this way: He was finally contacted by the staff at the state hospital and he went to see Ada. He said that she had contracted tuberculosis. She was on a respirator that was aiding her tortured breathing.

Ron asked the nurse a series of questions that started with, "Does she know what is going on?"

The quick reply was "No."

"Will she ever know what is going on?"

The nurse said, "No."

Ron followed up with, "Will she get any better?"

The nurse answered again, "No."

It was clear that Ada was in the last stage of her life and was only alive because of the aid of the machine she was hooked up to—the respirator—and the nutrition drip that supplied her body with fluid.

Ron then did something that he said sent the staff into near convulsions. He reached over and unplugged the respirator.

The nurse dashed out to get the release order allowing Ada to be taken off the respirator. The room went silent without the machine.

Ada died a day later.

She was buried the next Tuesday at Frazier Cemetery, next to Wilbur. Reverend Bob Evans officiated. Her six grandsons—Rick, Lanny Hicks, Mike, Deke, Brian, and I—were pallbearers. Rick buzzed into town that morning and borrowed a sports coat from me to wear at the funeral.

Nondescript church music was played in the background. Few came, but her brother Boon and sister Myrtle were there and were of note because of the conversation they had *during* the funeral service.

Boon told Myrtle that he didn't understand why Ada couldn't have given him and his wife, Harriet, one of her kids, especially since she didn't really take very good care of them. The whole time Boon was talking, Myrtle was trying to hush him. But he kept on going. He talked about how he and Harriet would have been fine with adopting one of the boys or even Lucy. He went on about how Little Charles had even died. Finally, Myrtle got him to stop, but even after all of the years that passed, it was still bothering him. Eventually, he and Harriet did adopt, not one of Ada's children but one of her granddaughters, Nancy, who was without a doubt Lucy's daughter in looks and temperament.

Uncle Ron

I was working at a Simon & Schuster subsidiary, Judy/Instructo, in Minneapolis in March of 1990. I had been working there a little more than three months when Shirley called to tell me that she had heard that Ron had robbed a bank in Pisgah. She faxed me the following newspaper article with the highlighted line: "Sass said the man came into the bank at about 9 a.m. and walked up to the first window with a paper bag, the teller saw a gun in the waste of the man's pants." Waste!

That article was from the daily *Nonpareil* that ran on Tuesday, March 6, 1990, leading with the headline "Drifter held in bank holdup."

> *PISGAH—A former Council Bluffs man accused of holding up a bank here Monday morning faces federal charges in connection with the armed robbery, according to authorities.*
>
> *Roland Keith Gillette, 59, whose last known address was in Texas, was arrested outside Omaha about an hour after the*

gunman held up the Iowa Savings Bank in this small Harrison county city, the FBI said.

Gillette was described as a drifter.

Harrison county Sheriff Merle Sass said Gillette has also lived in Missouri Valley, Logan, and Little Sioux. Gillette had been living in Texas for the past two years, he said.

Sass said he had his deputies looking for the bank robber immediately after being alerted by the bank. They were joined in the search for the man by the Iowa and Nebraska state patrols and city and county law enforcement officials in the area.

"It was a good thing we got the item out real fast," Sass said of his department's radio broadcast giving a description of the bank robber.

Sass said the man came into the bank at about 9 a.m. and walked up to the first window with a paper bag, the teller saw a gun in the waste of the man's pants.

The man told the teller to put all of the money in her drawer into the bag and then demanded that the teller next to her give him all of the money in her drawer also.

The man said not to "give him any trouble and not to follow him out of the bank and they would be all right." Sass said.

The man drove a pickup away from the bank and must have crossed into Nebraska on U.S. Highway 30, which leads into Blair, Neb., Sass said. He then headed south along U.S. Highway 75.

At about 10:20 a.m., a Douglas County, Neb. Sheriff's deputy, Gary Kirkle, spotted the pickup and stopped it outside Omaha in the area of U.S. Highway 75 and interstate 680 with help from the Nebraska State Patrol.

Gillette immediately surrendered and signed a form consenting to a search that recovered the money according to the FBI.

"I'm the one you're looking for. I have no gun. What you want is in the paper bag on the floorboard," Gillette told arresting officers Monday, according to an affidavit filed in U.S. District court in Des Moines by FBI Special Agent Charles Kempf.

Officers recovered $3,123 including twenty $10 bills that had prerecorded serial numbers, the affidavit said.

> Gillette appeared before a federal magistrate in Omaha and waived a removal hearing clearing the way for his transfer to Iowa for arraignment in Des Moines.
>
> The maximum penalty for federal bank robbery is up to 20 years in prison and up to $5,000 in fines.

So far as we know, it was Ron's last bank robbery. There may have been a liquor store or two after and some drug running in and out of Mexico, but that was the last bank robbery.

After serving his sentence, Ron moved to a small apartment in Woodbine. He said that had he known he was going to live so long, he would have taken care of himself. His emphysema and diabetes got the best of him; his body was broken down from years of misuse and neglect. He was found unconscious and rushed to the Immanuel Medical Center in Omaha, where he died on October 25, 2001, at the age of seventy—an age no one thought he would live to, including Ron.

Jack Hampton and Jack Peterson, both friends of Ron's, and four of his nephews—Mike Rife, Lanny Hicks, Deke Rife, and Brian Rife—carried his casket to the grave. He was buried in the Frazier Cemetery close to Wilbur. The family got together and bought him a gravestone.

Uncle Fred

Fred died peacefully on February 23, 2008, two weeks shy of his eighty-ninth birthday, at his Missouri Valley home. He is buried a few feet from Wilbur in the Frazier Cemetery, which is right next to the golf course they spent so many hours in together—laughing, arguing, golfing, and drinking.

Mom

Shirley died on November 22, 2015, after a long decline in health. In the end, she was suffering from dementia—she was in and out of consciousness and lucidity. She survived her siblings, and the last of Wilbur's siblings' spouses, before she passed away.

The last time I visited her was at the Longview Nursing Home in Missouri Valley, Iowa. My brother Deke, my son, Zain, and I visited her over the course of three days on Labor Day weekend that year. The first evening we arrived, Shirley didn't recognize me or Zain. She did recognize Deke. Deke let me know, jokingly, that she remembered him because he was her favorite. The next day, however, she thought Deke was Wilbur and even called him a son of a bitch once, so we knew for sure she thought Deke was Wilbur. She did remember Zain and me that day. We even got a glimpse of her acerbic sense of humor. At one point, she looked up at me and said, "You know, Douglas, Zain looks a lot like you did at that age." Then she grinned and continued, "But he's a lot better looking."

She was buried in Frazier Cemetery next to Wilbur Rife, and I gave the following eulogy at her funeral service:

"We have come to celebrate, celebrate the life of Shirley Inez Rasmussen Rife, the eighth of nine children born to Hans and Carrie Turner Rasmussen. She was born October 8, 1931.

"The name Shirley crested in popularity in 1935 when it was ranked number four. Her middle name Inez was never wildly popular, though it had its wave in 1918. Shirley means "bright meadow" and Inez means "pure." Those of you who knew her well can write your own joke.

"Reanna Rife, Tim's daughter, is named for Mom. In fact, when Tim was at the hospital the day Reanna was born, Mike came to see his newest granddaughter. Mike asked Tim, 'What did you name her?' Tim answered, 'Reanna Inez.' Mike said, 'I like Reanna, but I'm not sure about Inez.' Mom, who was standing next to Mike, gave him a sharp elbow and said with some colorful language—yes, she was like that—'Hey, Mike, that's my middle name!'

"And Mike said, 'Oh, I didn't know.' He's like that.

"Mom was born on a hardscrabble farm in windswept Custer County, South Dakota. Her mother was especially industrious—she canned over a thousand quarts of meat and vegetables every year. When Mom was still living on the farm, her job was to make pies—lots of pies for when the threshing crew came. They ate pie for breakfast, the coffee break, lunch, and the afternoon break. She would make up to seventeen or eighteen pies a day when the threshers were working. Dad used to say that the only thing that Mom knew how to cook was pie when they first married. She learned to add other dishes to her repertoire and learned well.

"Mom hated school for a lot of reasons—she was always embarrassed that she only had two blouses and two skirts that she alternated. So she quit school when she was in tenth grade and went to work in the tiny Cave Café in Custer. She met Wilbur Rife there, and they started dating, going to dances, and meeting after her shift for dinner.

"It wasn't until Mom and Dad were celebrating their twenty-fifth wedding anniversary when I realized that Mike, the little love child, was born before they were married.

"I said to Mom, 'Hey, Mom, I think you are celebrating the wrong year.' Mike was sitting close to me at the time and started laughing and said, 'Did you just figure that out?' Mike is like that.

"Mom just said, 'Honey, the first one can come anytime; the rest of them take nine months.'

"And then she said, 'Now shut up, we have a room full of people!'

"Mom was like that.

"This isn't about Dad, but he was a definite influence on her life. Because of him it went in a direction she had not planned. She always looked at her wedding day, April 14, as one of the three great American tragedies: April 14, 1865, Abraham Lincoln was shot at Ford's Theater; April 14, 1912, the Titanic hit an iceberg; April 14, 1949, our mom and dad got married.

"But she didn't hate the kids part—she loved all four of us, but her early experience made her *hate* men. She always said, 'If I could do it over again, I'd shack up and have my kids and kick Wilbur's ass to the curb.' Not exactly a Hallmark moment!

"But, don't tell me God doesn't have a good sense of humor. Mom hated men and she had four boys:

"Wilbur Michael Rife—named after Dad and Mom's brother. Clyde Mansel Rife—we know and love him as 'Deke,' named after Dad's two favorite people, his dad and his best friend. Brian Mark Rife—named after Dad's second favorite golfing buddy. Now my name was supposed to be Douglas Montgomery Rife, but Mom looked down at her little moon-faced newborn idiot and thought, He will never be able to spell a name with that many letters. So she named me Douglas Marlin. She was, at times, practical.

"We are a family of early adopters. Our family embraced divorce long before it became popular. The first divorce in the family was in 1865. So, Mom and Dad followed family tradition and divorced after twenty-six years and went their own ways.

"Mom, like most of us, was a contradiction:

"She was essentially a shy person who shied away from attention, parties, or crowds, yet ran a tavern.

"She was the world's worst housekeeper, yet kept a neat and flowered yard.

"As I said, she was a horrible housekeeper, yet made a living for a while cleaning houses. Now that is irony.

"Mom could be irascible and stubborn, even mean-spirited, saying nasty things about people, yet she always had an open heart and an open door policy when it came to sharing her home with family and friends who needed a place to stay, including my uncle Ron and his girlfriend Judy, who was a topless dancer. She even taught her to crochet. By the way, they stole all of our good towels when they left.

"We are all a collection of things we believe in, like or don't like:

"She hated Jay Leno—loved Johnny Carson.

"She was one of the original soda pop warriors, she hated Coke—loved Pepsi.

"She loved the color purple and hated the color yellow, even yellow flowers.

"She loved lap dogs—even the feisty ones like our little toy Manchester, Fritzy, even though he bit every person in the family, including her, but most especially Shelly! Even when he got too old to run, he would amble over to the door and catch some poor Jehovah's Witness off guard with a sharp bite. She always laughed. Mom was like that.

"Mom was a generous person who loved her family. She had a spark and a good and biting sense of humor. She had a warm and generous spirit and real friendships. She was loved. She was a mom, a grandmother, an aunt, a sister, a daughter, a great-grandmother, a cousin—and even a wife, too.

"Mom is gone now, but she is going to live in our hearts and memories. And so many things will make me think of her:

- When I see a double wedding ring quilt top
- When I see a container of garlic salt
- Or when I drive by a tavern that looks a little worn but friendly
- When I see a can of fizzing Pepsi
- When I see an unfiltered Pall Mall cigarette with an ash that is two inches long and ready to fall to the floor
- Or when I roll out egg noodles on Thanksgiving morning like so many people in this room did in the last few days
- And countless other things

"Mom gave me lots of salty advice like when I was a teenage boy and she said, 'Flies spread disease so keep yours closed.' She also said, 'Nobody likes change but wet babies.' And this change is going to be hard—a life without her—but so many reminders of her will make it a bit easier knowing that she is all around and always in our memories and always in our hearts."

After I spoke, my nephew, Shaun, got up to say a few words about her, too. His remarks weren't written down or recorded, but one of his stories sticks out in my mind.

When Shaun was a teenager, he had a close relationship with Shirley. He talked to her quite a bit, bummed cigarettes off her, and generally hung out at her house drinking Pepsi and musing about school, friends, and the world. He was searching for the right church at the time. He went to his grandmother for advice. Shirley said, "Well, honey, all churches are about the same. Pick any one you want to because the basic message for each church is nearly the same—just don't be an asshole."

And that was another example of her salty advice—her version of the golden rule.

Robyn Ann also stood up to say a word. Her story was about Shirely's unflinching generosity. Robyn Ann was in the process of buying a house and was $200 short, just $200 and she was only going to need the money for the closing. She had come to Shirely's bar to find Fred to see if she could borrow the money from her dad. When she asked, he pulled a wad of bills out of his pocket neatly folded in half and said, "I'm sorry, sis, I'm a little short." Robyn Ann was frustrated and walked to the end of the bar, and when retelling the story to Shirley, Shirley stopped her and said, "Hang on there, Robbie." She walked to a cabinet behind the bar, came back with a sack of money, and said, "Take what you need and pay me back when you get it."

Wilbur Michael "Mike" Rife

Mike passed away after a night of watching movies with his friends, who found him sitting in his chair the next morning. Mike was buried in Frazier Cemetery and I gave the following eulogy at his funeral service, February 16, 2019:

"We are gathered here today to morn and to celebrate the life of Wilbur Michael Rife. The name Wilbur is German and means resolute and brilliant. It had its peak in popularity just about the time our Dad, Wilbur Merle Rife, was born and then steadily and rapidly declined. The year Mike was born, only 486 boys in the entire U.S. were named Wilbur that year. Now Dad said our brother was named after *him*. Mom said he was named after *her* brother, Wilber. Their arguments started early and centered on things important and unimportant. Any excuse to disagree but it didn't matter anyway, since he didn't go by Wilbur. Most of us called him 'Michael' or 'Mike.' Our cousins on the Rife side, who are more like our siblings than cousins, called him 'Mickey.' And sometimes we *all* called him 'Dungerbonk,' which was the sound he made when he tripped over his own feet. Yes, Mike was tall, lanky, awkward, and a bit clumsy.

"Mike was born January 14, 1949, on his grandparent's windswept and hardscrabble farm in Custer County, South Dakota, during a snowstorm, at four o'clock in the morning. Dr. Calverd delivered him in the early morning hours with an assist from Mom's Mom, Carrie Rasmussen, who was a midwife. He was the heaviest of us four boys, weighing in at a few ounces shy of seven pounds. He was a cute, chubby, happy baby boy. And, he was a happy kid, too.

"Mike was introverted and one of his favorite activities was to read. He read voraciously. It seemed he always had his nose in a book. He liked Westerns. Often when our parents would argue, Mike would retreat to a corner and open up a paperback waiting for the battle to subside while he consumed a book by Louis L'Amour or Zane Grey or some other Western writer—trading the real life battle at home for the life of a gunfighter on the page. Since our parents fought a lot, Mike had plenty of time for reading.

"Mike was a gentle boy. But, like any big brother, Mike could get upset, but his punishments were a lot like his teasing. He would sit on you and tickle you until you peed your pants. No one laughed harder at that than he did.

"As kids we spent a lot of time in the summers at Uncle Fred and Aunt Amy's house in River Sioux. It was mystical in a way. We got to roam unfettered through the fields, swim at Baker's Lake, and walk the creeks. No one worried about us there. That's where we all learned how to ride bikes.

"Of course, even when he learned how to ride, he didn't necessarily understand the mechanics of the bike. In a bike race between Deke and Robyn Ann and Mike and Rhonda, from Ab's to Uncle Fred's, Rhonda's foot was caught in the spokes. Mike didn't understand what was going on with the back wheel or the front wheel as they scooted forward. Mike and Rhonda lost.

"We played in the abandoned two-room schoolhouse next to their house, climbed trees, and ate green apples. Of course, if you got caught eating green apples, Aunt Amy would put you in the cellar, our cousin Rhonda would stack tires on the door, so you were trapped with the spiders and insects. Like the oncoming stomachache after eating the green apples wasn't punishment enough. And we got pop and candy at Peasely's. It was unstructured and unsupervised fun—it was our Shangri-La.

"Sioux was populated by characters. Huck Peasley was a local who would show up with a bunch of freshly caught fish. Aunt Amy's mother, 'Granny' as she was called by everyone in the village, kept us in peach pie and always had an open door. She was there if we had a scrape that needed washed out or a cut that needed tended to. Then there was Floyd Smith, Granny's neighbor, who haunted us with stories of Raw Head and Bloody Bones, and Cousin Rick who teased us with stories of Tilly Witch and Miss Rat.

"Many times our call to go out and play was when one of our parents would open the door and shew us out and say, 'Pretend the wind is blowing you away.' We weren't supposed to come back in until it was dark. We were like feral cats. We were free.

"That kid's paradise ended on August 31, 1966, when Mike joined the Army. This decision more than any other defined and affected his life.

"He had his basic training at Fort Polk, in Louisiana; AIT at Fort Sill, Oklahoma, and jump school in Fort Benning, Georgia. He was part of the 82nd Airborne Fort Bragg, North Carolina. Mike served his nation in Vietnam from December 17, 1967 to January 11, 1969, as part of the 101st Airborne Division, Second Brigade. The TET Offensive started in February of 1968 and was some of the heaviest combat during the entire war.

"After the Vietnam War, Mike went to Topeka, Kansas, for therapy for PTSD. As part of the therapy, he journaled about his experiences in the Vietnam War. He gave me those journals.

"Mike wrote about just a few of the hardships he faced in the jungle, and I want to share a few excerpts, 'I remember crossing a lot of rivers and creeks and rice paddies and always having to pick leeches off afterwards. No matter how careful you were. They'd get on your legs and stomach and arms and back. The ants would bite the hell out of you and so would the centipedes. The things would be six to twelve inches long. They had venom that would make you sick and cause whatever area they bit to swell and go numb. The elephant grass cut our hands and arms and necks and faces. And you were constantly fighting the mosquitoes and bugs. You had to be on guard against being hit, always listening to the radio and keeping the volume down so that no one else but you could hear it. At night, at times it was so still it was spooky and the mist and fog would roll in where you couldn't see anything below you. You could watch it go between your feet and legs.'

"Mike longed for anything that tasted of home, writing, 'I got so tired of powdered, dehydrated, and canned food. What a guy wouldn't have given for fresh food. Meat or fruit, fresh milk or a catfish or carp or trout. A banana split or homemade apple pie or a homemade pie of any kind.'

"In another passage he wrote, 'I remember seeing green and orange tracers that morning for the first time and I was scared. I was hit by shrapnel that night and I felt a bullet pass through my hair. The bullets were all around us and the tracers looked like they were coming right at us.'

"Mike fought through his thirteen months of duty in Vietnam and made it, he lived.

"Mike was a good soldier—he was awarded the Army Commendation Medal (ARCOM) for consistent acts of heroism and meritorious service. He was also awarded the Bronze Star for heroic service in a combat zone. Mike mustered out September 8, 1969, with an honorable discharge.

"Though I was never in the service and never wore the uniform, I stand here as an American and as his brother and salute his service to our country.

"Mike was married at the Mount Olive Lutheran Church in Omaha, Nebraska. And from the union of that marriage was born on November 13, 1971, Timothy Michael Rife. Nothing made Mike more proud than his son. And later, his granddaughters, Haleigh, Reanna, Ericah, and then his great-granddaughter, Brecklyn. Mike was a devoted and loving father, grandfather, and great-father, proudly displaying pictures of his family around his home in Sioux.

"Mike went back to Sioux for the last decades of his life maybe as a way to relive some of the happy memories of his childhood spent there during those lost summers. Maybe as a way to escape.

"He moved into a historic house for our family. Our great-grandfather George Washington Henry Rife and his wife, Annie, lived there, as well as two of George's sisters and their husbands before him. Our grandfather Clyde lived there and so did our father and Uncle Fred as kids. Mike loved the house and died there this last Monday, February 11.

"Though Mike was seventy, his life now seems short. If there is a lesson in any of this, it is if you are staring at a piece of cake and wondering whether or not you should eat it—do it. If you have a bucket list of trips you are going to take someday, take the trip now.

"Eat the cake, take the trip. Eat the cake, take the trip. Don't wait.

"In memory of Wilbur Michael Rife:

> Sweet be thy rest O soldier brave
> Let angels guard thy hallowed grave
> And while the stars in Heaven flame
> Let glory wreath thy honored name."

Brian Mark Rife

The last time I saw Brian was at our Fourth of July family picnic at Deke's house in Des Moines. He told me that the body tells you when it is over and he said he knew he did not have many days left. He died four days later. Brian was buried in Frazier Cemetery and I gave the following eulogy at his funeral service:

"Brian asked me to write and deliver his eulogy at our brother Mike's funeral in February. In fact, we joked about it, neither one of us imagining it would happen this soon—let alone this very year. I told him that I was likely to outlive him since he was older and single. Married men live longer on average than single men. Sadly, the opposite is true for women—single women live longer. What does that say about living with a man?

"I was also reluctant to deliver the eulogy because at Mike's funeral, and this is the only time I have ever seen this happen, after I finished with Mike's eulogy, my cousin Rhonda popped up like a jack-in-the box with a rebuttal! A rebuttal—anyone else ever seen that? We'll see if she needs to set the record straight or has anything to refute today.

"I am also reluctant because this is going to be really tough to get through. Really tough. Brian was my first friend.

"Brian Mark Rife, was born in Omaha on September 7, 1955, just thirteen months before I was. Brian and I were inseparable as kids. In fact, many people thought we were twins since we were born so close together. I was, though, less like his twin and more like his shadow. I followed him everywhere. He was my buddy, as I said, he was my very first friend.

"When we were left alone on a Saturday night when we were as young as seven and eight, we'd spend hours peeling and cutting potatoes into stars and animal shapes and then frying them up with a big dollup of ketchup on the side of the heaping platter while we watched sci-fi movies like *The House on the Haunted Hill* with Vincent Price. We were always together.

"Or we'd get into Mom's car and pretend we were driving. Once we actually started it. Brian was on the steering wheel and I was on the gas pedal. We drove the car into the front porch and knew we were in trouble when we heard glass breaking. I stayed pressing on the gas—our tires whirring around throwing rocks behind us until Mom showed up and spanked us all the way to our bedroom. Usually, though, we just knocked the car our of gear and rolled backwards over the Rayburns' white picket fence.

"Or we'd douse Wonder bread in whipped eggs on Saturday morning to cook French toast. We made our own syrup with a cup of white sugar, a cup of brown sugar, and a cup of water. We'd take turns trying to light the pilot light on our gas stove until it went *poof* and the flame lit. Then we'd stand on an upside-down bucket or a chair to fry the battered bread, flipping it in the pan with our fingertips. We were always together.

"And every school day, Brian and I trudged together to cross 30th Street by ourselves to get to Florence Elementary, timing it so we could run across the busy street without being hit. It was like a live game of Frogger. But we were always together.

"The year Windsor Castle caught fire, the Queen of England described the year as annus horribilis. The annus horribilis for our family was 1957.

"That year, our house was nearly totaled when Deke, looking for a toy, caught the house alight with a candle. Much of the interior was gutted, and windows on the bedroom side and front of the house were blown out. It was not livable. Over the next two or three months, the crew Dad worked with at Howard Johnson's came to help repair and rebuild our house. Out of the ashes they made our home livable again.

"Once we moved back in, things got back to a sort of normalcy. In April of '58, Dad headed back to Greenland to the Thule Airforce Base to work heavy equipment. Things seemed like they were getting back to the way they were. But, on Wednesday, July 9 of that year, all of that was to change, and change for the worse.

"Most of us have a moment or maybe even several moments that change our lives. They are seminal moments that cause us to think differently or change the course of our lives, often in ways we can't foresee.

"July 9, 1958, was that moment not only for Brian but for our entire family.

"That afternoon, some neighbor boys came over to play. Deke and his friend were wrestling out in the front yard. In the scrimmage, I got pushed forward and fell on the front step face forward. When I hit the cement step, I bit through my lip, cutting open a gash about an inch and a half or so long. Blood started dripping down my face. I ran crying to Mom, who held a washrag against the cut to stop the bleeding. Mom loaded me into our car and headed to get the wound stitched up. Mom left Mike in charge.

"Mike and his friend kept playing. One of them had crawled up in the loft of our garage and got a gas can down. They had built a little fire out in the backyard, but it didn't flame up like they thought it was going to. So, they dumped gasoline on it. They stood back and struck matches and pitched them at the stack of stuff to see who could get a match to light it up—sort of a flaming basket.

"Mike had just turned to go inside the house to fix something for everyone to eat when the other boy struck a match that he didn't think had lit. He flicked the match behind him to discard it, not paying attention to either the gas can that was there or Brian who had walked up to see what was going on.

"What was thought to be an unlit match landed right in the gas can. Brian stumbled and fell toward the gas can just as the match flew in, and it exploded. Gas shot out of the mouth of the gas can onto Brian's face, setting his face aflame.

"Deke was sitting on top of the chicken coop. He heard the poof of the gas pouring up out of the can and looked in Brian's direction to see what had happened. When Brian cried out, Deke jumped off the chicken coup to see what he could do to help and landed on a broken jar, cutting open his foot.

"Mike screamed. 'Go tell the Rayburns we need help.' Deke hobbled as quickly as he could, his foot bleeding all the way over to the Rayburns. They called the rescue unit.

"Mike ran into the house to call for help from Jack and Leona Hampton. On the race out of the house, Mike grabbed a stick of butter. By the time Mike got back outside, Brian had fallen. Mike lifted him to his feet and began patting out the fire on Brian's face and applying the butter as pieces of Brian's skin came off into Mike's hands.

"Mom pulled up and could instantly see that something was wrong. She got home just as a rescue unit pulled up. Brian was standing in the yard, and she could see his face looked different.

"Mom could see there was no skin on his face. Brian looked like a ghost. He was standing somehow, but his body was limp.

"Deke and Brian were loaded into the back of the ambulance. Mike and I went with Leona Hampton.

"The doctors bandaged Brian and sent him home.

"Brian lay there like a tiny, still mummy. Only his eyes, nose holes, and a slit for his mouth weren't covered.

"Through the night, Brian just kept getting worse and worse. It was as if she could feel the life leaving his frail body. Occasionally, Mom would put her face next his mouth to check for his breath.

"At two in the morning, Leona Hampton drove Brian and Mom back to the hospital.

"As soon as they laid Brian down on a gurney, the nurses surrounded him and started rubbing him all over and getting the blood circulating. They were bringing him back from the brink of death.

"It had been a horrendous day. Brian was burnt beyond recognition, Mike's hands were burnt, Deke's foot was cut open, and it all started with my lip getting stitched up.

"Mom, who could be prone to hyperbolic expression, said, 'This has been the worst day of my life.' And it was not at all overstated.

"Brian made it—still in shock and blind for the next three days—but he made it.

"Over the next years Brain had a series of skin grafts. Each time he would come home from the hospital he would hop out of the car, his entire head bandaged. We'd all yell, 'Let's play mummy—you be the mummy.' He had the costume; he got the role. As if it were a British farce, he'd stretch out his arms and start chasing us—like nothing horrendous had happened.

"But it *had* affected him. He had nightmares.

"If we left the closet door open in our bedroom, he'd wake up in the middle night and instead of seeing a shirt hanging on a coat hanger, he saw a monster. He'd scream bloody murder and wake me from a sound sleep. I had to shut the door and he was relieved.

"Or if we left piles of clothing on the floor, he'd wake me up with a bloodcurdling scream that poisonous turtles were on the floor coming our way. I had to get up and kick the turtles under the bed before he could get back to sleep.

"And sometimes, when Brian was nervous, he would rock back and forth slapping his legs until we would lay our hands on top of his to stop him.

"While the accident and the skin grafts and the scars did change Brian, they did not define him.

"His personality defined him. Brian was warm, generous, and giving. He shared whatever he had with his friends and family.

"Brian loved games. He was an avid pitch player. He also loved to play foosball and had a table in his front room for a year—making it easy for him to get a spontaneous game at a moment's notice. And, as Derek and Shaun found out when they got snowed in Brian's house for three days, he could play for hours and hours, fueled by junk food and Pepsi.

"He was funny, too. He loved to tell jokes. In fact, he told and retold jokes the night of Mike's viewing in February: 'Where does a snowman put his money? A snowbank!' 'Who is a snowman's favorite relative? Antarctica.'

"Or he would like to deliver one-liners like this one he heard that night from Rick Schaefer, 'What does a school janitor say when he jumps out of a closet?' Then he would act out the punchline, 'Supplies!'

"Of course, he told jokes more risqué than that, but this is a family-friendly audience with a G rating. Brian wasn't really G rated.

"He also had a quick and sometimes biting wit.

"I remember when Mom was having her topless dancers in the bar, all the ministers in town, save the Catholic priest, decided they were going to make it their mission to talk her out of it. One by one they came to see Mom and tried to sway her. She was implacable. Finally, the last one to come was Pastor Fredricks, the Lutheran minister. He was shy and self-assuming. It was obvious that he was uncomfortable and didn't really want to be there. Nonetheless he made the trip out to our house. While he was there it started to rain, and it was a deluge of biblical proportions. We lived out at the Schwertley place outside of town. Our driveway was rocked and there was a turnaround three-quarters of the way up that was rocked, too. When Pastor Fredricks left, he backed up and missed the turnaround. We were sitting in the living room after he'd gone and could hear his wheels spinning. Mom barked, 'Get up and see what is going on.' We looked out the window and he was up to his axles in mud. 'You boys better go out and give him a push or he'll never leave.' So, out Brian and I went into the pouring rain. As we got to the car, Pastor Fredrick rolled down the window a crack and asked, 'Are you boys here to help me?' And Brian quipped, 'Yes, Pastor, doesn't the Lord work in strange and mysterious ways?'

"Brian also had a creative spirit. He wrote plays, like the *Emporium*, he wrote short stories, and he drew pictures, often caricatures of the people he knew. In fact, next to nearly every address in his address book is a caricature of the person.

"He also wrote poetry. This one was written and even published in the *Omaha World-Herald*:

> Silent, Secret Love
> Softly, saying I love you.
> Softly, so you don't hear.
> Wanting to kiss you.
> Wanting to hold you.
> Why haven't I told you?

Why do I keep it to myself?
When you are my everything.
When you are all I want!
Wonder if you'll ever know.
Wonder if you will ever be mine.
Watching your every move.
Watching all your actions.
Waiting for your touch.
Waiting for you to realize.
Silently, I confess.
Silently, my love you possess.

"Lastly, Brian was a collector. He collected character glasses, movies, CDs, antique lamps, Christmas decorations, artwork of all kinds, and photos.

"But mostly, he collected friends. Brian never had much money, but whatever he had he would share including his home—he had an open-door policy. His home was practically an inn for people who needed a place to stay. People, friends of his who needed a temporary place, moved in and out of his home. He was giving with all that he had. He had a generous and loving spirit.

"To some of us, he was a brother, a cousin, an uncle, but to all of us he was a friend, my first friend, and we are going to miss him."

About the Author

Douglas M. Rife has been developing products for classroom teachers and school administrators as a publisher and author for decades. His personal passion is American history which has led him to republish out of print local histories, volunteer as a docent, help to preserve local historic sites, and to assist in drafting legislation to protect cemeteries in his home state. He blogs about cemeteries at gravelyspeaking.com and has written more than twenty-five books for teachers who teach American and family history. Currently, Rife lives in Bloomington, Indiana, with his wife where they raised their three children.

www.ingramcontent.com/pod-product-compliance
Lightning Source LLC
Chambersburg PA
CBHW010929180426
43194CB00045B/2842